What Your Third Grader Needs to Know

FUNDAMENTALS OF A GOOD THIRD-GRADE EDUCATION

The Core Knowledge™ Series

Resource Books for Kindergarten Through Grade Six

A Delta Trade Paperback

THE CORE KNOWLEDGE SERIES

What Your Third Grader Needs to Know

FUNDAMENTALS OF A GOOD THIRD-GRADE EDUCATION
(Revised Edition)

Edited by

E. D. HIRSCH, JR.

A Delta Book
Published by
Bantam Dell Publishing
a division of
Random House, Inc.
1540 Broadway
New York, New York 10036

ISBN 0-385-33626-8

Reprinted by arrangement with Doubleday

Manufactured in the United States of America

Published simultaneously in Canada

June 2002

10 9 8 7 6

Editor-in-Chief of the Core Knowledge Series: E. D. Hirsch, Jr.

Text Editors: John Holdren, Susan Tyler Hitchcock

Art Editor: Tricia Emlet

Writers: John Hirsch (Math), Michele Josselyn (Visual Arts),
Mary Beth Klee (American History), Barbara Lachman (Music),
Deborah Mazzotta Prum (World History), Christiana Whittington (Music)

Artists and Photographers: Jonathan Fuqua, Dave Garbot, Steve Henry, Sara Holdren,
Phillip Jones, Bob Kirchman, GB McIntosh, Mary Michaela Murray, Meg West

Art Research and Permissions: Tricia Emlet

Text Permissions: Jeanne Nicholson Siler

Acknowledgments

This series has depended on the help, advice, and encouragement of more than two thousand people. Some of those singled out here already know the depth of our gratitude; others may be surprised to find themselves thanked publicly for help they gave quietly and freely. To helpers named and unnamed we are deeply grateful.

Advisors on Multiculturalism: Minerva Allen, Barbara Carey, Frank de Varona, Mick Fedullo, Dorothy Fields, Elizabeth Fox-Genovese, Marcia Galli, Dan Garner, Henry Louis Gates, Cheryl Kulas, Joseph C. Miller, Gerry Raining Bird, Connie Rocha, Dorothy Small, Sharon Stewart-Peregoy, Sterling Stuckey, Marlene Walking Bear, Lucille Watahomigie, Ramona Wilson

Advisors on Elementary Education: Joseph Adelson, Isobel Beck, Paul Bell, Carl Bereiter, David Bjorklund, Constance Jones, Elizabeth LaFuze, J. P. Lutz, Sandra Scarr, Nancy Stein, Phyllis Wilkin

Advisors on Subject Matter: Marilyn Jager Adams, Karima-Diane Alavi, Richard Anderson, Judith Birsh, Louis A. Bloomfield, Cheryl Cannard, Barbara Foorman, Paul Gagnon, David Geary, Andrew Gleason, Ted Hirsch, H. Wiley Hitchcock, Henry Holt, Blair Jones, Connie Juel, Eric Karell, Morton Keller, Joseph Kett, Charles Kimball, Mary Beth Klee, David Klein, Barbara Lachman, Karen Lang, Michael Lynch, Diane McGuinness, Sheelagh McGurn, John F. Miller, Joseph C. Miller, Jean Osborn, Vikas Pershad, Margaret Redd, Donna Rehorn, Gilbert Roy, Nancy Royal, Mark Rush, Janet Smith, Ralph Smith, Keith Stanovich, Paula Stanovich, Nancy Strother, David Summers, Nancy Summers, Marlene Thompson, James Trefil, Patricia Wattenmaker, Nancy Wayne, Christiana Whittington, Linda Williams Bevilacqua, Lois Williams

Writers and Editors: This revised edition involved a careful reconsideration of material in the first edition of this book and others in the series. In that spirit we acknowledge previous writers and current editorial staff at the Core Knowledge Foundation: Linda Bevilacqua, Nancy Bryson, Matthew Davis, Marie Hawthorne, Pamela C. Johnson, Blair Logwood Jones, Michael Marshall, James Miller, Elaine Moran, Kristen Moses, A. Brooke Russell, Peter Ryan, Lindley Shutz, Helen Storey, Souzanne Wright

Conferees, March 1990: Nola Bacci, Joan Baratz-Snowden, Thomasyne Beverley, Thomas Blackton, Angela Burkhalter, Monty Caldwell, Thomas M. Carroll, Laura Chapman, Carol Anne Collins, Lou Corsaro, Henry Cotton, Anne Coughlin, Arletta Dimberg, Debra P. Douglas, Patricia Edwards, Janet Elenbogen, Mick Fedullo, Michele

Fomalont, Mamon Gibson, Jean Haines, Barbara Hayes, Stephen Herzog, Helen Kelley, Brenda King, John King, Elizabeth LaFuze, Diana Lam, Nancy Lambert, Doris Langaster, Richard LaPointe, Lloyd Leverton, Madeline Long, Allen Luster, Joseph McGeehan, Janet McLin, Gloria McPhee, Marcia Mallard, William J. Maloney, Judith Matz, John Morabito, Robert Morrill, Roberta Morse, Karen Nathan, Dawn Nichols, Valeta Paige, Mary Perrin, Joseph Piazza, Jeanne Price, Marilyn Rauth, Judith Raybern, Mary Reese, Richard Rice, Wallace Saval, John Saxon, Jan Schwab, Ted Sharp, Diana Smith, Richard Smith, Trevanian Smith, Carol Stevens, Nancy Summers, Michael Terry, Robert Todd, Elois Veltman, Sharon Walker, Mary Ann Ward, Charles Whiten, Penny Williams, Clarke Worthington, Jane York

Schools: Special thanks to Three Oaks Elementary for piloting the original *Core Knowledge Sequence* in 1990. And thanks to the schools that have offered their advice and suggestions for improving the *Core Knowledge Sequence,* including (in alphabetical order): Academy Charter School (CO); Coleman Elementary (TX); Coral Reef Elementary (FL); Coronado Village Elementary (TX); Crooksville Elementary (OH); Crossroads Academy (NH); Gesher Jewish Day School (VA); Hawthorne Elementary (TX); Highland Heights Elementary (IN); Joella Good Elementary (FL); Mohegan School-CS 67 (NY); The Morse School (MA); Nichols Hills Elementary (OK); North East Elementary (MD); Ridge View Elementary (WA); R. N. Harris Elementary (NC); Southside Elementary (FL); Thomas Johnson Elementary (MD); Vienna Elementary (MD); Washington Core Knowledge School (CO). And to the many other schools teaching Core Knowledge—too many to name here, and some of whom we have yet to discover—our heartfelt thanks for "sharing the knowledge"!

Benefactors: The Brown Foundation, The Challenge Foundation, Mrs. E. D. Hirsch, Sr., The Walton Family Foundation

Our grateful acknowledgment to these persons does not imply that we have taken their (sometimes conflicting) advice in every case, or that each of them endorses all aspects of this project. Responsibility for final decisions rests with the editors alone. Suggestions for improvements are always welcome. We thank in advance those who send advice for revising and improving this series.

A Note to Teachers

Throughout, we have addressed explanations and suggested activities to "parents," but we consider teachers an important part of the audience for this book as well. We hope you will find it useful in your work with children, whether or not you teach in the growing network of Core Knowledge schools.

If you are interested in learning more about the work and ideas of teachers in Core Knowledge schools, please contact the Core Knowledge Foundation for more information: 801 East High Street, Charlottesville, VA 22902; 434-977-7550; or by e-mail: coreknow@coreknowledge.org. You will find lessons created by teachers in the Core Knowledge schools and other supporting materials developed by the foundation on our Web site: www.coreknowledge.org.

This book is dedicated to
Lucy Alexander Hirsch
Born March 20, 2000

Contents

I. Language and Literature

II. Geography and History

III. Visual Arts

IV. Music

V. Mathematics

VI. Science

Introduction
to the Revised Edition

This is a revision of the first edition of *What Your Third Grader Needs to Know*, first published in 1992. Almost nothing in that earlier book, which elicited wide praise and warm expressions of gratitude from teachers and parents, has become outdated. Why, then, revise the earlier book at all?

Because good things can be made better. In the intervening years since 1992, we at the Core Knowledge Foundation have had the benefit of a great deal of practical experience that can improve the contributions these Core Knowledge books can make to early education. We have learned from an ever-growing network of Core Knowledge schools. At this writing, we can build on the experiences of hundreds of schools across the nation that are following the Core Knowledge curriculum guidelines. We have also received many suggestions from parents who are using the books. And besides conducting our own research, we have continued to seek advice from subject-matter experts and multicultural advisors. All these activities have enabled us to field-test and refine the original *Core Knowledge Sequence*—the curriculum guidelines on which the Core Knowledge books are based.

What kind of knowledge and skills can your child be expected to learn at school in third grade? How can you help your child at home? These are questions we try to answer in this book. It presents a range of knowledge and skills—in literature, reading and writing, history and geography, visual arts, music, mathematics, and science—that should be at the core of an enriching, challenging third-grade education.

Because children and localities differ greatly across this big, diverse country, so do third-grade classrooms. But all communities, including classrooms, require some common ground for communication and learning. In this book, we present the specific shared knowledge that hundreds of parents and teachers across the nation have agreed upon for American third graders. This core is not a comprehensive prescription for everything that every third grader needs to know. Such a complete prescription would be rigid and undesirable. But the book does offer a solid common ground—about 50 percent of the curriculum—that will enable young students to become active, successful learners in their classroom community and later in the larger world we live in.

In this revised edition, we have retold some stories in more detail than before and placed a more engaging emphasis on the story in history. We have also included many color reproductions in the Visual Arts section. These improvements reflect contributions from many hands and minds. Our gratitude to all these advisors and contributors is great indeed.

A special acknowledgment is owed to the original director of the revision project, John

Holdren. He oversaw the research and consensus-building that led to the changes made in the underlying *Core Knowledge Sequence*. He sought and found excellent contributors to this revised edition. He devised ways to overcome what I and others had felt to be a shortcoming in the stories of the earlier edition—their too-great brevity and lack of narrative tension. He edited the contributions of our various writers and wrote considerable portions of the book. For all of these improvements, I owe a large debt of thanks to John Holdren. As is customary with a chief editor, however, I accept responsibility for any defects that may still be found, and I invite readers to send criticisms and suggestions to the Core Knowledge Foundation.

We hope you and your child will enjoy this book, and that it will help lay the foundations upon which to build a lifetime of learning.

E. D. Hirsch, Jr.

General Introduction
to the Core Knowledge Series

I. WHAT IS YOUR CHILD LEARNING IN SCHOOL?

A parent of identical twins sent me a letter in which she expressed concern that her children, who are in the same grade in the same school, are being taught completely different things. How can this be? Because they are in different classrooms; because the teachers in these classrooms have only the vaguest guidelines to follow; in short, because the school, like many in the United States, lacks a definite, specific curriculum.

Many parents would be surprised if they were to examine the curriculum of their child's elementary school. Ask to see your school's curriculum. Does it spell out, in clear and concrete terms, a core of specific content and skills all children at a particular grade level are expected to learn by the end of the school year?

Many curricula speak in general terms of vaguely defined skills, processes, and attitudes, often in an abstract, pseudotechnical language that calls, for example, for children to "analyze patterns and data," or "investigate the structure and dynamics of living systems," or "work cooperatively in a group." Such vagueness evades the central question: what is your child learning in school? It places unreasonable demands upon teachers and often results in years of schooling marred by repetitions and gaps. Yet another unit on dinosaurs or "pioneer days." *Charlotte's Web* for the third time. "You've never heard of the Bill of Rights?" "You've never been taught how to add two fractions with unlike denominators?"

When identical twins in two different classrooms in the same school have few academic experiences in common, that is cause for concern. When teachers in that school do not know what children in other classrooms are learning on the same grade level, much less in earlier and later grades, they cannot reliably predict that children will come prepared with a shared core of knowledge and skills. For an elementary school to be successful, teachers need a common vision of what they want their students to know and be able to do. They need to have *clear, specific learning goals*, as well as the sense of mutual accountability that comes from shared commitment to helping all children achieve those goals. Lacking both specific goals and mutual accountability, too many schools exist in a state of curricular incoherence, one result of which is that they fall far short of developing the full potential of our children.

To address this problem, I started the nonprofit Core Knowledge Foundation in 1986. This book and its companion volumes in the Core Knowledge Series are designed to give parents, teachers, and, through them, children a guide to clearly defined learning goals in the form of a carefully sequenced body of knowledge, based upon the specific content guidelines developed by the Core Knowledge Foundation (see below, "The Consensus Behind the *Core Knowledge Sequence*").

Core Knowledge is an attempt to define, in a coherent and sequential way, a body of widely used knowledge taken for granted by competent writers and speakers in the United States. Because this knowledge is taken for granted rather than being explained when it is used, it forms a necessary foundation for the higher-order reading, writing, and thinking skills that children need for academic and vocational success. The universal attainment of such knowledge should be a central aim of curricula in our elementary schools, just as it is currently the aim in all world-class educational systems.

For reasons explained in the next section, making sure that all young children in the United States possess a core of shared knowledge is a necessary step in developing a first-rate educational system.

II. WHY CORE KNOWLEDGE IS NEEDED

Learning builds on learning: children (and adults) gain new knowledge only by building on what they already know. It is essential to begin building solid foundations of knowledge in the early grades when children are most receptive because, for the vast majority of children, academic deficiencies from the first six grades can *permanently* impair the success of later learning. Poor performance of American students in middle and high schools can be traced to shortcomings inherited from elementary schools that have not imparted to children the knowledge and skills they need for further learning.

All of the highest-achieving and most egalitarian elementary school systems in the world (such as those in Sweden, France, and Japan) teach their children a specific core of knowledge in each of the first six grades, thus enabling all children to enter each new grade with a secure foundation for further learning. It is time American schools did so as well, for the following reasons.

(1) Commonly shared knowledge makes schooling more effective.

We know that the one-on-one tutorial is the most effective form of schooling, in part because a parent or teacher can provide tailor-made instruction for the individual child. But in a nontutorial situation—in, for example, a typical classroom with twenty-five or more students—the instructor cannot effectively impart new knowledge to all the students unless each one shares the background knowledge that the lesson is being built upon.

Consider this scenario: In third grade, Ms. Franklin is about to begin a unit on early explorers: Columbus, Magellan, and others. In her class, she has some students who were in Mr. Washington's second-grade class last year and some students who were in Ms. Johnson's second-grade class. She also has a few students who have moved from other towns. As Ms. Franklin begins the unit on explorers, she asks the children to look at a globe and use their fingers to trace a route across the Atlantic Ocean from Europe to North America. The students who had Mr. Washington look blankly at her: they didn't learn that last year. The students who had Ms. Johnson, however, eagerly point to the proper places on the globe. And two of the students who came from other towns pipe up and say, "Columbus and Magellan again? We did that last year."

When all the students in a class *do* share the relevant background knowledge, a classroom can begin to approach the effectiveness of a tutorial. Even when some children in a class do not have elements of the knowledge they were supposed to acquire in previous grades, the existence of a specifically defined core makes it possible for the teacher or parent to identify and fill the gaps, thus giving all students a chance to fulfill their potential in later grades.

(2) Commonly shared knowledge makes schooling more fair and democratic.

When all the children who enter a grade can be assumed to share some of the same building blocks of knowledge, and when the teacher knows exactly what those building blocks are, then all the students are empowered to learn. In our current system, children from disadvantaged backgrounds too often suffer from unmerited low expectations that translate into watered-down curricula. But if we specify the core of knowledge that all children should share, then we can guarantee equal access to that knowledge and compensate for the academic advantages some students are offered at home. In a Core Knowledge school, *all* children enjoy the benefits of important, challenging knowledge that will provide the foundation for successful later learning.

(3) Commonly shared knowledge helps create cooperation and solidarity in our schools and nation.

Diversity is a hallmark and strength of our nation. American classrooms are often, and increasingly, made up of students from a variety of cultural backgrounds, and those different cultures should be honored by all students. At the same time, education should create a *school-based* culture that is common and welcoming to all because it includes knowledge of many cultures and gives all students, no matter what their background, a common foundation for understanding our cultural diversity.

III. The Consensus Behind the Core Knowledge Sequence

The content in this and other volumes in the Core Knowledge Series is based on a document called the *Core Knowledge Sequence*, grade-by-grade guidelines of specific content in history, geography, mathematics, science, language arts, and fine arts. The *Sequence* is not meant to outline the whole of the school curriculum; rather, it offers specific guidelines to knowledge that can reasonably be expected to make up about *half* of any school's curriculum, thus leaving ample room for local requirements and emphases. Teaching a common core of knowledge, such as that articulated in the *Core Knowledge*

Sequence, is compatible with a variety of instructional methods and additional subject matters.

The *Core Knowledge Sequence* is the result of a long process of research and consensus-building undertaken by the Core Knowledge Foundation. Here is how we achieved the consensus behind the *Core Knowledge Sequence*.

First we analyzed the many reports issued by state departments of education and by professional organizations—such as the National Council of Teachers of Mathematics and the American Association for the Advancement of Science—that recommend general outcomes for elementary and secondary education. We also tabulated the knowledge and skills through grade six specified in the successful educational systems of several other countries, including France, Japan, Sweden, and West Germany.

In addition, we formed an advisory board on multiculturalism that proposed a specific knowledge of diverse cultural traditions that American children should all share as part of their school-based common culture. We sent the resulting materials to three independent groups of teachers, scholars, and scientists around the country, asking them to create a master list of the knowledge children should have by the end of grade six. About 150 teachers (including college professors, scientists, and administrators) were involved in this initial step.

These items were amalgamated into a master plan, and further groups of teachers and specialists were asked to agree on a grade-by-grade sequence of the items. That sequence was then sent to some one hundred educators and specialists, who participated in a national conference that was called to hammer out a working agreement on an appropriate core of knowledge for the first six grades.

This important meeting took place in March 1990. The conferees were elementary school teachers, curriculum specialists, scientists, science writers, officers of national organizations, representatives of ethnic groups, district superintendents, and school principals from across the country. A total of twenty-four working groups decided on revisions in the *Core Knowledge Sequence*. The resulting provisional *Sequence* was further fine-tuned during a year of implementation at a pioneering school, Three Oaks Elementary in Lee County, Florida.

In only a few years, many more schools—urban and rural, rich and poor, public and private—joined in the effort to teach Core Knowledge. Based largely on suggestions from these schools, the *Core Knowledge Sequence* has been significantly revised: it was extended to seventh and eighth grades; separate guidelines were added for kindergarten; and a few topics in other grades were added, omitted, or moved from one grade to another, in order to create an even more coherent sequence for learning. A *Core Knowledge Preschool Sequence* was first published in 1997.

The Core Knowledge Foundation continues to work with schools and advisors to fine-tune the *Sequence*. The revised editions of this and other books in the Core Knowledge Series reflect the revisions in the *Sequence*. Current editions of the *Core Knowledge Se-*

quence and the *Core Knowledge Preschool Sequence* may be ordered from the Core Knowledge Foundation; see the end of this Introduction for the address.

IV. THE NATURE OF THIS SERIES

The books in this series are designed to give a convenient and engaging introduction to the knowledge specified in the *Core Knowledge Sequence*. These are resource books, addressed primarily to parents, but which we hope will be useful tools for both parents and teachers. These books are not intended to replace the local curriculum or school textbooks, but rather to serve as aids to help children gain some of the important knowledge they will need to make progress in school and be effective in society.

Although we have made these books as accessible and useful as we can, parents and teachers should understand that they are not the only means by which the *Core Knowledge Sequence* can be imparted. The books represent a single version of the possibilities inherent in the *Sequence*, and a first step in the Core Knowledge reform effort. We hope that publishers will be stimulated to offer educational videos, computer software, games, alternative books, and other imaginative vehicles based on the *Core Knowledge Sequence*.

These books are not textbooks or workbooks, though they do suggest a variety of activities you can do with your child. In these books, we address your child directly, and occasionally ask questions to think about. The earliest books in the series are intended to be read aloud to children. Even as children become able to read the books on their own, we encourage parents to help their children read more actively by reading along with them and talking about what they are reading.

You and your child can read the sections of this book in any order, depending on your child's interests or depending on the topics your child is studying in school, which this book may sometimes complement or reinforce. You can skip from section to section and reread as much as your child likes.

We encourage you to think of this book as a guidebook that opens the way to many paths you and your child can explore. These paths may lead to the library, to many other good books, and, if possible, to plays, museums, concerts, and other opportunities for knowledge and enrichment. In short, this guidebook recommends places to visit and describes what is important in those places, but only you and your child can make the actual visit, travel the streets, and climb the steps.

V. WHAT YOU CAN DO TO HELP IMPROVE AMERICAN EDUCATION

The first step for parents and teachers who are committed to reform is to be skeptical about oversimplified slogans like "critical thinking" and "learning to learn." Such slogans are everywhere and, unfortunately for our schools, their partial insights have been elevated to the level of universal truths. For example: "What students learn is not important; rather, we must teach students to learn *how* to learn." "The child, not the academic subject, is the true focus of education." "Do not impose knowledge on children before they are developmentally ready to receive it." "Do not bog children down in mere facts, but rather, teach critical-thinking skills."

Who has not heard these sentiments, so admirable and humane, and—up to a point—so true? But these positive sentiments in favor of "thinking skills" and "higher understanding" have been turned into negative sentiments against the teaching of important knowledge. Those who have entered the teaching profession over the past forty years have been taught to scorn important knowledge as "mere facts" and to see the imparting of this knowledge as somehow injurious to children. Thus it has come about that many educators, armed with partially true slogans, have seemingly taken leave of common sense.

Many parents and teachers have come to the conclusion that elementary education must strike a better balance between the development of the whole child and the more limited but fundamental duty of the school to ensure that all children master a core of knowledge and skills essential to their competence as learners in later grades. But these parents and teachers cannot act on their convictions without an agreed-upon, concrete sequence of knowledge. Our main motivation in developing the *Core Knowledge Sequence* and this book series has been to give parents and teachers something concrete to work with.

It has been encouraging to see how many teachers, since the first volume in this series was published, have responded to the Core Knowledge reform effort. If you would like more information about the growing network of Core Knowledge schools, please contact the Core Knowledge Foundation at the address listed below.

Parents and teachers are urged to join in a grassroots effort to strengthen our elementary schools. Start in your own school and district. Insist that your school clearly state the core of *specific* knowledge and skills that each child in a grade must learn. Whether your school's core corresponds exactly to the Core Knowledge model is less important than the existence of *some* core—which, we hope, will be as solid, coherent, and challenging as the *Core Knowledge Sequence* has proved to be. Inform members of your community about the need for such a specific curriculum, and help make sure that your local school board members are independent-minded people who will insist that children have the benefit of a solid, specific, world-class curriculum in each grade.

Share the knowledge!

E. D. Hirsch, Jr.
Core Knowledge Foundation
801 East High Street
Charlottesville, VA 22902
coreknow@coreknowledge.org
www.coreknowledge.org

What Your Third Grader Needs to Know

FUNDAMENTALS OF A GOOD THIRD-GRADE EDUCATION

I.

Language
and
Literature

Reading, Writing, and Your Third Grader

The best way to nurture your child's reading and writing abilities is to provide rich literary experiences and find frequent and varied opportunities to work and play with language.

By the end of second grade, children have developed a reading vocabulary of familiar words and can decode the letter-sound patterns of many unfamiliar one- and two-syllable words. During third grade, as they increase their knowledge about words (including the concepts of syllables, prefixes, and suffixes), they put that knowledge to work, decoding unfamiliar multisyllabic words. If a child has not mastered the skill of decoding simple words, that practice should continue.

By third grade, the mental process of turning letters into sounds should be nearly automatic. This year, children focus more on meaning as they read. Their reading vocabulary expands tremendously, as does their ability to read longer and more complex literature. They read for information and begin to use nonfiction reference books like children's dictionaries and encyclopedias. They learn the distinction between fiction and nonfiction, and they read and enjoy longer and more complicated "chapter books."

In third grade, children continue to learn about language as they write it: identifying parts of speech, properly using punctuation, and recognizing sentence types. They begin to shape their own writing, understanding how paragraphs relate in a larger whole and exerting more control over vocabulary and structure.

Parents can do many things to help their children reach these new levels of understanding language:

Read aloud to your child. While third graders are beginning to read on their own, they also still enjoy listening. Continue reading aloud, both fiction and nonfiction, even as your child becomes an independent reader.

Have your child read aloud to you.

Visit the library with your child.

Encourage your child to write letters or keep a journal.

Play word games with your child. Scrabble, Hangman, Boggle, and other popular games that involve spelling, word recognition, and vocabulary development combine fun with language facility.

Find language wherever you go. Use road signs, advertising, magazines—the written word all around you—to keep your child thinking and talking about language.

Support your child's interests through reading. When your child shows an interest in something special—insects or baseball, Davy Crockett or ballet—go together to the library to find more to read on that subject.

The more a child reads and writes, the more fluent in language that child becomes. By using these strategies, you communicate the enjoyment of reading and writing and you help build the foundation for learning that will last a lifetime.

Suggested Resources

The American Heritage First Dictionary (Houghton Mifflin). Simple words, clear definitions, and ample visuals provide a helpful introduction to how a dictionary works.

E. D. Hirsch, Jr., *A First Dictionary of Cultural Literacy* (Houghton Mifflin). Some entries may be difficult for a third grader, but this book can serve as a single-volume encyclopedia of American culture.

Macmillan Dictionary for Children (Simon & Schuster). This dictionary offers 35,000 expanded entries with easy-to-read pronunciations, synonym lists, and color illustrations.

The World Book Student Discovery Encyclopedia (World Book Inc.). This multivolume reference is structured like a standard encyclopedia but designed and written so third graders can look things up and read entries easily.

Educators Publishing Service (EPS) is a mail-order company with good teacher-created resources including basic phonics, spelling, vocabulary development, reading comprehension, grammar, and composition skills. Write to EPS, 31 Smith Place, Cambridge, MA 02138-1089, call 800-435-7728, or visit www.epsbooks.com.

Literature

INTRODUCTION

This selection of poetry, stories, and myths can be read aloud or, in many cases, read independently by third graders. We hope you'll take it as a starting point in your search for more literature for your child to read and enjoy.

We have included both traditional and modern poetry. Poems can be silly, written for the sheer enjoyment of rhythm and rhyme, or they can be serious. Rhythm and rhyme make poetry the perfect literature for a third grader to memorize.

The stories selected here include classic folktales from many cultures and excerpts from great works of children's literature. Some of them have been chosen as literary links to topics elsewhere in the book. In the case of book-length works, we can provide only short excerpts, hoping that you and your child will read the rest on your own.

This book continues the effort, begun in previous books, to share the wealth of classical mythology. Since third graders learn about ancient Rome, several myths were chosen to convey a sense of Roman history. Likewise we offer some Norse mythology. Parents can coordinate readings about literature and history. Age-old myths also give parents the opportunity to discuss traditional virtues such as friendship, courage, and honesty.

Suggested Resources

For a frequently updated list of recommended children's books thematically linked to the subjects offered in this book and others in the Core Knowledge Series, consult *Resources to Build On* on the Core Knowledge Foundation Web site, at www.coreknowledge.org.

Favorite Poems Old and New, selected by Helen Ferris (Doubleday). One volume with more than seven hundred poems, including many perennial favorites.

William F. Russell, *Classic Myths to Read Aloud* (Crown Publishers). This book retells Greek and Roman myths in language with a suitably old-fashioned feel.

Spider, Cricket, and *Muse*. Colorful magazines, with intelligent material, that give children plenty of good monthly reading experiences with no advertising. *Spider*, for children aged six to nine, and *Cricket*, for children aged nine to fourteen, include stories, activities, and puzzles. *Muse*, sponsored by the Smithsonian Institution, offers science articles for children aged eight to fourteen. To subscribe to any of these, write the Cricket Magazine Group, Box 7499, Red Oak, IA 51591, call (800) 827-0227, or visit www.cricketmag.com.

Poetry

Adventures of Isabel
by Ogden Nash

Isabel met an enormous bear,
Isabel, Isabel didn't care;
The bear was hungry, the bear was ravenous,
The bear's big mouth was cruel and cavernous.
The bear said, Isabel, glad to meet you,
How do, Isabel, now I'll eat you!
Isabel, Isabel, didn't worry,
Isabel didn't scream or scurry.
She washed her hands and she straightened her hair up,
Then Isabel quietly ate the bear up.

Once in a night as black as pitch
Isabel met a wicked old witch.
The witch's face was cross and wrinkled,
The witch's gums with teeth were sprinkled.
Ho, ho, Isabel! the old witch crowed,
I'll turn you into an ugly toad!
Isabel, Isabel, didn't worry,
Isabel didn't scream or scurry,
She showed no rage and she showed no rancor,
But she turned the witch into milk and drank her.

Isabel met a hideous giant,
Isabel continued self-reliant.
The giant was hairy, the giant was horrid,
He had one eye in the middle of his forehead.
Good morning, Isabel, the giant said,
I'll grind your bones to make my bread.
Isabel, Isabel, didn't worry,
Isabel didn't scream or scurry,
She nibbled the Zwieback she always fed off,
And when it was gone, she cut the giant's head off.

Isabel met a troublesome doctor,
He punched and he poked till he really shocked her.
The doctor's talk was of coughs and chills
And the doctor's satchel bulged with pills.
The doctor said unto Isabel,
Swallow this, it will make you well.
Isabel, Isabel, didn't worry,
Isabel didn't scream or scurry.
She took those pills from the pill concocter,
And Isabel calmly cured the doctor.

By Myself
by Eloise Greenfield

When I'm by myself
And I close my eyes
I'm a twin
I'm a dimple in a chin
I'm a room full of toys
I'm a squeaky noise
I'm a gospel song
I'm a gong
I'm a leaf turning red
I'm a loaf of brown bread
I'm a whatever I want to be
An anything I care to be
And when I open my eyes
What I care to be
Is me

Catch a Little Rhyme
by Eve Merriam

Once upon a time
I caught a little rhyme

I set it on the floor
but it ran right out the door

I chased it on my bicycle
but it melted to an icicle

I scooped it up in my hat
but it turned into a cat

I caught it by the tail
but it stretched into a whale

I followed it in a boat
but it changed into a goat

When I fed it tin and paper
it became a tall skyscraper

Then it grew into a kite
and flew far out of sight . . .

Dream Variations
by Langston Hughes

To fling my arms wide
In some place of the sun,
To whirl and to dance
Till the white day is done.
Then rest at cool evening
Beneath a tall tree
While night comes on gently,
   Dark like me—
That is my dream!

To fling my arms wide
In the face of the sun,
Dance! Whirl! Whirl!
Till the quick day is done.
Rest at pale evening . . .
A tall, slim tree . . .
Night coming tenderly
   Black like me.

Knoxville, Tennessee
by Nikki Giovanni

I always like summer
best
you can eat fresh corn
from daddy's garden
and okra
and greens
and cabbage
and lots of
barbecue
and buttermilk
and homemade ice-cream
at the church picnic
and listen to
gospel music
outside
at the church
homecoming
and go to the mountains with
your grandmother
and go barefooted
and be warm
all the time
not only when you go to bed
and sleep

The Crocodile
by Lewis Carroll

How doth the little crocodile
   Improve his shining tail,
And pour the waters of the Nile
   On every golden scale!

How cheerfully he seems to grin!
   How neatly spreads his claws,
And welcomes little fishes in
   With gently smiling jaws!

Lewis Carroll borrowed the rhythm and rhyme for "The Crocodile" from a serious poem written by Isaac Watts, called "Against Idleness and Mischief," which began like this:

How doth the little busy bee
   Improve each shining hour,
And gather honey all the day,
   From every opening flower!

How skillfully she builds her cell!
   How neat she spreads the wax!
And labours hard to store it well
   With the sweet food she makes.

When you compare the two poems, you see that Carroll was up to some mischief himself!

Trees
by Sergeant Joyce Kilmer

I think that I shall never see
A poem lovely as a tree.

A tree whose hungry mouth is pressed
Against the earth's sweet flowing breast;

A tree that looks at God all day,
And lifts her leafy arms to pray;

A tree that may in summer wear
A nest of robins in her hair;

Upon whose bosom snow has lain,
Who intimately lives with rain.

Poems are made by fools like me,
But only God can make a tree.

For Want of a Nail
(traditional Mother Goose rhyme) .

For want of a nail, the shoe was lost,
For want of the shoe, the horse was lost,
For want of a horse, the rider was lost,
For want of a rider, the battle was lost,
For want of the battle, the kingdom was lost,
And all for the want of a horseshoe nail.

Jimmy Jet and His TV Set
by Shel Silverstein

I'll tell you the story of Jimmy Jet—
And you know what I tell you is true.
He loved to watch his TV set
Almost as much as you.

He watched all day, he watched all night
Till he grew pale and lean,
From "The Early Show" to "The Late Late Show"
And all the shows between.

He watched till his eyes were frozen wide,
And his bottom grew into his chair.
And his chin turned into a tuning dial,
And antennae grew out of his hair.

And his brains turned into TV tubes,
And his face to a TV screen.
And two knobs saying "VERT." and "HORIZ."
Grew where his ears had been.

And he grew a plug that looked like a tail
So we plugged in little Jim.
And now instead of him watching TV
We all sit around and watch him.

First Thanksgiving of All

by Nancy Byrd Turner

Peace and Mercy and Jonathan,
And Patience (very small),
Stood by the table giving thanks
The first Thanksgiving of all.
There was very little for them to
eat,
Nothing special and nothing
sweet;
Only bread and a little broth,
And a bit of fruit (and no
tablecloth);
But Peace and Mercy and
Jonathan
And Patience, in a row,
Stood up and asked a blessing on
Thanksgiving, long ago.

Thankful they were their ship had
come
Safely across the sea;
Thankful they were for hearth and
home,
And kin and company;
They were glad of broth to go with
their bread,
Glad their apples were round and
red,
Glad of mayflowers they would bring
Out of the woods again next spring.
So Peace and Mercy and Jonathan,
And Patience (very small),
Stood up gratefully giving thanks
The first Thanksgiving of all.

Eletelephony
by Laura Richards

Once there was an elephant,
Who tried to use the telephant—
No! No! I mean an elephone
Who tried to use the telephone—
(Dear me! I am not certain quite
That even now I've got it right.)

Howe'er it was, he got his trunk
Entangled in the telephunk;
The more he tried to get it free,
The louder buzzed the telephee—
(I fear I'd better drop the song
Of elephop and telephong!)

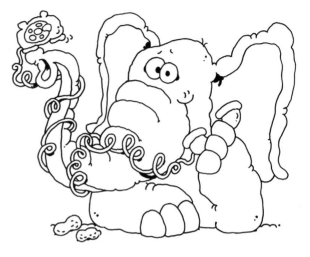

Father William
by Lewis Carroll

"You are old, Father William," the young man said,
"And your hair has become very white;
And yet you incessantly stand on your head—
Do you think, at your age, it is right?"

"In my youth," Father William replied to his son,
"I feared it might injure the brain;
But now that I'm perfectly sure I have none,
Why, I do it again and again."

"You are old," said the youth, "as I mentioned before,
And have grown most uncommonly fat;

Yet you turned a back somersault in at the door—
    Pray, what is the reason of that?"

"In my youth," said the sage, as he shook his gray locks,
    "I kept all my limbs very supple
By the use of this ointment—one shilling the box—
    Allow me to sell you a couple?"

"You are old," said the youth, "and your jaws are too weak
    For anything tougher than suet;
Yet you finished the goose, with the bones and the beak—
    Pray how did you manage to do it?"

"In my youth," said his father, "I took to the law,
    And argued each case with my wife;
And the muscular strength which it gave to my jaw
    Has lasted the rest of my life."

"You are old," said the youth, "one
        would hardly suppose
    That your eye was as steady as ever;
Yet you balanced an eel on the end
        of your nose—
    What made you so awfully clever?"

"I have answered three questions, and that is enough,"
    Said his father. "Don't give yourself airs!
Do you think I can listen all day to such stuff?
    Be off, or I'll kick you downstairs!"

Stories

Alice's Adventures in Wonderland
(adapted from Lewis Carroll's original)

In 1865, the English author Lewis Carroll—whose real name was Charles Dodgson—intro-duced the world to a girl named Alice and the strange and funny world of Wonderland. Alice's Adventures in Wonderland was so popular that Carroll wrote another book, called Through the Looking-Glass and What Alice Found There.

Alice was beginning to get very tired of sitting by her sister on the bank and of hav-ing nothing to do: once or twice she had peeped into the book her sister was reading, but it had no pictures or conversations in it, "and what is the use of a book," thought Alice, "without pictures or conversations?"

So she was considering, in her own mind (as well as she could, for the hot day made her feel very sleepy and stupid), whether the pleasure of making a daisy-chain would be worth the trouble of get-ting up and picking the daisies, when suddenly a White Rabbit with pink eyes ran close by her.

There was nothing so *very* remarkable in that; nor did Alice think it so *very* much out of the way to hear the Rabbit say to itself, "Oh dear! Oh dear! I shall be too late!" But when the Rabbit actually *took a watch out of its waistcoat-pocket*, and looked at it, and then hurried on, Alice started to her feet, and burning with curiosity, she ran across the field af-ter it, and was just in time to see it pop down a large rabbit-hole under the hedge.

The White Rabbit.

In another moment down went Alice after it, never once considering how in the world she was to get out again.

The rabbit-hole dipped suddenly down, so suddenly that Alice found herself falling down what seemed to be a very deep well.

Either the well was very deep, or she fell very slowly, for she had plenty of time as she went down to look about her, and to wonder what was going to happen next. She looked at the sides of the well, and noticed that they were filled with cupboards and bookshelves.

"Well!" thought Alice to herself. "After such a fall as this, I shall think nothing of tum-bling down stairs!"

Down, down, down. Would the fall *never* come to an end? "I wonder how many miles I've fallen by this time?" she said aloud. "I must be getting somewhere near the center of the earth. Let me see: that would be four thousand miles down, I think. I wonder if I shall fall right *through* the earth! How funny it'll seem to come out among the people that walk with their heads downwards! I shall have to ask them what the name of the country is. Please, Ma'am, is this New Zealand? Or Australia?"

She felt that she was dozing off when suddenly, thump! thump! down she came upon a heap of sticks and dry leaves.

Alice was not a bit hurt. She looked up: before her was another long passage, and the White Rabbit was hurrying down it. Away Alice went like the wind, and was just in time to hear the Rabbit say, as it turned a corner, "Oh my ears and whiskers, how late it's getting!" She was close behind it when she turned the corner, but the Rabbit was no longer to be seen. She found herself in a long, low hall.

There were doors all around the hall, but they were all locked. Alice sadly wondered how she was ever to get out again. Suddenly she came upon a little three-legged table, all made of solid glass; there was nothing on it but a tiny golden key. But alas! It would not open any of the doors. However, Alice then came upon a low curtain she had not noticed before, and behind it was a little door about fifteen inches high. She tried the little golden key in the lock, and it fitted!

The door led into a small passage, not much larger than a rat-hole. Alice knelt down and looked along the passage into the loveliest garden you ever saw. How she longed to get out of that dark hall, and wander about among those beds of bright flowers and those cool fountains, but she could not even get her head through the doorway.

There seemed to be no use in waiting by the little door, so she went back to the table. This time she found a little bottle on it ("which certainly was not here before," said Alice), and tied round the neck of the bottle was a paper label with the words "DRINK ME" printed in large letters.

It was all very well to say "Drink me," but the wise little Alice was not going to do *that* in a hurry: "No, I'll look first," she said, "and see whether it's marked '*poison*,' or not." However, this bottle was *not* marked "poison," so Alice ventured to taste it, and finding it very nice (it had, in fact, a sort of mixed flavor of cherry-tart, custard, pineapple, roast turkey, toffee, and hot buttered toast), she very soon finished it off.

"What a curious feeling!" said Alice, who was shutting up like a telescope. She was now only ten inches high, the right size for going through the little door into that lovely garden. But alas for poor Alice! When she got to the door, she found she had forgotten the little golden key, and when she went back to the table for it, she found she could not possibly reach it. The poor little thing sat down and cried, but soon her eye fell on a little glass box that was under the table: she opened it, and found in it a very small cake, on which the words "EAT ME" were beautifully marked in currants. "Well, I'll eat it," said Alice, and very soon finished off the cake.

"Curiouser and curiouser!" cried Alice (for she was so much surprised that she quite forgot how to speak good English). "Now I'm opening out like the largest telescope that ever was! Good-bye feet!" Her head struck against the roof of the hall: in fact she was now rather more than nine feet high, and she at once took up the little golden key and hurried to the garden door.

Poor Alice! It was as much as she could do, lying down on one side, to look through into the garden with one eye; but to get through was more hopeless than ever: she sat down and began to cry again. She went on, shedding gallons of tears, until there was a large pool around her, about four inches deep and reaching half down the hall.

After a time she heard a pattering of feet in the distance, and she hastily dried her eyes to see what was coming. It was the White Rabbit returning, splendidly dressed, with a pair of white kid gloves in one hand and a large fan in the other. He was muttering to himself, "Oh! The Duchess! Oh! *Won't* she be a savage if I've kept her waiting!"

Alice felt so desperate that she was ready to ask help of any one; so when the Rabbit came near her, she began, in a low, timid voice, "If you please, sir—" The Rabbit started violently, dropped the white kid gloves and the fan, and scurried away into the darkness as fast as he could go.

"Dear, dear!" said Alice. "How queer everything is today!" As she said this, she looked down at her hands, and was surprised to see that she had put on one of the Rabbit's little white kid gloves. "How *can* I have done that?" she thought. "I must be growing small again." She was shrinking rapidly, and in another moment, splash! She was up to her chin in salt water. She was in the pool of tears which she had wept when she was nine feet high.

Alice soon makes her way to dry ground and once again encounters the White Rabbit. But the Rabbit eludes her, leaving Alice—who has shrunk again—to wander until she comes upon a caterpillar, sitting upon a mushroom and smoking a kind of pipe called a hookah.

Alice stretched herself up on tiptoe and peeped over the edge of the mushroom, and her eyes immediately met those of a large blue caterpillar. The Caterpillar and Alice looked at each other for some time in silence. At last the Caterpillar took the hookah out of its mouth, and addressed her in a languid, sleepy voice.

The Caterpillar and Alice.

"Who are *you*?" said the Caterpillar.

Alice replied, rather shyly, "I—I hardly know, sir, just at present—at least I know who I *was* when I got up this morning, but I think I must have been changed several times since then."

"What do you mean by that?" said the Caterpillar sternly. "Explain yourself!"

"I can't explain *myself*, I'm afraid, sir," said Alice, "because I'm not myself, you see."

"I don't see," said the Caterpillar.

"I'm afraid I can't put it more clearly," Alice replied, "for being so many different sizes in one day is very confusing."

"It isn't," said the Caterpillar.

Alice felt a little irritated at the Caterpillar's making such *very* short remarks. As the Caterpillar seemed to be in a *very* unpleasant state of mind, she turned away.

"Come back!" the Caterpillar called after her. "I've something important to say!"

This sounded promising, so Alice turned and came back again.

"Keep your temper," said the Caterpillar.

"Is that all?" said Alice, swallowing down her anger as well as she could.

"Are you content now?" said the Caterpillar.

"Well, I should like to be a *little* larger, sir, if you wouldn't mind," said Alice: "three inches is such a wretched height to be."

"It is a very good height indeed!" said the Caterpillar, rearing itself up angrily as it spoke (it was exactly three inches high). "You'll get used to it in time," he said, and began smoking again.

In a minute or two the Caterpillar took the hookah out of its mouth, and yawned once or twice, and shook itself. Then it got down off the mushroom and crawled away into the grass, remarking as it went, "One side will make you grow taller, and the other side will make you grow shorter."

"One side of *what*? The other side of *what*?" thought Alice to herself.

"Of the mushroom," said the Caterpillar, just as if she had asked it aloud; and in another moment it was out of sight.

Alice stretched her arms around the mushroom and broke off a bit of the edge with each hand. Very carefully, she nibbled first at one and then at the other, and after some violent rising and shrinking, managed to bring herself back to her usual height.

Alice wandered until she came upon a cat—the Cheshire Cat—sitting on a bough of a tree and grinning from ear to ear.

"Cheshire Puss," she began, rather timidly, "would you tell me, please, which way I ought to walk from here?"

"That depends a good deal on where you want to get to," said the Cat.

"I don't care much where—" said Alice.

"Then it doesn't matter which way you go," said the Cat.

"—so long as I get *somewhere*," Alice added.

"Oh, you're sure to do that," said the Cat, "if you only walk long enough."

Alice tried another question. "What sort of people live about here?"

"In *that* direction," said the Cat, waving its right paw round, "lives a Hatter, and in *that* direction," waving the other paw, "lives a March Hare. Visit either you like: they're both mad."

"But I don't want to go among mad people," Alice remarked.

"Oh, you can't help that," said the Cat. "We're all mad here." Then it vanished slowly, beginning with the end of the tail, and ending with the grin, which remained some time after the rest of it had gone.

"Well! A grin without a cat! It's the most curious thing!" thought Alice.

She had not gone far before she came upon a house, with a table set out under a tree in front of the house. The March Hare and the Mad Hatter were having tea at it; a Dormouse was sitting between them, fast asleep. The table was a large one, but the three were all crowded together at one corner of it. "No room! No room!" they cried out when they saw Alice coming.

"There's *plenty* of room!" said Alice indignantly, and she sat down in a large arm chair at one end of the table.

What a tea party!

"Have some wine," said the March Hare.

Alice looked all round the table. "I don't see any wine," she remarked.

"There isn't any," said the March Hare.

"Then it wasn't very civil of you to offer it," said Alice angrily.

"It wasn't very civil of you to sit down without being invited," said the March Hare.

The Hatter had been looking at Alice for some time and said, "Why is a raven like a writing desk?"

"Riddles! We shall have some fun now!" thought Alice. "I believe I can guess that," she added aloud.

"Do you mean that you think you can find out the answer to it?" said the March Hare.

"Exactly so," said Alice.

"Then you should say what you mean," the March Hare went on.

"I do," Alice replied. "At least—at least I mean what I say—that's the same thing, you know."

"Not the same thing a bit!" said the Hatter. "Why, you might just as well say that 'I see what I eat' is the same thing as 'I eat what I see'!"

"You might just as well say," added the Dormouse, which seemed to be talking in its sleep, "that 'I breathe when I sleep' is the same thing as 'I sleep when I breathe'!"

"It *is* the same thing with you," said the Hatter. Then he turned to Alice again and asked, "Have you guessed the riddle yet?"

"No, I give it up," Alice replied. "What's the answer?"

"I haven't the slightest idea," said the Hatter.

"Nor I," said the March Hare.

"This," thought Alice, "is the stupidest tea-party I ever was at in all my life!"

Alice wanders into many more adventures in Wonderland. She meets a walking, talking deck of cards, ruled by a furious Queen of Hearts, who responds to everyone by shouting, "Off with your head!"—including Alice! You'll enjoy reading about the Queen and Alice in the full book of Alice's Adventures in Wonderland.

Aladdin and the Wonderful Lamp

This story and the next one, "Ali Baba and the Forty Thieves," come from a book called A Thousand and One Nights. It begins with the story of a cruel sultan in Persia who chose a new wife every day and killed her before the next morning. A clever young woman, Scheherazade [shuh-HAIR-uh-zahd], outwitted him. When it came her turn to be the wife of the sultan, she began telling him stories so fascinating that he could not wait to hear the next. By the time she had told him 1001 stories, he had fallen in love with her, and so he spared her life. The Russian composer Rimsky-Korsakov wrote musical pieces about Scheherazade and her stories. You can learn more about them in the music section of this book, on page 195.

There was once an idle, good-for-nothing boy called Aladdin. When his father, the tailor, died, Aladdin's mother took up spinning to earn their living.

One day a stranger approached Aladdin.

"Tell me, my son," said the stranger. "Are you not the son of the tailor?"

Aladdin answered yes, and the stranger threw his arms around him. "My dear nephew!" he cried. "Your father was my brother! And now I learn he is dead!"

Aladdin introduced the man to his mother, who had never in her life heard that her husband had a brother. She received him kindly, though, and when the man promised to set Aladdin up in business as a merchant, she believed him.

But the stranger was really a magician from faraway Africa. He had come to China in search of a magic lamp, known to give all the riches anyone could imagine. To find the

Aladdin was delighted. He rubbed the lamp and commanded the genie to prepare a wedding in princely style. Slaves brought him rich clothes, sweet perfumes, and a splendid horse, which he rode to the wedding. Slaves threw gold pieces into the hands of all the people who lined the streets to see him. He commanded the genie to build a palace right next to the home of the sultan, with kitchens full of golden dishes and stables full of handsome horses. Finally, at Aladdin's request, the genie spread a thick carpet from the sultan's home to Aladdin's palace so his bride's feet would not have to touch the earth.

When the sultan saw such magnificence, he was sure that Aladdin was the right husband for his daughter. They celebrated their wedding with a feast and music that lasted all day and all night. Aladdin thought that his life could not be more perfect.

But danger lurked afar. The magician caught wind of Aladdin's good fortune. "That lazy boy? Surely this must be the magic of the lamp," he said, and he whisked himself back to China. He dressed himself as a poor peddler and carried a few shiny lamps in a basket. As he walked by Aladdin's palace, he shouted, "New lamps for old!"

It just so happened that on that morning, Aladdin had gone out hunting. His wife, the princess, heard the voice from the street. "We have that ugly old lamp," she thought. "I would gladly trade it for a shiny new one." With that, she handed over Aladdin's lamp to the disguised magician.

Immediately, the magician rubbed the lamp and the genie appeared.

"Take Aladdin's palace and all that it contains," commanded the magician. "Set it down in my country of Africa."

"I hear and I obey," said the genie.

The next morning, when the sultan looked out the window, both the palace and his daughter had disappeared. He sent his soldiers out, and they dragged Aladdin before the sultan. "Find my daughter!" he stormed. "If you fail, you die!"

Poor Aladdin wandered far from the city. He walked beside a river and rubbed his hands, wondering what to do. The genie of the ring appeared once more, asking, "What do you wish?"

"Bring my palace and my beloved wife home to me," asked Aladdin.

"Alas," said the genie, "that duty belongs only to the genie of the lamp."

"Then take me to be with my wife."

Instantly, Aladdin found himself in Africa. His wife greeted him joyfully. When Aladdin heard her story, he knew that the magician had used the lamp to work his evil deed. They hit on a plan to get back the lamp.

While Aladdin kept out of sight, the princess treated the magician to a fine supper. Into his cup of wine, she slipped a poison powder. No sooner had the magician swallowed one gulp of wine than he fell on the floor, dead.

Aladdin ran in and discovered the lamp, hidden inside the magician's sleeve. He rubbed it and the monstrous genie appeared. "What do you wish?" the genie thundered.

"Take this building with all it contains," commanded Aladdin, pointing to the palace. "Carry it to China and set it down beside the sultan's home."

"I hear and I obey," replied the genie, and the palace was lifted up into the air.

The next morning, when the sultan arose and looked out the window, he was overjoyed to see his daughter and her palace once again. He ordered a month of celebrations. From then on, Aladdin lived with the princess in peace and pleasure and safety. When the old sultan died, Aladdin took his throne and ruled justly over all people, rich and poor.

Ali Baba and the Forty Thieves

Here is another story told by Scheherazade to the Persian sultan to save her life and collected in A Thousand and One Nights.

Many years ago there lived two brothers in Persia, Cassim and Ali Baba. The elder brother had married the daughter of a rich merchant and lived very well. But Ali Baba had married a poor woman and barely had enough to get by.

One day, as Ali Baba was coming home from cutting wood, a troop of horsemen came riding at full speed toward him. Hiding in the bushes, he watched as the horsemen, who numbered forty, climbed off their horses. Each heaved onto the ground a heavy saddlebag, and Ali Baba began to understand that these were thieves hiding their treasure.

One stood in front of a steep rock. "Open, sesame!" he cried, and a doorway appeared in the rock. The robbers entered and the door shut behind them. Ali Baba waited quietly. Then the door opened again. The leader of the thieves counted all the men as they passed by him, then cried, "Shut, sesame!" The door in the rock closed.

When the robbers were out of sight, Ali Baba tried the magic trick for himself. "Open, sesame!" he called, and the door opened.

Inside was a huge room, filled with bags of treasure and heaps of coins. Ali Baba picked up a few bags of coins—just a few—then he said the magic words that opened the door again. "Open, sesame!" Once out of the cave, he said, "Shut, sesame!" The door in the rock closed.

Ali Baba hurried home. To his poor wife, a few bags of coins were a treasure. "Let me weigh the money, to know how much we have," she said.

"Just be sure to keep our secret," Ali Baba said.

His wife ran to Cassim's house to borrow a scale with which to weigh the coins.

"What would my poor sister-in-law need to weigh?" wondered Cassim's wife. She secretly rubbed some wax on the bottom of the scale. When Ali Baba's wife returned it, a shiny gold coin stayed stuck to the wax. "Do they have so much gold that they must weigh it?" Cassim exclaimed when he heard what had happened.

Now, Cassim was rich, but he was also jealous. Early the next morning he went to his brother and demanded to know where the gold coin came from. Ali Baba told him. "I will go and fetch some treasure for myself," said Cassim.

Cassim remembered to say, "Open, sesame!" To his joy, the door opened wide, showing bags of treasure and heaps of coins. He filled ten bags as full as he could. He was so excited he forgot the magic words. "Open, barley!" he cried. "Open, oats!" But nothing he said opened the door. He was locked inside the cave of treasure.

At noon, the robbers returned to their cave. They spoke the magic words and the door in the rock opened. Cassim tried to hide, but he could not escape from forty thieves. They cut Cassim's body into four quarters and hung them inside the cave.

By nighttime, Cassim's wife was worried. Ali Baba knew where to find his brother. He went to the rock and spoke the magic words: "Open, sesame!" Then he found his worst fears to be true. He wrapped what was left of his brother's body in cloth, laid the bundle on the back of his mule, covered them with branches, and carried them back to his brother's house.

A smart young slave girl named Morgiana worked for Cassim and his wife. When she heard what Ali Baba had brought home, she agreed to help him keep it secret. She ran to the druggist's, asking for strong medicine. "My master is sick unto death," she said. "He cannot eat or speak." Having heard that, no one was surprised to hear the next day that Cassim had died and that his brother, Ali Baba, had moved into his house to console the widow and take care of unfinished business.

Now Morgiana considered Ali Baba her master, and she willingly helped him carry out his plan. She ran to the cobbler's and put two gold pieces into his hand. "I have a task for you, but it must be kept a secret," she said. She led him blindfolded to Cassim's house. She asked him to sew Cassim's body back together, so that he might be buried without anyone knowing what had happened to him. She gave the cobbler a third piece of gold for his trouble and led him blindfolded back home again.

When the forty thieves found Cassim's body missing, they knew that someone still

knew the secret of how to get into their cave. They went from person to person throughout the town, trying to discover who it was. One thief happened on the cobbler, who was
working at the crack of dawn.

"How can you see your work?" asked the thief. "It is scarcely light."

"I have very good eyes," said the cobbler. "Yesterday I sewed together a dead body in a
room much darker than this."

"Aha!" thought the thief. To the cobbler he said, "You must be joking. Show me the
house where you did such a strange job."

"I was blindfolded," said the cobbler, "but I think I can remember the way." He walked
down the street, counting his steps as he went, and stopped at Cassim's doorstep.

The thief gave the cobbler a gold piece, thanked him, and sent him on his way. When
he asked the neighbors, the thief learned that Ali Baba had recently lost his brother yet
come into great riches. The thief was sure that Ali Baba was the man who had discovered the way into the cave. He marked Ali Baba's door with chalk.

But smart Morgiana noticed the chalk marks on the door. "Either an enemy plans to
do my master wrong or a boy has been playing tricks," she thought. "Either way, it is best
to guard against all possible evil." She fetched a piece of chalk and marked three other
doors near her master's.

When the thief returned, he was confused by all the chalk marks. In a rage, his leader
killed him on the spot. He sent another thief to find the cobbler, who pointed out Ali
Baba's house, which this thief marked with red chalk.

But Morgiana was watching. She marked all the doors up and down the street with red
chalk, too. Again the leader, infuriated, killed this man on the spot.

The leader decided to follow the cobbler by himself. He made no marks on Ali Baba's
door. He just looked at it very carefully, so he would remember it. He went back to his
fellow thieves and told them his new plan.

"Bring nineteen mules," he said. "To each mule, attach two earthen jars, big enough
for a man to fit in. Put oil in only one of those jars." And do you know what he did with
the other thirty-seven jars? He made the thieves crawl into them!

The leader of the thieves led the nineteen mules carrying thirty-eight jars right up to
Ali Baba's door. "Sir, I have some oil to sell at market tomorrow," he told Ali Baba. "Might
I stay the night with you?" Ali Baba told Morgiana to show the man to a room and feed
him. As the man left the mules behind, he whispered to the thieves in hiding, "I'll be
back at midnight. Come out when you hear my voice."

As Morgiana was making soup for the stranger, her lamp went out. "All I need is a little oil for the lamp, just enough to finish cooking," she said to herself. "I can borrow a bit
from those jars belonging to the stranger."

So she went outside and cautiously opened the first jar. As she did so, a voice whispered, "Is it time?"

"No, not yet, be patient," she answered, wondering. She went from jar to jar, hearing a voice from each and always answering the same way, until she finally came to the jar of oil. The smart girl went back to her kitchen, lit the lamp, then built a great fire of wood, upon which she set a huge black kettle and filled it with oil from the jar outside. She heated that oil until it was boiling, then poured some into each of the jars, killing the thieves inside the jars, one by one. When the leader found out, he ran away into the night, afraid for his own life.

When Morgiana told Ali Baba what had happened, he was so grateful he offered her her freedom. She thanked him, asking that she be allowed to continue living with him and his family.

But that is still not the end of the story! The leader of the forty thieves came back to town many weeks later, hoping for revenge. He learned that the son of Cassim owned a shop. He brought treasures from his secret cave and pretended to be a merchant, too. In that way he became friends with the nephew of Ali Baba.

One night, not knowing who this new merchant really was, Ali Baba invited him to dinner. "Thank you, no," the man answered. "My doctor says I must eat no salt."

"Who is this difficult man who eats no salt?" asked Morgiana.

"He is our new friend," Ali Baba answered.

But Morgiana looked closely and recognized him. Looking even more closely, she saw a dagger hidden in his robe.

Knowing that danger might befall her master, Morgiana dressed like a dancing girl and offered to entertain the visitor after dinner. She danced with grace and spirit. She swept a jeweled dagger through the air as part of the art of her dance. As the leader of the thieves reached to give the dancer a coin of gold, Morgiana plunged the dagger into his heart.

"What have you done?" cried Ali Baba. "You have murdered my new friend!"

"Nay, master, I have saved your life," answered Morgiana. She drew back the guest's robe and revealed his hidden dagger.

Again Morgiana had saved the life of Ali Baba. Since she already had her freedom, he found something even more wonderful to give her in thanks. He said that she could marry his nephew, who truly loved her. So Morgiana joined the family of Ali Baba and shared the fortunes of his house.

The Hunting of the Great Bear

This story comes from the Iroquois people, Native Americans who lived in the eastern part of today's United States, on land that we now call New York, Pennsylvania, and Ohio.

There were four hunters who were brothers. No hunters were as good as they were at following a trail. Once they began tracking their quarry, they never gave up.

One day, in the time when the cold nights return, an urgent message came to the four hunters. A great bear had appeared at a village nearby, so large and powerful that many of the villagers thought it must be some kind of monster. The people of the village were afraid.

Picking up their spears and calling to their small dog, the four hunters set forth for that village. As they came closer, they noticed how quiet the woods were. There were no signs of rabbits or deer. Even the birds were silent. They found where the great bear had reared up on hind legs and made deep scratches on a pine tree to mark its territory. The tallest of the brothers tried to touch the highest scratch mark with the tip of his spear.

"It is as the people feared," the first brother said. "This one we are to hunt is Nyah-gwaheh, a monster bear."

"The Nyah-gwaheh has special magic, but that magic will do the bear no good if we find its track," said the second brother.

"I have always heard that from the old people," said the third brother. "The Nyah-gwaheh can only chase a hunter who has not yet found its trail. When you find its trail and begin to chase it, then it must run from you."

"Brothers," said the fourth, the fattest and laziest, "did we bring along enough food to eat? It may take a long time to catch this big bear. I'm feeling hungry."

Before long, the four hunters and their small dog reached the village. It was a sad sight to see. There was no fire burning in the center of the village, and the doors of all the long-houses were closed. No game hung from the racks; no skins were stretched for tanning. All the people looked hungry.

The elder of the village appeared.

"Uncle," said the tallest brother, "we have come to help you get rid of the monster."

Then the fattest and laziest brother spoke. "Uncle, is there some food we can eat? Can we find a place to rest before we start chasing this big bear?"

The second hunter shook his head and smiled. "My brother is only joking, Uncle," he said. "We are going now to pick up the monster bear's trail."

"I am not sure you can do that, nephews," the elder said. "Though we find tracks closer and closer to the doors of our lodges each morning, whenever we try to follow those tracks they disappear."

The third hunter knelt down and patted the head of their small dog. "Uncle," he said, "that is because they do not have a dog such as ours." He pointed to the two black spots above the eyes of the small dog. "Four-Eyes can see any tracks, even those many days old."

"May Creator's protection be with you," said the elder.

"I think we should have something to eat first," said the fourth hunter, but his brothers did not listen.

The four hunters walked, following their little dog, who kept lifting up its head, as if to look around with its four eyes.

"Brothers," the fattest and laziest hunter complained, "don't you think we should rest? We've been walking a long time." But his brothers paid no attention to him. Though they could see no tracks, they could feel the presence of the Nyah-gwaheh. They knew that if they did not soon find its trail, the monster bear would circle around them, and then they would be the hunted ones.

The fattest and laziest brother decided to eat while they walked. He opened his pemmican pouch, and shook out the strips of meat and berries he had pounded with maple sugar and dried in the sun. Pale squirming things fell out instead. The magic of the Nyah-gwaheh had changed the food into worms.

"Look what that bear did to my pemmican!" the fattest and laziest brother shouted. "Now I'm getting angry."

Meanwhile, like a giant shadow, the Nyah-gwaheh was moving through the trees. Its huge teeth shone; its eyes flashed red. Soon it would be behind them, on their trail.

Just then, though, the little dog lifted its head and yelped.

"Eh-heh!" the first brother called.

"Four-Eyes has found the trail," shouted the second brother.

"We have the track of the Nyah-gwaheh," said the third brother.

"Big Bear," the fattest and laziest one yelled, "we are after you now!"

Fear filled the heart of the great bear for the first time, and it began to run. As it broke from the cover of the pines, the four hunters saw it, a gigantic shape, so white as to appear almost naked. The great bear's strides were long and swifter than a deer's. The four hunters and their little dog were swift as well. The trail led through swamps and thickets. It was easy for the hunters to follow, for the bear pushed everything aside as it ran, even knocking down big trees. They came to a mountain and followed the trail higher and higher, every now and then catching a glimpse of their quarry over the next rise.

But the lazy hunter was getting tired of running. He pretended to fall and twist his ankle. "Brothers," he called, "I have sprained my ankle. You must carry me."

His brothers did as he asked, two of them carrying him while the third carried his spear. They ran more slowly now, but they were not falling any farther behind. The day turned into night, yet they could still see the white shape ahead of them. They were at the top of the mountain now. The bear was tiring, but so were they. Four-Eyes, the little dog, was close behind the great bear, nipping at its tail as it ran.

The fattest and laziest brother asked to be put down. "I think my leg has gotten better," he said. Fresh and rested, he dashed ahead of the others. Just as the great bear turned to bite at the little dog, the fattest and laziest brother thrust his spear into the heart of the Nyah-gwaheh. The monster bear fell dead.

By the time the other brothers caught up, the fattest and laziest one had built a fire and was cutting up the bear.

"Come on, brothers," he said. "Let's eat. All this running has made me hungry!"

So they cooked the meat of the great bear, and its fat sizzled as it dripped from their fire. They ate until even the fattest and laziest brother leaned back in contentment. Just then, though, the first brother looked down.

"Brothers," the second brother exclaimed, "look below us!"

"We aren't on a mountaintop at all," said the third brother. "We are up in the sky."

Below them, thousands of lights sparkled in the darkness. The great bear had indeed been magical, and they had followed it up into the heavens.

Just then their little dog yipped twice. There, where they had piled the bones of their feast, the bear was coming back to life. It rose to its feet and began to run again, the dog close on its heels. Grabbing up their spears, the four hunters again began to chase the great bear across the skies.

So it was, as the old people say, and so it still is. Each autumn the hunters chase the Great Bear across the skies and kill it. As they cut it up for meat, the blood of the bear falls from the sky and colors the leaves of the maple trees scarlet. As they cook the meat, the dripping fat bleaches the grass white.

If you look in the nighttime skies as the seasons change, you can read this story. The Great Bear is the shape some call the Big Dipper, which rotates around the North Star. During the summer, you can see the hunters and their small dog (just barely) in the Dipper's handle, running close behind the Great Bear. When autumn comes, the constellation seems to turn upside down. Then, the old people say, the lazy hunter has killed the bear. As more moons pass (which is how the old people talk about months going by), the constellations revolve. The bear slowly rises back on its feet, and the chase begins again.

Gone Is Gone

This story comes from Bohemia, which was in the Czech Republic, part of eastern Europe. It is sometimes called "The Story of a Man Who Wanted to Do Housework."

Once there was a man named Fritzl. He had a wife named Liesi. They had a little baby, Kinndli by name, and Spitz, their dog. They had one cow, two goats, three pigs, and a dozen geese. They lived on a patch of land, and that's where they worked.

Fritzl had to plow the ground, sow the seeds, and hoe the weeds. He had to cut the hay and rake it, too, and stack it up in bunches in the sun.

Liesi had the house to clean, the soup to cook, the butter to churn, the barnyard and the baby to care for. They both worked hard, but Fritzl always thought that he worked harder. Evenings when he came home from the field, he sat down and said, "Hu! Little do you know, Liesi, what a man's work is like."

"Mine is none too easy," said Liesi.

"None too easy!" cried Fritzl. "All you do is putter and potter around the house a bit."

"Nay, if you think so," said Liesi, "we'll take it turn and turn about tomorrow. I will do your work, and you can do mine."

So the next morning, there was Liesi at peep of day, striding out across the fields. And Fritzl, where was he? He was in the kitchen, frying a string of juicy sausages, lost in pleasant thoughts.

"A mug of apple cider with my sausage," he was thinking. "That would be just the thing." Fritzl went down into the cellar where there was a big barrel full of cider.

But hulla! What was that noise up in the kitchen! When Fritzl reached the top of the stairs, there was that Spitz-dog dashing out of the kitchen door with the string of juicy sausages.

"What's gone is gone," said Fritzl, shrugging his shoulders.

But the cider, now! Had he put the cork back in the barrel? With big fast steps Fritzl went to look, but it was too late, for the cider had run all over the cellar.

"What's gone is gone," said Fritzl, scratching his head.

Now it was time to churn the butter. Fritzl filled the churn with good rich cream, took it under a tree, and began to churn with all his might. His little Kinndli was out there, playing Moo-cow among the daisies. "This is pleasant, now," thought Fritzl. "But what about the cow? I've forgotten all about her this morning."

With big fast steps Fritzl ran to the barn, carrying a bucket of cool water for the cow.

The poor creature's tongue was hanging out of her mouth for thirst. She was hungry, too, so Fritzl took her from the barn to the green, grassy meadow.

But then Fritzl thought about Kinndli. She would surely get into trouble if he went all the way out to the meadow. Better keep the cow on the roof. Fritzl's house was not covered with shingles or tin or tile—it was covered with moss and sod, and a fine crop of grass and flowers grew there. The house was built into the side of a hill, so Fritzl took the cow up the little hill and onto the roof. The cow was soon munching away, so Fritzl went back to his churning.

But hulla! Kinndli was climbing up on the churn, and the churn was tipping! And now there on the grass lay Kinndli, all covered with half-churned cream and butter.

"What's gone is gone," said Fritzl, blinking his blue eyes.

The sun had climbed high up into the heavens. Noontime it was, no dinner made. Fritzl hurried off to the garden. He gathered potatoes and onions, carrots and cabbages, beets and beans, turnips, parsley, and celery. "That will make a good soup," he said, his arms so full of vegetables he could not close the garden gate behind him. He sat down in the kitchen and began cutting and paring away. How the man did work!

But now there was a great noise above him. Fritzl jumped to his feet. "That cow," he said. "She's sliding around on the roof. She might slip off and break her neck."

Up on the roof went Fritzl once more, this time with loops of heavy rope. He took one end of the rope and tied it around the cow's middle. The other end he dropped down the chimney and pulled through the fireplace. Then he took that end of the rope and tied it around his own middle. "That will keep the cow from falling off the roof," he said, chuckling.

He heaped sticks on the fireplace and set a big kettle of water over it. "We'll soon have a good big soup," he said. He put in the vegetables. He put in the bacon. He started to light the fire—but that he never did, for just then, with a bump and a thump, the cow slipped over the edge of the roof, and Fritzl was whisked up into the chimney. There he dangled, poor man, and couldn't get up and couldn't get down.

Before long, there came Liesi home from the

fields. But hulla! What was that hanging over the edge of the roof? It was the cow, half-choked, with her eyes bulging and her tongue hanging out. Liesi cut the rope and let the poor cow down.

Now Liesi saw the garden with the gate wide open. There were the pigs and the goats and all the geese, too, full to bursting, but the garden, alas! was empty.

Liesi walked on and saw the churn upturned and Kinndli there in the sun, stiff and sticky with dried cream and butter.

Liesi hurried on and saw the Spitz-dog on the grass, full of sausages and looking none too well.

Liesi looked at the cellar. There was cider all over the floor and halfway up the stairs.

Liesi looked in the kitchen. The floor was piled high with peelings and littered with pots and pans.

At last Liesi saw the fireplace. Hulla! What was that in the soup kettle? Two arms were waving, two legs were kicking, and a weak gurgle was coming up out of the water.

"What can this mean?" cried Liesi. Poor Fritzl, for as soon as the cow's rope had been cut, he had dropped down the chimney—crash! splash!—right into the kettle of soup.

Liesi pulled and tugged, and there, dripping and spluttering, with a cabbage leaf in his hair, celery in his pocket, and a sprig of parsley in his ear, was Fritzl.

"Is that the way you keep house?" she asked.

"Oh, Liesi," sputtered Fritzl. "You're right. That work of yours is none too easy."

"It's hard at first," said Liesi, "but tomorrow you will do better."

"Nay, nay," cried Fritzl. "Gone is gone, and so is my housework from this day on. Please, Liesi, let me go back to my work in the fields, and never more will I say that my work is harder than yours."

"If that's your promise," said Liesi, "we can surely live in peace and happiness forever." And that they did.

The Little Match Girl

This is one of many well-known fairy tales written by Hans Christian Andersen, who lived in Denmark during the 1800s.

It was terribly cold and nearly dark on the last evening of the old year. Snow was falling fast, and yet a poor little girl, with bare head and naked feet, roamed through the streets.

It is true she had had on a pair of slippers when she left home, but they were not of much use. They had belonged to her mother, and were so large that she had lost them in running across the street to escape the carriages. She found one, but a boy seized the other and ran away with it. So the little girl went on, her little naked feet blue with the cold.

In an old apron she carried matches. She held a bundle of them in her hands. No one had bought any matches from her the whole day. Shivering with cold and hunger, she crept along. The snowflakes fell on her hair, which hung in lovely curls on her shoulders.

Lights were shining from every window, and there was a fine smell of roast goose in the air. The little girl remembered that it was New Year's Eve. Between two houses, she huddled herself together, but she could not keep out the cold. She dared not go home, for she had sold no matches and could not take home even a penny of money. Her father would certainly beat her. Besides, it was almost as cold at home as here, for the wind howled through, even though the holes in the walls and windows had been stopped up with straw and rags.

Her little hands were almost frozen. Perhaps a burning match might warm her fingers. She drew one out. *Scratch!* How it sputtered as it burned! It gave a warm, bright light, like a little candle, as she held her hand over it. It was really a wonderful light. It seemed to the little girl that she was sitting by a large iron stove, with polished brass feet and pretty brass ornaments. It seemed so beautifully warm that she stretched out her feet as if to warm them. But then the flame of the match went out, the stove vanished, and she had only the half-burned match in her hand.

She rubbed another match on the wall. It burst into flame. Where its light fell, the little girl could see through the wall to a table, covered with a snowy-white tablecloth, with splendid dishes and a steaming roast goose, stuffed with apples and plums. What was still more wonderful, the goose jumped down from the dish with a knife and fork stuck into its breast and waddled across the floor to the little girl. Then the match went out, and there remained nothing but the cold wall before her.

She lit another match, and she found herself sitting under a beautiful Christmas tree, with thousands of candles and twinkling decorations. The little girl stretched her hand out. Then the match went out.

At that, the Christmas lights began to rise up into the sky. They rose higher and higher, until they looked to the little girl like the stars in the sky. Then she saw a star fall, leaving behind it a bright streak of fire. "Someone is dying," thought the little girl, for her grandmother, the only person who had ever loved her and who was now dead, had told her that when a star falls, a soul is on its way to heaven.

The little girl struck a match and light shone all around her. In the brightness stood her grandmother, clear and shining, kind and loving.

"Grandmother," cried the girl. "I know you will vanish like the warm stove, the roast goose, and the Christmas tree. Take me with you." She made haste to light the whole bundle of matches. They glowed with a light that was brighter than the noonday sun, and her grandmother appeared more beautiful than ever. She took the little girl in her arms, and they both flew upward in brightness and joy, far above the earth, where there was no cold or hunger or pain.

In the dawn of the morning, there lay the poor little girl with pale cheeks and smiling mouth, leaning against the wall. She had been frozen to death on the last evening of the old year. Now the new year's sun rose and shone upon her. The child still sat, in the stiffness of death, holding the bundle of burned matches.

"She tried to warm herself," said some. No one imagined what beautiful things she had seen, nor into what glory she had entered with her grandmother on New Year's Day.

The People Could Fly

This story was shared among African American slaves for a long time before anyone ever wrote it down. It has many different versions.

They say that these people could fly. Long ago in Africa, some of them would shout a few magic words and lift themselves into the air like crows, flapping their black wings. They say that when these people were put on the ships as slaves, they had to fold those wings. There was no room for flying on those cramped ships. And they say that when these people were put to work in the fields, they lost the freedom to spread their wings. They could not even imagine flying.

But not all of them forgot the magic words.

One afternoon the sun was so hot it seemed to singe the hair on their heads. They had been picking cotton since sunup without a rest. One young woman, Sarah, was carrying her child on her back and was feeling so weary she fainted.

"Back to work," the overseer snarled. "There is no time for rest!" He raised his whip in warning.

All the other slaves stopped to watch him. Sarah staggered to her feet, her child on her back, and began to pick again. Sarah fell again. The overseer snapped his whip at her, and Sarah rose a second time.

An old man came to Sarah through the rows of cotton. He looked both ways, then whispered something in her ear. Sarah looked both ways and passed the message on. The whispering spread from slave to slave as swiftly as a breeze, and the overseer never no-ticed. The slaves kept working.

But Sarah's baby began to whimper and cry, and Sarah stopped to comfort him. The overseer rode toward her. Just as his whip was about to lash her back, that same old man shouted those magic words, remembered from so long ago.

With those words, Sarah began to rise. She spread her arms. They felt like wings. She rose above the overseer's whip like an eagle.

Wheeling his horse around, the overseer bellowed, "Who shouted? What did he say?" All the other slaves stayed quiet and kept busy, but they knew Sarah had flown to free-dom.

The sun was so hot that others began to fall. The overseer cracked his whip at one man, but before that whip made contact, another shout rang out. The weary slave rose into the air. Then the overseer saw a woman crumpled over nearby, and he raised his whip to strike her. Once again those magic words rang out, and the woman rose up into the air.

As each slave fainted with the heat, the overseer raised his whip. Each time he did, the slave would rise up into the air. Then the overseer saw the old man, his mouth ready to shout.

"Seize that old man," the overseer shouted, raising his whip.

The old man looked the overseer in the eye. "Now" was all he said. With that one word, all the people cir-cled round and joined hands. Chanting the magic words, they slowly rose. They flew above the field and far out of reach of the overseer.

They say those slaves flew back to Africa. We don't really know. But we remem-ber, and we still whisper this story to all those who try, in their hearts and minds, to lift their wings and fly.

Three Words of Wisdom

This story comes from the border territory between the Southwest United States and Mexico.

There were once three men who lived in the country. Two had large families, and one had only his wife and a son who wanted to be a priest. No matter the number of mouths to feed, though, their crops failed year after year. Their families were starving. They decided to find jobs in the city.

Just a few miles from town, they ran into an old man who asked if he might travel with them. They asked if he knew of any work. He answered, "In my lifetime, I have gathered heaps of gold. I don't have a family, so I will share it with you. You may have either my coins or my golden wisdom."

The men with large families asked for the money, but the man with the small family asked for the wisdom.

The old man divided his gold coins between the two men. To the third, he said, "Here are my words of wisdom: Don't take shortcuts. Don't ask about what does not concern you. And don't jump too quickly to conclusions."

The two men scolded their friend for his stupidity. "You can't feed your family with wisdom." And they all set off for home.

As they left the main road to take a shortcut through the forest, the third man said, "Remember what the old man said? *Don't take any shortcuts.*" But the two men ignored him and plunged into the woods. There they were attacked by bandits, who took their money and their lives.

Unaware of his friends' fate, the third man traveled on toward the city. As night fell, he reached a huge ranch where a rancher lived, starved for good company.

What a feast this man served! Our traveler had never seen more succulent meat, the fruit like gems, candles glistening overhead. Washing down the last sweet mouthful, our traveler began to ask where such riches came from, but then he remembered the old man's words: *Don't ask about what doesn't concern you.* He kept still.

The rancher saw his guest swallow his question. Lifting the cover from the last banquet platter, he revealed the head of a man! "You are very wise," he said, "for this is what happened to the last man who asked how I made my riches. All of my life, I have waited for someone simply to accept me as I am, to share in my gifts without asking how I got them. Now that I have seen your wisdom, I will gladly share them with you!"

The rancher led our traveler to the window, saying, "All of this and all that lives and grows here are yours to use, whenever you are in need."

Our traveler woke the next morning to find a cart and donkey loaded down with more food and money than he could ever ask for. He couldn't wait to get home.

He approached his house quietly, hoping to surprise his wife and son. He peeked into the window and nearly choked with rage! His wife was embracing a priest! He started to howl with anger, but then he remembered the old man's words of wisdom: *Don't jump to conclusions.*

Trying to calm himself, he knocked on the door. His wife turned to the priest and said, "Perhaps it is your father." During the traveler's long absence, his son had become a priest! Our traveler greeted his family as a wise man would, and the three lived happily ever after.

William Tell

The people of Switzerland have told this legend for a long time. No one knows if William Tell was a real man. His story may be a way of telling about an actual rebellion that took place around 1300.

Many years ago a cruel governor named Gessler ruled over the people of Switzerland. He taxed them heavily, so nothing could be bought or sold unless the governor received some of the money. Many people who did nothing wrong were put into prison for a long time. The Swiss people were unhappy indeed.

One day Gessler set up a tall pole in the public square of the town called Altdorf. Atop that pole he put his own cap, announcing that all citizens must uncover their heads as they passed by the cap, or else they would be put to death. Guards stood in the square day and night to see that the order was obeyed.

Now, there lived in a small village not far away a famous hunter by the name of William Tell. No one in all the land could shoot with bow and arrow as well as he could.

One morning Tell took his little son, Walter, with him into Altdorf on business. He heard the news about Gessler's order, but he could not bring himself to bare his head to a cap atop a pole.

"Take off your hat and bow!" a guard commanded.

"Why should I bow to a cap on a pole?" asked William Tell.

"This man will not uncover his head as he passes by your cap," the guards reported to Gessler.

"You are said to be the best shot in the mountains," said Gessler to William Tell. "I will design a punishment just for you." He sent a soldier to an orchard for an apple. "Place this fruit upon the head of your son," said Gessler. "Then walk a hundred yards away and shoot that apple with your bow and arrow."

Tell begged the tyrant to come up with another punishment.

"Obey my order!" roared Gessler.

Walter took his place, with the apple atop his head. Tell drew an arrow from his quiver. He slowly fit the arrow to the bow and raised them to his shoulder.

"Shoot, Father," said young Walter firmly. "I am not afraid. I am staying still."

Tell pulled back his bowstring. *Ping!* The arrow flew through the air. It pierced the apple, which dropped in two pieces onto the ground. The people watching shouted for joy.

As William Tell rushed to embrace his son, a second arrow fell from under his coat.

"What did you plan for that second arrow?" asked Gessler angrily.

"That arrow was for your heart, you tyrant!" William Tell responded. "If I had hurt my beloved son, you can be sure I would not have missed the mark a second time."

Legend has it that, in the years to come, William Tell did send an arrow through the heart of Gessler—and set the people of Switzerland free.

The River Bank
(adapted from Kenneth Grahame's original)

This episode of The Wind in the Willows *will give you a taste of the wonderful book by Kenneth Grahame, published in 1908. Grahame was born in Scotland in 1859. He worked as a banker and lived in England most of his life. If you enjoy this story, you will like the whole book, full of the antics of little animals in the English countryside, including Toad, who loves his speedy motorcar.*

The Mole had been working very hard all the morning, spring-cleaning his little home. Spring was moving in the air above and in the earth below and around him, penetrating even his dark and lowly little house.

But suddenly, he bolted out of the house without even waiting to put on his coat. "Hang spring-cleaning!" he said. Something up above was calling him, and he made for the steep little tunnel. He scraped and scratched and scrabbled and scrooged, working busily with his little paws and muttering to himself, "Up we go!" till at last, pop! his snout came out into the sunlight and he found himself rolling in the warm grass of a great meadow.

The sunshine struck hot on his fur, soft breezes caressed his heated brow, and the carol of happy birds sounded almost like a shout. He thought his happiness was complete when suddenly he stood by the edge of a full-fed river. Never in his life had he seen a river before. He was bewitched, entranced, fascinated. By the side of the river he trotted, and, when tired at last, he sat on the bank, while the river still chattered on to him.

A dark hole in the bank opposite, just above the water's edge, caught his eye. As he gazed, something seemed to twinkle down in the heart of it, vanished, then twinkled once more like a tiny star. As he looked, it winked at him, and so declared itself to be an eye; and a small face began gradually to grow up round it, like a frame round a picture.

A brown little face, with whiskers.

Small neat ears and thick silky hair.

It was the Water Rat!

"Would you like to come over?" inquired the Rat. He stooped and unfastened a rope and hauled on it, then lightly stepped into a little boat, just the size for two animals.

"Now then, step lively!" said the Rat, and the Mole to his surprise found himself in the stern of a real boat.

"Do you know, I've never been in a boat before in all my life?" said the Mole.

"What?" cried the Rat. "What have you been doing, then? Believe me, my young friend, there is *nothing*—absolutely nothing—half so much worth doing as simply messing about in boats."

"Look ahead, Rat!" cried the Mole suddenly.

It was too late. The boat struck the bank full tilt. The joyous oarsman lay on his back at the bottom of the boat, his heels in the air. The Rat picked himself up with a pleasant laugh. He tied the boat to his dock, climbed into his hole, and in a few moments reappeared with a fat lunch basket.

"Shove that under your feet," he said to the Mole. He untied the boat and took to his oars again.

"What's inside it?" asked the Mole.

"There's cold chicken inside it," replied the Rat; "coldtonguecoldhamcoldbeef-pickledgherkinssaladfrenchrollscresssandwichespottedmeatgingerbeerlemonadesodawater—"

"Oh, stop, stop," cried the Mole. "This is too much!"

"Do you really think so? It's only what I always take on these little trips."

The Mole, absorbed in the new life he was entering upon, the sparkle, the scents and the sounds and the sunlight, trailed a paw in the water and dreamed long waking dreams.

"What lies over there?" he asked, waving a paw.

"That? Oh, that's just the Wild Wood," said the Rat. "We don't go there very much, we river-bankers."

"Aren't they—aren't they very *nice* people in there?" said the Mole.

"W-e-ll," said the Rat. "The squirrels are all right. And the rabbits—some of 'em, but rabbits are a mixed lot. And then there's Badger. He lives right in the heart of it; wouldn't live anywhere else. Dear old Badger! Nobody interferes with him."

"And beyond the Wild Wood?" asked the Mole. "Where it's all blue and dim?"

"Beyond the Wild Wood comes the Wide World," said the Rat. "And that's something that doesn't matter, to either you or me. I've never been there, and I'm never going, nor you either, if you've got any sense at all. Don't ever refer to it again, please. Now then! Here's our backwater at last, where we're going to lunch."

The Rat brought the boat alongside the bank, tied her up, helped the Mole ashore, and swung out the lunch basket. The Mole emptied the lunch basket, gasping, "Oh my! Oh my!" at each new item. When all was ready, the Rat said, "Now, pitch in, old fellow!"

The afternoon sun was getting low as the Rat rowed gently homewards. The Mole was very full of lunch, and already quite at home in a boat (so he thought). He began to feel more and more jealous of Rat, rowing so strongly and easily along, and he imagined that he could do it every bit as well. He jumped up and seized the oars, so suddenly that the Rat, who was gazing out over the water and saying poetry-things to himself, was taken by surprise and fell backward off his seat with his legs in the air for the second time. The Mole grabbed the oars with entire confidence.

"Stop it, you silly fool!" cried the Rat. "It's not as easy as it looks! You'll have us over!"

The Mole flung the oars back. He missed the water altogether, and he found himself lying on the top of the tumbled Rat. He made a grab at the side of the boat, and *sploosh!* Over went the boat, and he found himself in the river.

The Rat hauled the Mole out of the water, a squashy lump of misery.

Limp and dejected, the Mole took his seat in the stern of the boat again. "Ratty, my generous friend! I am very sorry indeed for my foolish conduct."

"That's all right," responded the Rat cheerily. "What's a little wet to a Water Rat? Look here, I really think you had better stay with me for a little time. I'll teach you to row and to swim."

The Mole was so touched by his kind manner of speaking that he could find no voice to answer him; and he had to brush away a tear or two with the back of his paw.

When they got home, the Rat made a bright fire in the parlor and told the Mole river stories till suppertime. A terribly sleepy Mole had to be escorted upstairs, to the best bedroom, where he laid his head on his pillow in great peace and contentment, knowing that his newfound friend the River was lapping the sill of his window.

The days grew longer and full of interest as the spring became summer. Mole learned to swim and to row, and, with his ear to the reed stems, he caught something of what the wind went whispering so constantly among them.

Mythology

Gods, Heroes, and Tricksters from Scandinavia

In the World History section of this book, you can read about the Vikings. The Vikings were also called Norsemen, from a word meaning "north." They came from the lands in northwest Europe called Scandinavia, which today includes the countries of Sweden, Denmark, and Norway. Can you find those countries on a map?

Like the ancient Greeks and Romans, the Vikings told stories to explain things like how the world began, or why we have different seasons, or what happens to people after they die. We don't believe these stories, but we still enjoy them. We call these stories *myths*.

Norse Gods and Goddesses

The Norse gods lived in a land called Asgard, ruled by the chief god, Odin (also called Woden). The Vikings believed that the world began when Odin and his brothers fought and killed a terrible frost giant. The earth was made out of the giant's body, the oceans out of his blood, the mountains out of his bones, and the trees out of his hair.

Odin was very wise, but he wanted to be wiser. He once went to the Well of Wisdom and sacrificed one of his eyes to drink of its water. That is why many pictures of Odin show him with one empty eye socket.

Maidens called the Valkyries [VAL-keer-eez] waited on Odin. When a Viking warrior was killed in battle, one of the Valkyries picked up the dead warrior and carried him on her swift warhorse to Valhalla, a great palace in Asgard. In Valhalla, the honored warriors lived forever, fighting by day and feasting by night.

Odin, the greatest of all the gods in Norse mythology.

Odin's oldest son, Thor, was the god of thunder. Two goats pulled his chariot through the sky. When he swung his mighty hammer, thunderbolts flew and rain fell onto the earth.

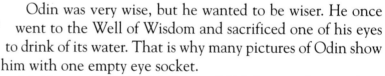

The German composer Richard Wagner [RICK-kart VAHG-ner] wrote a series of operas based on Norse myths called *The Ring of the Nibelung* [NEE-beh-loong]. One passage, "The Ride of the Valkyries," has been used in movies and on TV.

While the Norse gods lived above the clouds, dwarfs and trolls lived in dark, secret caves. A hag named Hel ruled the underworld, where spirits went after death. From her name comes the word "hell."

Four of the days of the week are named after Norse gods. The day we call Wednesday comes from "Woden's Day." From Tyr, the Norse god of war, comes "Tyr's Day," which is our Tuesday. Friday comes from "Freya's Day," after the Norse goddess of love and beauty. Which day of the week do you think might be "Thor's Day"?

Thor, son of Odin, the Norse god of thunder.

The World Tree and the End of the World

The Vikings believed that a giant "world tree" called Yggdrasill [IG-druh-sil] held up the universe. Yggdrasill had three roots. One root stretched to the land of ice. One root reached to Asgard, the land of the gods. And one root stretched to the land of the giants. Three sisters who lived beside the tree controlled everyone's past, present, and future. A giant serpent chewed at the roots of the tree. One day the tree would fall and bring down the world, causing a second great battle between the gods and the giants. The Vikings predicted that the giants would win this battle. The world would be destroyed, then begin again—but this time, everything would be perfect.

Loki and the Gifts for the Gods

Here is a Norse myth about a god named Loki, the son of a giant and a god, who loved to cause mischief. Odin invited him to the great feasts of the gods, even though he was always playing tricks on them.

Thor's wife, Sif, had long, golden hair that shimmered like a field of ripe barley grain. Loki knew how much Thor admired his wife's hair. Still, one night as she was sleeping, Loki crept into her room and cut off all of Sif's golden hair!

Loki cuts off Sif's golden hair while she is fast asleep.

Imagine Thor's surprise when he awakened the next morning to find his beautiful wife with nothing but fuzz on her head! Thor knew instantly who had played this trick on him. Thunderbolts seemed to shoot out of his angry eyes at Loki.

"Spare me, Thor!" cried Loki. "I know just where to go to ask for long locks of golden hair, even more beautiful than those Sif had before."

Loki traveled beneath the earth, where dwarfs lived in secret caves and hideaways. The dwarfs were so ugly Loki did not even want to look at them, but they were the best craftsmen in all the world.

"What do you want with us?" the dwarfs grumbled. They were never friendly to anyone.

"Dear dwarfs, I have come with a mission from the gods in Asgard," Loki said. "Only you can work this magic."

The only thing that could turn a dwarf even half-friendly was flattery. Loki wondered how much the dwarfs would give him. "First, Odin needs a spear that will never miss its mark," he said. "Second, the gods need a ship that can sail both land and sea." The dwarfs grunted and grumbled, but Loki kept on. "And third, beautiful Sif, wife of Thor, needs hair spun of the finest gold, and magic, so that it comes alive as soon as it touches her head."

The dwarfs could not resist the challenge. They worked all night and day and the next night, too. They made all three of the things that Loki asked for. He tucked the spear under his arm. He folded the ship up and put it in his pocket. He took the hair of pure gold, more beautiful than any human hair could ever be, and draped it across his shoulder. He winked at the dwarfs—that was the only thank-you he gave them—and in a flash he was gone.

On his way back to Asgard, Loki met two more dwarfs, the brothers Brokk and Sindri. "See these gifts?" he said, showing off. "I'll bet you can't make anything better, and you can cut off my head if I'm wrong!"

To answer Loki's challenge, Brokk and Sindri created three more gifts fit for the gods. They made a fierce boar with golden bristles. They made a shining golden ring. Then Brokk worked the bellows and Sindri hammered iron on the anvil and together they made a massive hammer. "We'll put magic into it," one brother told the other, "so it will always hit its mark and return to the one who threw it."

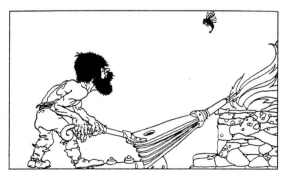

Loki, in the shape of a gadfly, pesters Brokk the dwarf as he works the bellows.

Loki worried that he would lose the bet. He turned himself into a gadfly and buzzed around their faces. Brokk swatted the fly away from his eyes as he made the hammer's handle, and it came out a bit too short. Loki grabbed the gifts and fled to Asgard, with an angry dwarf close after him.

When Sif received the golden hair, she was overjoyed. Magically, it attached to her head, just as if it had grown there. Odin, greatest of all the gods and father to Thor, took the spear for his own. Odin also claimed the ring, which had the magic power to make eight more rings every ninth night. Another god claimed the golden boar, believing it better than a horse for riding through the darkness. All the gods of Asgard marveled over the ship, seeing that the wind would fill its sails whenever they wished to travel.

Then Thor picked up the hammer and swung it high above his head. All the gods said it was the best gift of all, because it could defeat the giants. Brokk grinned at Loki, sure now that he had won the bet and getting ready to cut off Loki's head.

"But only my head!" cried Loki. "Not one inch of my neck shall you have!" It was a silly argument, but the gods agreed with Loki.

Enraged, Brokk sewed Loki's lips shut with a leather thong. The gods laughed a deep, thunderous laugh. They were thankful for all Loki had brought them, but they were also happy to have his mouth shut for a little while. As Loki scampered away, struggling to open his lips, Thor forgave him for the mischief that had started this whole adventure.

Myths from Ancient Greece and Rome

Jason and the Golden Fleece

Here is an ancient Greek myth about the hero named Jason. Jason was raised by a centaur, half man and half horse. His adventures fill a whole book, called The Golden Fleece.

One day long ago a centaur sat on the bank of a river, speaking to a handsome young man. "You are now twenty years old," said the centaur, who had raised this man from childhood. "The time has come for you to reclaim the kingdom that your stepuncle, Pelias, stole from your father. Go, and may the gods be with you."

Jason and the centaur who raised him.

Wearing a leopard's skin and sandals tied with golden strings, Jason set out for the kingdom of his stepuncle. He waded across a river, and one of his sandals came loose. When Jason arrived wearing only one sandal, it worried Pelias. A wise man had long ago predicted that he would lose his kingdom to a man with one shoe.

Pelias kept his worries secret, though. He said that Jason should rule the country. "First there is something that you must do," said Pelias. "Bring me the golden fleece, and I will make you king."

Pelias believed he had given Jason an impossible assignment. Many years before, Hermes, the messenger of the gods, had saved a boy from drowning by sending a large golden ram to carry him across the sea. In thanks, the boy had sacrificed the ram to the gods and nailed its golden fleece high upon an oak tree.

Jason gathered the bravest heroes of the land and set sail in quest of the golden fleece. He named his ship *Argo* and his crew the Argonauts. At every island they passed, they met with danger and adventure. They sailed safely through a narrow strait where two huge rocks moved back and forth in the water and crushed anything between them. They finally arrived at the island where the golden fleece hung.

When the island's king heard what Jason and the Argonauts were after, he said, "I will give you the fleece after you prove your powers. In my fields, you will find two brass bulls. Hitch those bulls to a plow and use them to sow the teeth of a dragon in my fields."

This king, like Pelias before him, felt certain that he had given Jason an impossible assignment. He knew that the brass bulls were wild and strong and difficult to handle. He also knew that when dragon's teeth are planted, iron men spring up out of the earth ready to attack.

The king's beautiful daughter, Medea, had already fallen in love with Jason. She was ready to do anything—even use her magic spells—to help him. "Here is some magic ointment," she said to Jason. "Rub it on your body, your sword, and your shield. Then nothing can harm you. And remember: When you have sowed the dragon's teeth, throw a great stone among the warriors. Then they will destroy each other."

Strengthened through Medea's magic, Jason wrestled the bulls to the ground, yoked them to a plow, and drove them through the field. The plow cut a deep furrow in the soil. Into that furrow, Jason sowed the dragon's teeth. When the army of iron men sprang up out of the earth, he threw a stone among them. The men turned upon each other, and when the battle was over, Jason was the only man left alive.

The king was furious. "The golden fleece hangs high on a tree, guarded by a giant dragon," he said. "Go and get it for yourself."

Medea charms the serpent who guards the golden fleece.

Again the king believed he had given Jason an impossible task, but again Medea helped Jason. They approached the fearful dragon, coiled at the foot of the tree. Medea began to sing. At the sound of her voice, the dragon's eyes grew heavy. Slowly, the creature lowered its head and fell asleep.

"Hurry," Medea whispered. Jason reached up and took hold of the precious treasure. As he and Medea fled, they heard a horrible roar as the dragon awoke and found its treasure stolen.

The *Argo* awaited them. With a wild leap, Jason and Medea were on board. The Argonauts rowed the ship swiftly, leaving the monster spitting fire behind them.

Jason's stepuncle had never expected to see him again, but the young hero sailed back victorious. Through bravery and magic, he had won the golden fleece.

Perseus and Medusa

This ancient myth describes the Gorgons, who were frightening female monsters with snakes for hair.

There was once a lovely young woman, so lovely that Zeus himself, the king of the gods, fell in love with her. Together they had a son, named Perseus. The father of the young woman was horrified, because it had been predicted that he would be killed by his own grandson. So he put his daughter and her baby boy into a chest and threw them into the sea.

They floated for many days and finally washed up on an island shore, where they made a home. Perseus grew up to be a strong and handsome young man.

Now, the king of the island was also cruel. He wanted Perseus's mother all to himself. He assigned Perseus to a great adventure, but he really intended a task so difficult that Perseus would not survive.

"Bring me the head of Medusa," said the king.

"Medusa?" asked Perseus in wonder. Medusa was a Gorgon, a hideous monster with a head full of snakes. She turned a man to stone the minute he looked her in the eye. No one could approach Medusa, let alone cut her head off! But Perseus accepted the challenge.

Zeus sent his messenger, Hermes, with gifts for Perseus.

"Your father has sent me from Mount Olympus, home of the gods, with three things," said Hermes. "From Athena, the goddess of wisdom, here is a bright brass shield. From Hades, the god of the underworld, here is a helmet to make you invisible. And from me, here is a sword that cuts through anything with one stroke." Then Hermes took the winged sandals off his feet and gave them to Perseus.

With gifts from the gods, Perseus felt even braver. He thanked Hermes, and through him all the gods, including great Zeus. "But where will I find this monster Medusa?" he asked.

"You must put that question to the Three Gray Sisters," said Hermes. "These three women share a single eye. They live together in a deep, dark cave at the western edge of the world."

Perseus traveled for days and nights until he came to a twilight land. There he stood at the opening of a deep, dark cave and listened as the Three Gray Sisters mumbled among themselves.

"Someone is coming," said the first sister. "I can feel him."

"Someone is coming," said the second sister. "I can hear him."

"Someone is coming," said the third sister. "I can see him with my eye."

"Give me the eye," said the first.

"No, me," said the second, "so I can see, too!"

Perseus steals the eye
from the Three Gray Sisters.

As they struggled over the one eye they shared, Perseus grabbed it. A howl shot up from all three sisters when they realized that not one of them had the precious eye anymore.

"Never fear, good women," said Perseus. "I will return your eye as long as you tell me where I will find the Gorgon Medusa."

The sisters told Perseus how to find Medusa. With Hermes's sandals on his feet, he flew over land and sea to the land of the Gorgons. There they were, three massive monsters, lying asleep. The biggest and most horrible one was Medusa.

Perseus put on the helmet of invisibility so that Medusa would not see him coming. He held up the bright shield so that his gaze would not meet hers and yet he could see her face, reflected as in a mirror. Aided by Hermes's winged sandals, he approached the Gorgon, raised the sword, and, with one swing, cut the head off the horrible Medusa. The snakes on her head hissed in pain. Perseus shoved her head into a goatskin pouch and instantly flew away.

Returning to the island where the cruel king kept his mother, Perseus approached the throne.

"Just as I suspected," said the king with a smile. "You have come back empty-handed."

Perseus shows Medusa's head to the evil king, who instantly turns to stone.

"On the contrary," said Perseus. "I have done what you commanded." He pulled Medusa's head out of the goatskin bag. Even in death, with her eyes wide open, the Gorgon had her powers. The evil king looked her straight in the eye and turned to stone.

Cupid and Psyche

Have you ever seen Cupid, that little boy with wings, on a Valentine's Day card? To the ancient Romans, Cupid was a god. Here is a myth about how he fell in love with a woman.

Once there was a king who had three daughters. The youngest, named Psyche [SY-kee], was the most beautiful of all—so beautiful, in fact, that people began to say she was even more beautiful than Venus, the goddess of beauty.

When Venus heard these claims, she was filled with jealousy. She went to her son, Cupid, and said, "Shoot the girl with one of your arrows and make her fall in love with the ugliest man on earth."

Obediently, Cupid took his bow and arrow and flew down to Earth. Just as he was taking aim to shoot Psyche, his finger slipped. He pricked himself with his own arrow and fell in love with Psyche.

Cupid sent a message to Psyche's family, saying that the gods wished her to climb a mountain and marry the husband that they had chosen for her—a terrible monster. Psyche bravely climbed the mountain, feeling a warm wind surround her. Suddenly, she found herself in a magnificent palace. She saw no one, but she heard friendly voices, promising her every desire. She fell asleep, surrounded by sweet music. While she slept, Cupid visited her. She knew her husband only in her dreams. He stayed all night, but left before morning's light. Night after night, Psyche felt her husband come to her in the darkness and leave before morning's light.

One night Psyche asked her husband why he came in darkness. "Why should you wish to see me?" he answered. "I love you, and all I ask is that you love me." Still, Psyche grew more curious. Who was her husband? What did he look like? Why did he hide? Was he indeed a terrible monster?

One night she stayed awake. She waited until she felt him lying by her side, then she lit a lamp. What she saw was no monster, but the lovely face of Cupid himself. Her hand trembled with delight, and a drop of hot oil fell from the lamp onto Cupid's shoulder and awoke him.

"I asked only for your trust," he said sadly. "When trust is gone, love must depart." And away flew Cupid, home to Venus, who scolded him for falling in love with a mere woman.

Psyche dares to look at her husband.

The moment Cupid flew away, the magnificent palace vanished. Night and day Psyche wandered, searching for her lost love. At last she went to the temple of Venus herself. "You dare to come seeking a husband, you ugly girl?" Venus cried. She showed Psyche a huge pile of grain—wheat, millet, barley, and lentils. "Separate this grain by morning." Venus laughed, then disappeared.

Psyche knew the task was impossible. Then, looking through her tears, she noticed a seed moving, then another, and then many more. An army of ants had come to her aid, each carrying a seed and dividing the seeds into separate piles.

Venus was furious to find the work done. "Your next task will not be so easy," she said. "Take this box into the underworld and ask the queen of that realm, Proserpina [pro-SUR-pi-nah], to send me a little of her beauty."

The underworld? No mortal could return. Suddenly, a voice spoke to her. "Take a coin to the boatman who will carry you across the river to the underworld. Take a cake to calm the mean three-headed dog who guards the underworld. And this above all: once Proserpina has placed beauty in the box, do not open it."

Following the mysterious voice, Psyche journeyed safely to the underworld, and Proserpina sent a box of beauty back with her to Venus.

But Psyche could not help wondering what was inside the box. She lifted the lid and peeked inside. A deep sleep came over her, and Psyche fell senseless to the ground.

Meanwhile, Cupid's love for Psyche had grown stronger than ever. Finding her lying on the ground, he took the sleep from her body. "See what curiosity gets you?" Cupid said, smiling, as she awoke.

While Psyche delivered the box to Venus, Cupid begged Jupiter, the king of the gods, to bless their marriage. Jupiter invited Psyche to drink ambrosia of the gods, and she became immortal. In the marriage of Cupid and Psyche, Love and the Soul (which is what the word "psyche" means today) were united at last and forever.

The Sword of Damocles

This story comes to us from ancient Rome. Many people still use the phrase "sword of Damocles" to speak of danger that is always present.

Damocles [da-mo-KLEES] looked with envy on his friend Dionysius [die-oh-NIS-ee-us], the king of Syracuse. He believed that the king had a very good life—all the riches and all the power that anyone could imagine.

"You think I'm lucky?" Dionysius said to him one day. "If you think so, let's trade places. You sit here, on the throne, for just one day and see if you still think I'm lucky."

Damocles eagerly accepted his friend's invitation. He ordered servants to bring him fine robes and a great banquet of food. He ordered expensive wine and fine music as he dined. He sat back, sure that he was the happiest man in the world.

Then he looked up. He caught his breath in fear. Above his head, a sword dangled from the ceiling attached by a single strand of horse's hair. Damocles could not speak, could not eat, could not enjoy the music. He could not even move.

"What is the matter, my friend?" asked Dionysius.

"How can I conduct my life with that sword hanging above me?" Damocles said.

"How indeed?" answered Dionysius. "And now you know how it feels to be king. That sword hangs over my head every minute of every day. There is always the chance the thread will break. An advisor may turn on me or an enemy spy may attack me. Even I might make an unwise decision that brings my downfall. The privilege of power brings dangers."

Damon and Pythias

Here is a story told by the ancient Roman writer Cicero as an example of true friendship.

Dionysius, the king of Syracuse, heard rumors that a young man named Pythias [PITH-ee-us] was making speeches and telling people to question whether he, or any king, should have so much power. He called Pythias before him. The young man arrived with his best friend, Damon, by his side.

"You dare to stand before the king without bowing?" barked Dionysius when he saw the two men before him.

"I believe that all people are equal," Pythias boldly stated. "No man should have absolute power over another."

"Who do you think you are, to speak such a philosophy and spread it among my people?" Dionysius raged.

"I speak the truth," Pythias answered bravely. "There can be nothing wrong with that."
Dionysius was outraged. "You risk punishment, even death, by speaking like that."

"My philosophy teaches me patience. I have no fear of punishment, or even death."

"We shall see what your philosophy provides you in prison," roared Dionysius. He commanded his soldiers to seize Pythias and lock him in the caverns of Syracuse until he promised never to contradict the king again.

Pythias stood strong and tall. "I cannot make that promise, and so I will accept that punishment," he said. "But may I first go home to tell my family and put my household in order?"

"Do you think I'm stupid?" shouted the king. "If I let you go, you will never return!"

Then up stepped Damon. "Put me in the cell until he returns."

"I will agree to this plan," said the king, "but if Pythias does not return in three days, Damon will be executed."

"I trust my friend," said Damon.

So Pythias traveled to his home, and Damon sat in the deep, dark cell alone. Two days came and went. On the morning of the third, Dionysius ordered Damon brought before him.

"Your friend has not returned," he bellowed. "You know what that means? It means your death!"

"I trust my friend," Damon repeated. "Something has delayed him. He will come back. I am sure of it."

At sundown, the soldiers led Damon to the place where he would be put to death. Dionysius watched with a sneer on his face. "What do you say of your friend now?" he asked.

"I trust my friend," Damon replied.

Pythias arrives just in time.

Just then Pythias rushed in, his clothing torn and his face bruised and dirty. "Thank the gods you are safe," he said to Damon. "My ship was wrecked in a

storm. Thieves attacked me on the road. But I did not give up, and I finally made it here. Now I am ready to take my punishment."

Seeing such friendship, Dionysius learned an important lesson. He revoked Damon's death sentence, freed Pythias, and asked the two men to teach him how to be such a good friend, too.

Androcles and the Lion

The ancient Romans thought it great sport to watch men fight wild animals to the death. This fight has a surprise ending.

Androcles [AN-droh-clees] was a Roman slave who escaped his master and ran away. He was delighted with his freedom but uncertain how he could make it on his own. As night fell, he found a cave carved naturally out of the hillside. He crept into the cool darkness, lay down, and fell asleep.

Suddenly, he awoke, hearing the loud roar of a lion nearby. It was no dream—it was a real lion, looking straight into the cave. Androcles shrank back, fearful for his life, watching the lion's every move.

Then he noticed that the lion was suffering. It was roaring in pain. The great beast limped into the cave and flopped down. It lifted its right front paw and licked it.

Androcles took a step toward the lion. The big cat gave him a sad look, as if asking for help. Androcles crouched next to the lion. He saw a thorn stuck in the middle of its paw. Gently, he pulled the thorn out. The lion looked him in the eye again and purred.

That was the beginning of a warm friendship between Androcles and the lion. They lived together in the cave and slept side by side, keeping each other warm.

But one day Roman soldiers discovered Androcles. The law of Rome said that runaway slaves must be punished, so Androcles was captured and shut into a prison cell in the city of Rome.

For ten days, Androcles sat alone in prison, fed nothing but water and crusts of stale bread. Then a soldier announced that he was to meet his death in the Colosseum.

Androcles knew what that meant. Runaway slaves were often made to fight vicious lions before crowds of Roman citizens. He knew, as he walked the path from the prison to the Colosseum, that he would soon die.

The crowd cheered as Androcles stepped into the arena. They cheered even more loudly as the lion appeared on the other side. Androcles walked into the ring and bravely faced his death.

Then he and the lion recognized each other. To the amazement of the crowd, instead of attacking, the lion began licking the slave's face—and the slave began stroking the lion!

The crowd cheered even more. "Free the slave! Free the lion!" they were yelling, and the emperor agreed. Androcles and the lion lived a long life together in the city of Rome.

Horatius at the Bridge

This famous story about a Roman hero has stayed with us in part because the English poet Thomas Macaulay wrote a book called Lays of Ancient Rome, *which included a poem about Horatius's acts of heroism. In the telling of this story, we quote some of the best verses from the poem.*

Lucius Tarquinius, the last of the Roman kings, was so cruel that the people called him Tarquin the Tyrant. Finally, they banded together and sent him out of Rome. Forced out of power, Tarquin visited Lars Porsena, king of the Etruscans, who lived to the north of Rome. Tarquin convinced Lars Porsena to assemble a huge army, much larger and more powerful than the Roman army, and attack Rome.

There was only one way for them to enter the city of Rome, over a small wooden bridge across the Tiber River. A soldier named Horatius guarded that bridge. When he saw the Etruscans preparing to attack his city, he came up with a plan.

He and two others would cross the bridge and fight off the Etruscans as they came down the narrow path toward the bridge. As they fought, Horatius suggested, the Romans could tear apart the bridge, making it impossible for the Etruscans to cross and storm the city.

> "Horatius," quoth the Consul,
>   "As thou sayest, so let it be."
> And straight against that great array
>   Forth went the dauntless Three.
> For Romans in Rome's quarrel
>   Spared neither land nor gold,
> Nor son nor wife, nor limb nor life,
>   In the brave days of old.

While the three soldiers held the Etruscans back, others chopped away at the wooden bridge. Just before the bridge fell into the river, Horatius commanded his two helpers to cross to the Roman side. He remained, fighting off the Etruscans until he could do so no longer. Then, praying to the Tiber River to take good care of him, Horatius dove into the water.

Every Roman soldier held his breath, afraid he had seen the last of brave Horatius. Then the crest of his helmet surfaced above the river, and all cheered. The current was high, the river was fast, and Horatius, wearing heavy armor, had to struggle to survive.

> And now he feels the bottom;
>   Now on dry earth he stands;
> Now round him throng the Fathers
>   To press his gory hands;
> And now, with shouts and clapping,
>   And noise of weeping loud,
> He enters through the River-Gate,
>   Borne by the joyous crowd.

Thanks to Horatius at the bridge, Tarquin and the Etruscans could not enter Rome. For many generations after, men and women told the story of how Horatius saved the city of Rome in the brave days of old.

Learning About Literature

Biography and Autobiography

A *biography* is the true story of a person's life.

Suppose you wanted to write the life story of someone you know. You could talk to her and ask her questions about what happened in her life. You could find out about her from her parents, relatives, and friends who know her well. If she had old letters and scrapbooks, you could learn from them, too.

But suppose you wanted to write the life story of someone who lived two hundred years ago. You could use writing that she and other people left behind, like old letters, diaries, and newspaper articles. You would have to read carefully and remember all that you learned, then turn that information into a story about the person's life.

A person is likely to tell her own life story differently than someone else would tell it. When a person chooses to write her own life story, it is called an *autobiography*. The prefix "auto-" means "self." An "autograph" is your name written by yourself. Something "automatic" works by itself. So an "autobiography" is a biography you write yourself.

We read autobiographies to learn about what people did and about the times in which they lived. For example, you might read the famous autobiography of a Dutch girl named Anne Frank, who wrote about what happened when she and her family hid from the Nazis by living in a tiny attic room. Or you could read another famous autobiography by Frederick Douglass, who wrote about his experiences as a slave.

Fiction and Nonfiction

Fiction means stories that did not actually happen, such as fairy tales and myths or made-up stories like *Alice's Adventures in Wonderland* or *Charlotte's Web*. Fiction can be so close to the truth that it seems real, or it can be so fantastic that it could never happen. When you make up a story, you are creating fiction.

Nonfiction, on the other hand, is all about true things—people who really lived and the things they really did. A biography is nonfiction. An autobiography is nonfiction. History is nonfiction. Articles in the newspaper and a science report are nonfiction, too. When you tell someone what you did on your summer vacation, you are creating nonfiction.

There is an old saying that "truth is stranger than fiction." Do you think that's true?

Sayings and Phrases

Note to parents: *Every culture has phrases and proverbs that make no sense when carried over literally into another culture. Their meanings come from metaphor and custom, not from literal definitions. The sayings and phrases in this section may be familiar to many children who have heard them at home. Their inclusion has been singled out for gratitude by parents and teachers who work with children from home cultures other than that of literate American English.*

Actions speak louder than words.

This saying reminds us that what people say does not always show what they think, while what people do reveals their thoughts or beliefs more clearly.

"Dad says he hates cats—even Jojo!" Stewart shook his head.

"But last night," Tracy said, "I saw Dad kiss the top of Jojo's head when he thought no one was looking."

"Maybe he really loves Jojo, but he keeps it a secret. Actions speak louder than words!"

His bark is worse than his bite.

People use this saying to describe a person who speaks angrily or threatens but may not be truly dangerous.

"Mr. Kreckle sure is a grouch," Jason said.

"Yeah," Mickey said. "They should call him 'principaddle'!"

"You two are so silly," Miyaka said. "Mr. Kreckle would never  paddle anybody. He might get mad easily, but he's really a nice man. His bark is worse than his bite!"

Beat around the bush

People use this phrase to mean that someone is avoiding direct discussion of a difficult subject by talking instead about related subjects that are less important.

"So how'd you do on your math test, Carlos?" Mr. Ramos asked.

Carlos cleared his throat. "Three kids were late for class, so the teacher didn't start the test until ten minutes after the hour began."

Carlos's father looked at his son, waiting for an answer to his question.

"I was supposed to bring in three pencils," Carlos said. "I forgot."

"Didn't you say you were going to grade the test in class, Carlos?" said Mr. Ramos. He was getting impatient.

"I don't know how that teacher expects us to finish twenty problems when we only have forty minutes."

Mr. Ramos got up and put his arm around Carlos's shoulder. "Come on, Carlos. Stop beating around the bush. Tell me how you did on your math test."

Beggars can't be choosers.

People use this saying to mean that when you are in a weak or disadvantaged position, you shouldn't be picky about the help that may be offered—even if it isn't exactly the sort of help you want.

"I didn't have time to eat breakfast," Janel said, "and I'm starving. But the only thing left in the cafeteria is spinach salad—yuk!"

"Beggars can't be choosers, Janel," Nikki said. "Looks like you'll have to eat something healthful for a change."

Clean bill of health

People use this phrase to express that something is in perfect shape.

Latasha worked for an hour on her math homework. She went over every problem and did her best to make sure every answer was correct. When she was finished, she showed it to her mother, who said, "You've certainly improved in math, Latasha. You did all of these equations perfectly! This homework gets a clean bill of health."

Cold shoulder

People use this phrase to mean that someone is acting unfriendly.

"Ever since I told Daryl he should lose some weight, he pretends he doesn't know me," Christina said. "I said 'hi' to him at recess, and he just walked away."

"Maybe it's the way you said it," Sara said. "If you told me I looked like a hippopotamus, I'd give you the cold shoulder, too!"

A feather in your cap

This expression indicates a person has done something to make him or her proud.

Camille loved to play the violin. She practiced every day. One day during orchestra rehearsal, the string section was playing a piece that Camille had practiced carefully.

"Camille, let me hear that measure again," said the orchestra conductor.

Camille played the measure perfectly.

"Beautiful!" the conductor said. "You deserve to be first chair in next week's concert. That will be a feather in your cap."

Last straw

This phrase describes the moment when things have gone too far one way and just have to change. It comes from a legend about a man who piled straw on his camel's back, one piece at a time. Even though each piece of straw was light, one piece was the "last straw" that broke the camel's back.

"What's wrong, Paul?" Lenny asked. "Do you need any help?"

Paul was kneeling down next to his bicycle, trying to remove his front tire, which had gone flat. "Just leave me alone," he snapped. "First I fell off my bike on the way to school and skinned my elbow. Then, once I got to math class, I remembered that I left my homework at home. Then Bob Banks tripped me when we were playing basketball, and I bruised my knee. And now I have a flat tire. This is the last straw!"

Let bygones be bygones.

People use this saying to mean letting go of whatever is bothering you so it becomes a thing of the past.

"I can't believe the teacher gave me a C on my science homework last week!" Tyrone banged his desk with his fist. "It makes me so mad!"

"Come on, Tyrone, that was last week! You just got an A on this week's homework," Janine said. "Let bygones be bygones!"

One rotten apple spoils the whole barrel.

This saying means that one bad thing can spoil everything connected with it.

  Mr. Small's class was known as the best-behaved class in the school. One day a new boy joined the class. He was noisy and rude, but he was also funny. Soon the other kids in Mr. Small's class started talking and laughing and becoming rowdy. Mr. Small just shook his head and said, "One rotten apple spoils the whole barrel!"

On its last legs

People use this phrase to say that something is about to die or is too worn out to be repaired.

"This has been a good old truck," Mr. Johnson said to his grandson, Vincent. They drove down the bumpy dirt road, and the truck sputtered and groaned. "I've had it for nearly twenty years."

Vincent was amazed to hear that the truck was older than he was.

"But you hear those noises it's making, Vincent?" The old man shook his head. "I'm afraid this truck is on its last legs."

Rule the roost

People use this phrase to describe a person who bosses other people around. It comes from the way a rooster acts in a chicken house, or "roost."

Katie and June were watching television in their living room. When Janice came in from playing, she ran in front of her sisters and changed the channel.

"Hey!" Katie said. "We were here first."

"Too bad," Janice said. "I'm the oldest."

"You may be the oldest," June said, "but that doesn't mean you rule the roost!"

The show must go on.

This saying means that no matter what happens, things will continue as planned.

"We can't play in the championship next Saturday," Karen said to her coach. "Lisa sprained her ankle, Cecilia has the mumps, and Jenny has to go away for the weekend. They're the best soccer players on the team. We'll lose without them."

"We've been practicing all season," answered her coach. "We're not giving up. The show must go on!"

Touch and go

This phrase describes a situation that is so difficult, no one knows how it will turn out.

Harold had been training to be a tightrope walker, but today was his first day to perform for an audience. He took his first steps steadily and slowly, using a long pole to keep his balance. When he got to the middle, he looked down for a moment. He felt himself teeter. The crowd gasped. Then, just in time, he regained his balance. The rest of his steps were strong and sure.

Later Harold said, "Everything was fine until I looked down. For a few seconds there, it was touch and go."

When in Rome, do as the Romans do.

This saying suggests that when you are in an unfamiliar situation, it's good to behave like others around you.

After a day at her new school, Clarisse called Morgan, her best friend from the old school. "You're not going to believe this, Morgan," she said. "They all pile their backpacks up outside the classroom door."

"They do?" Morgan said. "We never do that here at our school."

"I know," Clarisse said. "I wanted to keep mine with me, but when I saw what everyone else was doing, I took out my books and left it outside. When in Rome, do as the Romans do."

Learning About Language

Let's Write a Report

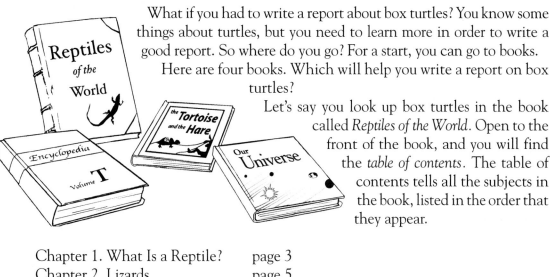

What if you had to write a report about box turtles? You know some things about turtles, but you need to learn more in order to write a good report. So where do you go? For a start, you can go to books. Here are four books. Which will help you write a report on box turtles?

Let's say you look up box turtles in the book called *Reptiles of the World*. Open to the front of the book, and you will find the *table of contents*. The table of contents tells all the subjects in the book, listed in the order that they appear.

What page will you turn to in order to learn about turtles? For the chapter on turtles, you will go to page 26. Since turtles are reptiles, you might also want to read the chapters on reptiles. On what pages can you find those chapters?

You can also use the *index* of a book to look up subjects that interest you. The index is always at the back of the book, and it gives an alphabetical list of everything in the book. Indexes help you find subjects that might not be named in the table of contents.

To do some reading for your report on box turtles, what page will you turn to?

There are other books that can give you information about box turtles. One very helpful kind of book is an *encyclopedia*. Encyclopedias give information about famous people, places, things, ideas, events in history, and more.

To find out about box turtles in the encyclopedia, open the volume marked "B" and look for "box turtles." But maybe you can't find that topic. Try looking in the volume marked "T" for "turtles." That article might include something about box turtles.

Some encyclopedias come on a disk that you use in a computer. With these, you just type in a word—like "turtle"—and the computer helps you search for information.

Dictionaries explain words. They show how to spell a word correctly, how to divide it into syllables, how to pronounce it (using symbols that stand for sounds), and what it means. Dictionaries also tell what part of speech a word is.

If you were reading a book and saw the word "flabbergast," where would you look to find out what it means? In a dictionary, under the letter "F." Say—what *does* "flabbergast" mean? Why not look it up?

After you have read about box turtles, you'll need to plan your report. Let's say you have three big ideas you want to write about:

1. What box turtles look like
2. Where box turtles live
3. What box turtles eat

You could write one *paragraph* about each of these big ideas.

A paragraph is a group of sentences all written about the same idea. It's a good idea to start a paragraph with a sentence that states the *topic*, or

a paragraph

topic sentence

indent

Box turtles are omnivores, which means they eat both plants and animals. Box turtles eat leaves and fruit. They also eat insects, earthworms, and slugs.

examples

the main idea, of the paragraph. Then you can write a few more sentences to explain the idea and give examples.

Every time you start writing about a new idea, you should begin a new paragraph. How do you show that it is a new paragraph? You *indent*. See the space at the beginning of this paragraph, before the word "Every"? When you make a space like that, you're indenting.

Let's Write a Letter

Today a lot of people use computers to send e-mail, but there are times when you will want to write a letter—to thank someone for a present, to send someone an invitation, or to make a formal request or statement, such as a letter to your city's mayor, suggesting your idea for a name for the new city park.

Writing a letter is different from writing a report. It's a lot more like talking. Still, there are a few rules to follow.

- Begin by writing a *heading,* which tells your address and the date.
- Write a *greeting* to the person you're addressing. The greeting is like saying hello.
- Write the *body* of your letter in paragraphs. Indent each new paragraph.
- End your letter with a *closing* (such as "Sincerely" or "Your friend"). Then write your *signature*—your name in handwriting.

What's a Sentence?

You know sentences. You speak and write them all the time. A sentence is a group of words that expresses a complete thought. Every sentence has a *subject* and a *predicate*.

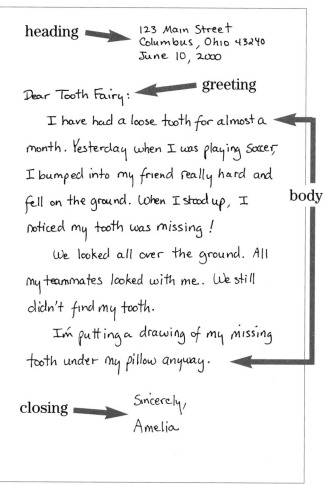

heading → 123 Main Street
Columbus, Ohio 43240
June 10, 2000

Dear Tooth Fairy: ← greeting

I have had a loose tooth for almost a month. Yesterday when I was playing soccer, I bumped into my friend really hard and fell on the ground. When I stood up, I noticed my tooth was missing!

We looked all over the ground. All my teammates looked with me. We still didn't find my tooth.

I'm putting a drawing of my missing tooth under my pillow anyway. ← body

closing → Sincerely,
Amelia

Is this a sentence?

Four fresh figs

No, something is missing. Is this a sentence?

Grow in my grandmother's garden

No, something is missing here, too. But if you put them together, you can make a complete sentence.

Four fresh figs grow in my grandmother's garden.

subject   predicate

Now look at the subject and predicate in this sentence:

Six silly spiders sing songs in the shower.

subject   predicate

Can you find the subject and predicate in this sentence?

Seven small sea horses swim south in summer.

Here's a sentence with something missing. This has a predicate, but it needs a subject.

Eight enormous _____ eat doughnuts every morning.

What's the predicate? It's *eat doughnuts every morning.* Now you make this a complete sentence. Choose a subject. *Eight enormous whats?*

Every sentence begins with a capital letter. Do you remember other times when you use a capital letter? Capital letters start proper nouns, like names of people and places: for example, **George Washington** and **United States.** You capitalize the main words in titles of books: for example, **Little House in the Big Woods.** You capitalize holidays, days of the week, and months of the year: for example, **Hanukkah, Wednesday,** and **January.** And you always use a capital letter for the word that stands for yourself: **I.**

What Kind of Sentence Is It?

Now let's find out about three different kinds of sentences. You make up these kinds of sentences every day. The three basic kinds of sentences are:

- declarative
- interrogative
- imperative

Let's start with this sentence:

Julia took her pet alligator for a walk.

That's called a *declarative* sentence because it *declares* or makes a statement about Julia and her pet.

If Julia's friend visited and found her not at home, she might use an *interrogative* sentence, which is a sentence that asks a question.

Did Julia take her pet alligator for a walk?

Interrogative sentences end with a question mark.

If Julia was sleeping late and had been ignoring her pet, then Julia's mother might use *imperative* sentences, which are sentences that make requests or give commands.

Wake up! Take your pet alligator for a walk.

Both of these are imperative sentences. Look at the first one again: *Wake up!* Where is the subject in that sentence? You don't see a subject, but we say that the subject, "you," is understood. In most imperative sentences, the "you" is understood, such as in *Stop!* or *Please sit down.*

If Julia took her pet alligator for a walk to the park, then the people who saw her might use *exclamatory statements*, which are incomplete sentences that show strong feeling:

Help! An alligator! What a crazy girl!

Exclamatory statements often end with exclamation marks!

Parts of Speech

Let's review the *parts of speech* you already know and find out about some new ones.

Nouns

Can you find the *nouns* in this sentence?

My brother put on his bathing suit, mask, and fins, but he forgot to bring a beach umbrella.

Remember, a noun names a person, place, or thing. Here is the sentence again with the nouns printed in color.

My brother put on his bathing suit, mask, and fins, but he forgot to bring a beach umbrella.

Adjectives

Do you remember what *adjectives* do? Here's a hint. Look at this sentence, with the adjectives printed in color:

On cold mornings, Michiko likes to cuddle up in her soft, fuzzy, purple blanket.

Adjectives are words that describe. Adjectives include words like *cold, soft, fuzzy,* and *purple,* as well as *long, big, scary,* and *beautiful.* Can you think of three adjectives to describe a puppy? How about an elephant?

There are three special adjectives you use all the time, called *articles* (or "determiners"). The articles are

a   an   the

You might say, "Please hand me a glass," but if you wanted a certain glass, you would say, "Please hand me the glass." If you felt hungry for an apple, just any old apple, you might say, "I would like an apple." But if you wanted to eat a certain apple—the big juicy red one on the counter—you might say, "I would like the apple." Notice that you use *a* before words that begin with a consonant, but *an* before words that begin with a vowel. You say "a glass," but "an apple."

Verbs

Can you think of a good word to fill in the blanks in each of these sentences?

José _____ fast.

Alison _____ the basketball.

For the first sentence, did you come up with something like *runs, walks,* or *eats?* For the second sentence, did you say something like *shot, dribbled,* or *passed?*

Words like *runs*, *walks*, *shot*, and *dribbled* show actions. Words that express action are *verbs*. Can you find three verbs in this sentence?

Henry carries his backpack and shouts to his friends while he rides his bicycle to school.

Adverbs

We use *adverbs* to add something to a verb. Adverbs describe the verb. For example, you could say,

Liz showed us her trophy.

What is the verb in that sentence? It's *showed*. So *how* did Liz show us her trophy? You could say,

Liz proudly showed us her trophy.

Or you could say,

Liz secretly showed us her trophy.

Proudly and *secretly* are adverbs. They each tell us something about the verb, *showed*. Most adverbs end with the letters *-ly*, such as:

quickly	slowly	suddenly
quietly	politely	carefully

Here are two sentences. First find the verb. Then think of a good adverb to tell something more about the verb.

The cat crept toward the mouse.

I asked for permission to leave the room.

Now, can you find the adjectives and the adverbs in this sentence? Adjectives first, then adverbs.

Melanie proudly showed her mother the fuzzy pink petunias that she had carefully planted in the garden.

Pronouns

Do you like to talk about yourself? Most people do! What do you call yourself when you do? Sometimes you use your name, but most of the time you use *pronouns*. You call yourself "I" and "me," depending on what you are saying. *I* and *me* are both pronouns.

Pronouns are words that stand for nouns. *He*, *she*, *it*, and *they* are pronouns. Here's a sentence without any pronouns:

*James asked Sarah to tell James when Sarah was going to come
over to James's house.*

Would you ever say or write a sentence like that? No! You would use pronouns, like this:

*James asked Sarah to tell him when she was going to come over
to his house.*

When you read that sentence, you understand that the pronouns *him* and *his* stand for "James" and the pronoun *she* stands for "Sarah."

More About Verbs

Some words help express action. They are called *helping verbs*, like:

does ride	*will* shout	*have* brought	*is* diving
has carried	*had* broken	*was* throwing	*am* thinking

Let's Punctuate!

Writing isn't just words and letters. All those little squiggles and symbols—like , ? ! . "—mean something, too.

Some punctuation marks come at the end of a sentence.

That last sentence ended with—what?—a *period.*

What other punctuation marks can end a sentence?

That last sentence, which was a question, ended with—what?—a *question mark.*

There is one more punctuation mark that can end a sentence!

What punctuation mark ended that sentence? It ended with an *exclamation mark.* When a sentence ends with one of those, you know it's about something exciting.

The *comma* is a punctuation mark that comes inside a sentence. Consider the comma in these sentences:

I was born on March 30, 1995.

A comma always comes between the date and the year.

I live in Oshkosh, Wisconsin.

A comma always comes between the names of a city and a state.

My favorite animals are earthworms, moles, and eagles.

Commas always separate words in a series.

Yes, I know that my favorite animals are strange!

Commas always come after the words "Yes" or "No" at the start of a sentence.

The *apostrophe* is a punctuation mark that comes inside a word. It has two different jobs.

An apostrophe can show *possession*.

Emily's scarecrow costume

my puppy's name

Even when the word is plural and ends in *-s*, you add an apostrophe and an *s* to make it possessive:

five crabs's claws

(Some people just add an apostrophe to show possession with a word ending in *-s*. They would write "five crabs' claws," and they would be right, too.)

An apostrophe is also used to make *contractions*, when two words come together to make one.

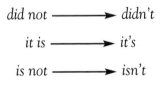

did not ⟶ *didn't*

it is ⟶ *it's*

is not ⟶ *isn't*

In contractions, the apostrophe stands for a letter that has been dropped. In the contractions above, what letters do the apostrophes stand for?

Just Say No Once

Here are two good sentences, easy to understand.

I didn't eat lunch today.

I ate no lunch today.

But what would it mean if somebody said:

I didn't eat no lunch today.

Would it mean that the person ate *no lunch*, or that the person *did* eat lunch? It's confusing, isn't it?

The third sentence has a *double negative*: both "didn't" (which stands for "did not") and "no lunch" are negatives. If you say you did not not do something, that can only mean you really did it. Double negatives are confusing, and it's best not to use them.

Prefixes and Suffixes

Prefixes attach to the beginning of words to change their meanings.

> *re-* means "again":
> *refill* means "fill again"
> *reread* means "read again"

> *un-* means "not":
> *unfriendly* means "not friendly"
> *unpleasant* means "not pleasant"

> *un-* can also mean the opposite or reverse of an action:
> *untie* means the reverse of "tie"
> *unlock* means the reverse of "lock"

> *dis-* means "not":
> *dishonest* means "not honest"
> *disobey* means "not obey"

> *dis-* can also mean the opposite or reverse of an action:
> *disappear* means the opposite of "appear"
> *dismount* means the reverse of "mount"

See if you can find an example of your own for each of these prefixes.

Suffixes attach to the end of words to change their meanings.

> *-er* and *-or* change verbs to nouns naming people:
> sing + -er ⟶ *singer*
> paint + -er ⟶ *painter*

> *-less* makes an adjective meaning without that noun:
> hope + less ⟶ *hopeless*
> fear + less ⟶ *fearless*

> *-ly* turns an adjective into an adverb:
> quick + ly ⟶ *quickly*
> calm + ly ⟶ *calmly*

Can you find another example for each of these three suffixes?

They Sound Alike, but They're Different

Can you solve this riddle?

Why was six afraid of seven?

Answer: Because seven eight nine!

This riddle works because the words "eight" and "ate" sound alike, even though they mean different things.

Words that have the same sound but different spellings and meanings are called *homophones*. "Eight" and "ate" are homophones. Can you think of some others? What is the word for a female deer, and what word is its homophone? "Doe" and "dough." Here's a silly sentence with two pairs of homophones:

We went *by* the store to *buy* a *whole* doughnut *hole*.

Can you make up a sentence with a pair of homophones?

Sometimes you just have to memorize the different words and their spellings. Here are a few to memorize.

Where are the bears? *They're there*, in *their* cave.

they're ⟶ "they are"

there ⟶ "in that place"

their ⟶ "belonging to them"

You're sure *your* hair is three feet long?

you're ⟶ "you are"

your ⟶ "belonging to you"

Look at that polar bear. I wonder if Icecube is *its* name and if *it's* cold in that icy water.

its ⟶ "belonging to it"

it's ⟶ "it is"

Here are two more sentences. Can you find the homophones?

Come over here so you can hear the bird better.

Those two tortoises are creeping too slowly to win the race.

Shorten Up with Abbreviations

Sometimes it's useful to find a short way to write a word that is used often. For instance, we use the word "Mister" so often that we abbreviate it as "Mr." When you see the abbreviation "Mr.," you still say the whole word, "Mister." Here are some common abbreviations.

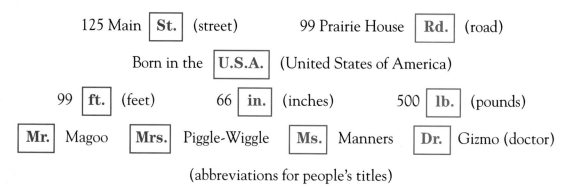

125 Main St. (street)   99 Prairie House Rd. (road)

Born in the U.S.A. (United States of America)

99 ft. (feet)   66 in. (inches)   500 lb. (pounds)

Mr. Magoo   Mrs. Piggle-Wiggle   Ms. Manners   Dr. Gizmo (doctor)

(abbreviations for people's titles)

II.

Geography and History

INTRODUCTION

As anyone knows who has witnessed children's fascination with dinosaurs, knights in armor, or pioneers on the prairie, young children are interested in other people, places, and times. The idea is not for the child to achieve deep historical knowledge, but for him or her to become familiar with people, words, and ideas so that, even years later, the child can say, "I know something about that."

Learning history is not simply a matter of recalling facts—although getting a firm mental grip on certain dates, such as 1607 and 1776, is important. Dates reinforce a sense of chronology and establish a foundation for more sophisticated historical understanding in years to come.

By third grade, children are ready to make more subtle connections among historical facts. They are beginning to understand how ideas cause change. Still, the best history teaching emphasizes the story. In some cases, it's hard—and perhaps not entirely necessary—to separate history from legend, as in the story of Romulus and Remus. We encourage parents and teachers to find art, drama, music, and literature that help children learn about history, too.

A special emphasis should be placed on learning geography. The elementary years are the best years in which to establish a lasting familiarity with the main features of world geography, such as the continents, the larger countries, the major rivers and mountains, and the major cities of the world. Especially when learned in connection with interesting stories, these features and places will stay with a person throughout life. Knowledge can be reinforced through work with maps—drawing, coloring, and playful practice at identifying place-names. Maps offer children a foundation for understanding how geography influences world politics and economics.

Suggested Resources

Alison Cooper, Adriano Nardi, Antonella Meucci, and Daniela de Luca, *The Children's Pictorial Atlas of the World* (Barron's Educational Series). This atlas includes colorful maps, useful legends, and economic and cultural features, written for nine-year-olds and up.

Roy Burrell, *Oxford First Ancient History* (Oxford University Press, 1994). Amply illustrated, this book covers ancient history from the Stone Age through the fall of Rome, interspersing factual chapters with narratives.

Joy Hakim, *The First Americans* and *Making Thirteen Colonies*, Books One and Two of A History of US series (Oxford University Press). The first two in a series of ten about American history, these engaging books are targeted for middle school readers.

Appleseeds. One of several Cobblestone magazines offering intelligent approaches to history for young readers, this one for second, third, and fourth graders. Write to Cobblestone Publishing, 30 Grove St., Peterborough, NH 03458, call 800-821-0115, or visit www.cobblestonepub.com.

World Geography

Let's see how many geographical facts you already know.

- What continent do you live on?
- What country do you live in?
- What state do you live in?

Was that easy? Well, we're just getting started. Now look at the map.

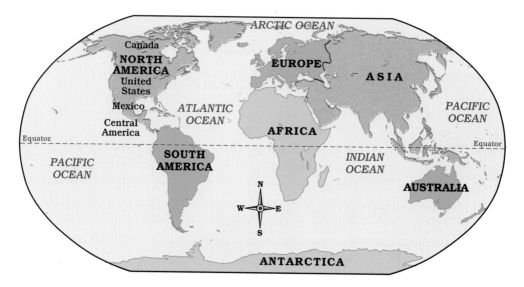

- Where is the compass rose on this map? What do N, E, S, and W stand for?
- Which way is north? South? East? West?
- Can you point to and name the world's seven continents?
- Can you point to and name the world's four big oceans?

Did you get all seven continents? And how about the four big oceans?
Now, can you point to these on the map?

- Canada
- United States
- Mexico
- Central America

- the equator
- the Northern Hemisphere
- the Southern Hemisphere

Do you have a globe? If you do, see if you can find the North Pole and the South Pole.
That's the whole quiz. How did you do?

Look at the Legend

Look at the map of Canada below. See the box in the corner? That's the map's *legend*. The legend explains the symbols used on the map. For example, it shows that a dotted line marks the *boundary* (or dividing line) between provinces, while a solid line marks the boundary between countries.

Maps often have bar scales to help you read distances. For example, the scale on this map shows that 1 inch equals a little less than 800 miles. If you traveled the full length of the boundary between Alaska and the Yukon Territory, how far would you travel? You can estimate your answer by using this map and a ruler. It's a little more than an inch, right? That represents about 800 miles.

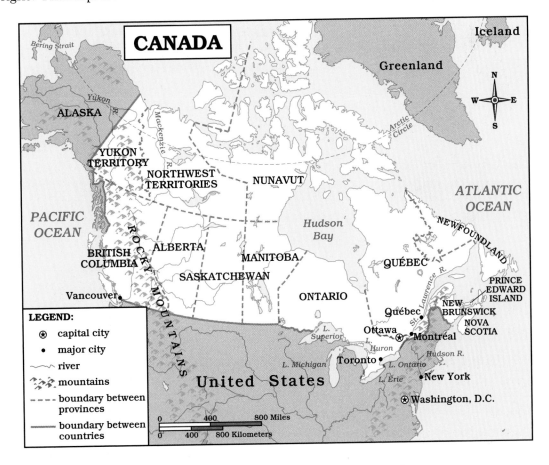

Great Rivers of the World

Many of the world's great civilizations—ancient Mesopotamia, Egypt, India, and China—started near a river. When rivers flood and recede, they leave behind rich soil.

Providing water and building rich soil, rivers help people grow lots of food. Where plenty of food can grow, civilization develops.

Rivers make a difference in the lives of all who live near them. People travel on rivers, bathe in rivers, drink water from rivers, and use river water in their fields and orchards. Water in rivers is fresh water. Ocean water is salt water, which people can't use to drink or water crops.

Rivers flow through every continent of the world. Every river begins as a little stream, at a starting point called the river's *source*. Several streams, called *tributaries*, flow together and join to make a river. A really big river might have a tributary that is also big enough to be considered a river. For example, the Mississippi River has many tributaries. The Missouri River, the Ohio River, the Tennessee River, and the Arkansas River (to name just a few) all flow into the Mississippi and make up a *river system*.

When it rains or snows, some water soaks into the ground, but some runs into rivers. In other words, rivers *drain* the land. The area of land drained by a river system is called a *drainage basin* or, for short, a *basin*. ("Basin" is another word for "sink.") The drainage

---

Some Geography Words

channel = a body of water connecting two larger bodies of water
  The Yucatán Channel connects the Gulf of Mexico and the Caribbean Sea.

isthmus = a narrow strip of land connecting two larger areas of land
  The Isthmus of Panama is a narrow strip of land connecting Central America and South America. Long ago, ships had to sail all the way around the southern tip of South America, but now they pass through the Panama Canal, which was dug through the Isthmus of Panama.

plateau = a high, flat area of land
  Some Native American tribes made their homes on plateaus in western North America.

reservoir = a lake created by humans for storing water
  The ancient Egyptians, living near the Nile River, built some of the world's first reservoirs.

strait = a narrow body of water connecting two larger bodies of water
  The Strait of Gibraltar connects the Atlantic Ocean and the Mediterranean Sea.

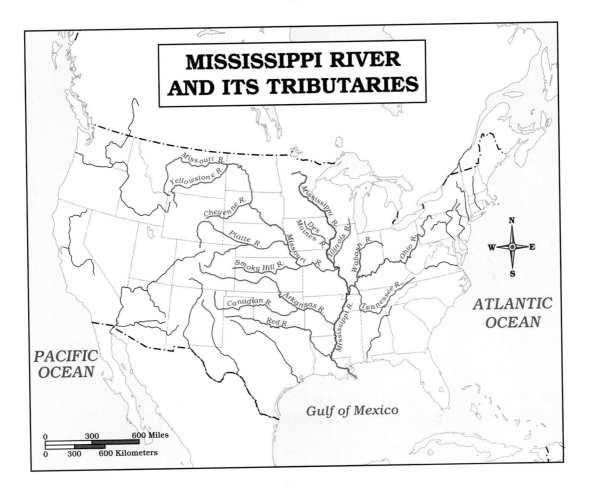

basin of a big river like the Mississippi is huge. With so many tributaries flowing into it, the Mississippi River drains almost half the land of the United States.

At its mouth, a river pours out into the ocean or some other big body of water. The Mississippi River empties into the Gulf of Mexico.

Let's visit the great rivers of the world. Use the map here to locate each river, but also look on a big world map or globe.

Rivers of Asia

The Yellow and the Yangtze In China, where these two rivers flow, people call them by different names. The Yellow River is called the Huang He. The Yangtze River is called the Chang Jiang, which means "long river." The Yangtze is more than three thousand miles long, flowing from the high mountains of Tibet all the way across China into the East China Sea.

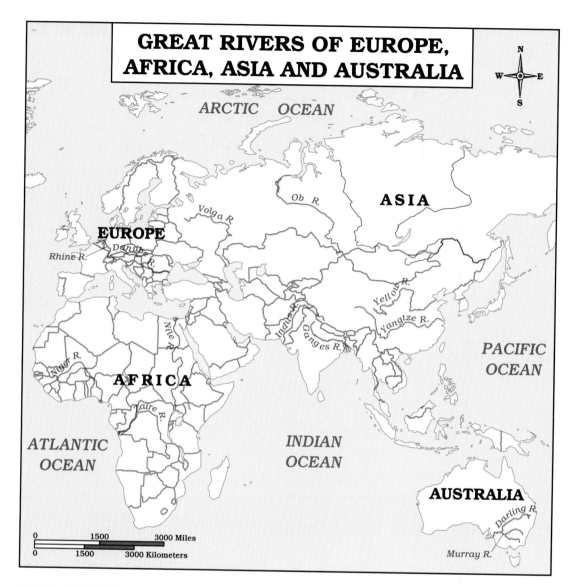

GREAT RIVERS OF EUROPE, AFRICA, ASIA AND AUSTRALIA

ARCTIC OCEAN

ASIA

Ob R.

EUROPE

Volga R.

Rhine R.

Danub

R.

Yellow R.

Nile R.

Indus R.

Ganges R.

Yangtze R.

PACIFIC OCEAN

Niger R.

AFRICA

Laire R.

ATLANTIC OCEAN

INDIAN OCEAN

AUSTRALIA

Darling R.

Murray R.

0   1500   3000 Miles
0   1500   3000 Kilometers

This boat, called a junk, is sailing on the Yellow River in China.

The Ob If you go to Siberia in northern Russia in wintertime, you will find the Ob River frozen solid. If you go in springtime, you might see the Ob River overflowing its banks. Its drainage basin fills up as the snow and ice melt.

The Ganges The Ganges River flows through India and Bangladesh. The source of the Ganges is in an icy cave, high in the Himalaya Mountains.

The Ganges is a holy river to people of the Hindu faith. Every year many thousands of Hindus come to bathe and pray in its waters.

The Indus Thousands of years ago, the great civilization of ancient India started along the Indus River. The Indus is still an important river, but the country through which it flows is now called Pakistan. Along the Indus River valley, people grow corn, rice, and dates.

---

delta = a fan-shaped deposit of sand and mud at the mouth of a river
The Ganges River widens into a broad delta as it flows into the Indian Ocean.

Rivers of Africa

The Nile What is the longest river in the world? It's the Nile. The Nile flows north through Egypt and empties into the Mediterranean Sea. Egypt is so hot and dry that most Egyptians live close to the Nile. In southern Egypt, the huge Aswan High Dam creates a reservoir and controls the flow of the Nile.

The Aswan High Dam, which controls the flow of the Nile River, was built in the 1960s.

The Zaire Imagine traveling on the Zaire River through the rain forest of central Africa. You could not travel on some stretches of the river because of dangerous waterfalls. The path of the Zaire makes a big loop. It empties into the Atlantic Ocean.

The Niger The Niger River travels through four nations in western Africa: Guinea,

Mali, Niger, and Nigeria. Some of Africa's great ancient kingdoms developed near the Niger.

Rivers of Europe

The Volga The Volga River is the longest in Europe, beginning north of Moscow, Russia's capital city, and flowing into the Caspian Sea. The Russian people call it Mother Volga. All along the Volga, people have built canals and reservoirs to make it easier to travel on it and use its water.

The Danube River flows past farms and villages in Austria.

The Danube The Danube River flows through eastern Europe, from Germany to the Black Sea. If you visit in winter, you can ice-skate on the Danube. In 1867, the Austrian composer Johann Strauss composed a lovely waltz about this river, called "On the Beautiful Blue Danube."

The Rhine The Rhine River starts high in the Alps in Switzerland, then flows north through or along the borders of Liechtenstein, Austria, Germany, France, and the Netherlands. It empties into the North Sea. Parts of the Rhine have been dug wide and deep to make canals for big barges that carry timber, iron, coal, and grain.

Rivers of Australia

Let's go "down under" and visit the continent of Australia.

The Darling and the Murray In the southeastern part of the country, the Darling River

joins the Murray River. The Murray then flows south into the Indian Ocean. The people in southeastern Australia use the Murray's water for irrigation. Sometimes they use so much water the river dries up.

Do you recognize this animal with webbed feet, fur, and a bill like a duck? It's a duck-billed platypus. Platypuses live in Australia, along the banks of the Darling and Murray Rivers.

Rivers of South America

The Amazon The world's second longest river, the Amazon starts in the Andes Mountains in Peru and flows through the rain forest jungle in Brazil. It has the largest drainage basin in the world: 2,700,000 square miles of land drain into the Amazon!

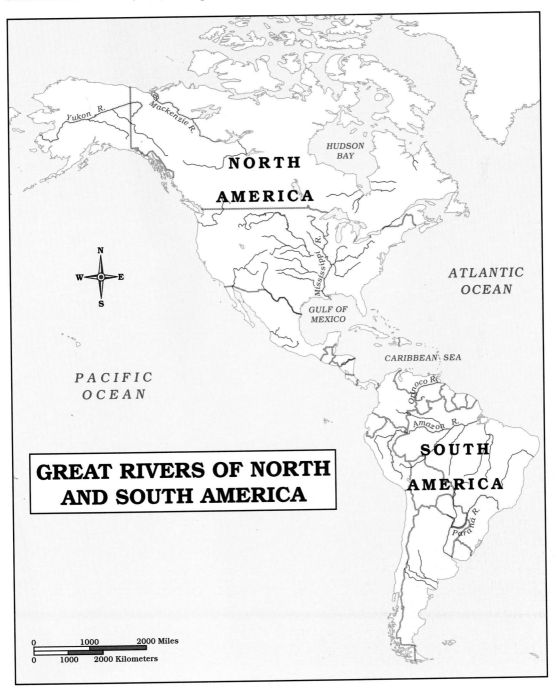

GREAT RIVERS OF NORTH AND SOUTH AMERICA

Look how well this family balances in their canoe as they paddle on the Amazon River in Brazil.

The Paraná If we go to Buenos Aires, the capital of Argentina, we find ourselves at the mouth of the Paraná River. The Paraná is so wide and deep that ocean freighters can travel four hundred miles up the river. The Paraná begins high up in the mountains and spreads into a wide delta as it empties into the Atlantic Ocean.

The Orinoco The Orinoco River flows through Venezuela into the Caribbean Sea. Christopher Columbus probably sailed into the mouth of the Orinoco in 1498. Today you can travel up one of the tributaries of the Orinoco and visit Angel Falls, the world's highest waterfall.

Rivers of North America

The Mississippi Climb aboard this big paddleboat. The paddle wheel turns to make the boat move. We're going to ride down the Mississippi, the most important river in the United States. Big tributary rivers flow into the Mississippi, including the Missouri from the northwest and the Ohio from the northeast. The Mississippi River spreads into a wide delta in the state of Louisiana.

The Mississippi River has been given many names. Native Americans called it "gathering of waters," since so many tributaries flowed into it. That is probably the original meaning of the name we now use.

The *Creole Queen,* a paddleboat on the Mississippi River.

The Mackenzie Canada's Mackenzie River flows north into the Arctic Ocean. It was named for Sir Alexander Mackenzie, the first explorer to travel from its source to its mouth.

The Yukon The Yukon River begins in the Canadian Rocky Mountains, just as the Mackenzie does, but it flows west through Alaska. The entire river stays frozen from October to June. Salmon like to swim through its cold, fresh water.

Salmon swim almost two thousand miles up the Yukon River to spawn, or lay their eggs.

World History

Ancient Rome

Do you remember the saying "When in Rome, do as the Romans do"? It's in the Language and Literature section of this book. When people use that saying today, they aren't really talking about the great city in Italy, are they? Here's another saying: "Rome wasn't built in a day." Again, when people use that saying today, they aren't really referring to Rome. Instead they mean, "Be patient. It takes a long time to complete a great task."

These and other sayings about Rome are still around because Rome is still important to us. Like the civilization of ancient Greece, ancient Rome still affects us today. In our laws and government, in the design of many buildings, in our calendar, even in many words of the English language, ancient Rome lives on in these modern times.

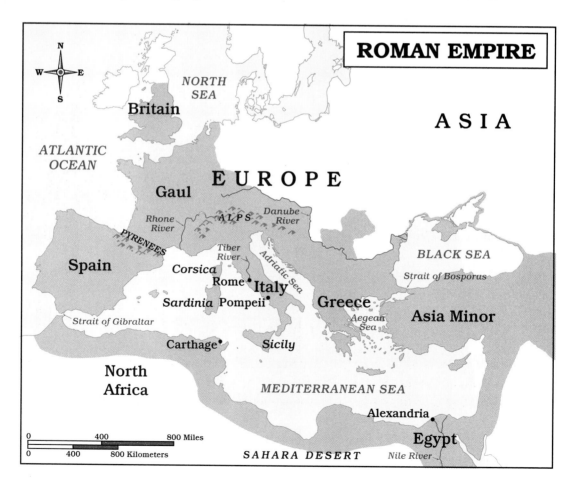

The Legend of How Rome Began

Almost three thousand years ago, people chose seven hills above the Tiber River in Italy as a good place to build their little huts and to farm the land. Those villages grew together into the city called Rome. As Rome grew, its army conquered other countries. The boundaries of Rome's empire spread. At its biggest and strongest, the Roman Empire included most of today's Europe and some of Africa and the Middle East as well. Sixty million people lived under Roman rule, many of them far from the city of Rome, in places that we now call Great Britain, Germany, France, Spain, Greece, Egypt, and Turkey.

The ancient Romans believed that they were born to rule the world. They told a story about how their city was founded by two brothers, Romulus and Remus.

In the legend, there was a jealous king who feared that if his niece had children, they might grow up and conquer him. To make sure that she never had any children, the jealous king made his niece become a priestess. That way she would devote herself to the gods and never marry any man.

Imagine the king's anger when his niece gave birth to twin boys, Romulus and Remus. She explained that the father of these two boys was not a man but Mars, the Roman god of war. The angry king put the babies into a basket and threw them into the Tiber River to drown.

Legend has it that Rome was founded by two brothers, Romulus and Remus, who were raised by a wolf.

But Romulus and Remus were rescued from the river by a mother wolf. She took them back to her lair and fed them as if they were her own babies. When a shepherd happened by and saw the two boys, he took them to his village and cared for them until they grew to be men.

Romulus and Remus agreed that they should start a city. As brothers will do, though, they argued over many things. Where would they put the city? Who would be its ruler? During one terrible argument, Romulus killed Remus.

Romulus went on to build his city on the seven hills overlooking the Tiber River. The city took its name from his: Rome. He ruled as king for many years. Then one night, in the midst of a huge thunderstorm, Romulus disappeared. The Romans believed that he became a god.

As with most legends, there is some truth in the story about Romulus and Remus. As early as 950 B.C., almost three thousand years ago, shepherds and farmers lived on those

Talking About Time in History

When we talk about ancient history, we're going back a long time, sometimes more than 2,000 years. That means we're going back to the year with the number 1, or even back further. How do we number those years more than 2,000 years ago?

We give years their dates based on the birthday of Jesus, whom Christians call Christ, starting to count from the year Jesus was born. The years before Christ was born are called B.C., which stands for "before Christ." If we say Rome was founded in the year 753 B.C., we mean 753 years before Jesus was born.

Every date after Jesus' birth is called A.D., which stands for *anno Domini*, or "in the year of the Lord" in Latin, the language of the Romans. "In the year of the Lord" is another way of saying "after Christ." If you were born in 1995, then another way to name your birth year is A.D. 1995, meaning that you were born 1,995 years after the birth of Jesus.

hills overlooking the Tiber River. About two hundred years later, around 750 B.C., those communities joined to form the one city of Rome.

Religion, Roman Style

Like the ancient Greeks, the ancient Romans worshiped many gods and goddesses. The Romans believed that their gods and goddesses looked and acted like people but held powers greater than any human being. Like the Greeks, the Romans built temples in which they worshiped their gods. They carved beautiful statues to show what they thought their gods looked like. Today in some museums we can see those statues, and in the city of Rome, we can see the ruins of those temples.

Also like the Greeks, the ancient Romans believed that different gods ruled different parts of their world. The king of all the gods, who ruled the sky, was named Jupiter by the Romans. He acted a lot like the Greek god Zeus. The Romans believed that Neptune ruled the sea, just as the Greeks believed in Poseidon.

Romans performed ceremonies to please the gods. They would pray, offer food and wine, and sacrifice animals such as sheep or goats. These ceremonies took place at home, led by the head of the household, or at temples, led by the priests.

The ancient Romans also believed that godlike spirits lived in nature. When birds flew overhead, Romans saw them as messengers from the gods. Priests would watch the way birds flew and decide what the gods were saying.

Rome's Powerful Location

What made Rome so powerful? One answer is location. Let's look at the map on page 88. First find the country we now call Italy. It is a peninsula, shaped like a boot, sticking out into the Mediterranean Sea. Its long eastern coastline edges the Adriatic Sea. Now find Rome. What are the advantages of its location?

Rome sits at a crossroads on both land and sea. It is on a river, so boats can leave Rome and reach the Mediterranean Sea. It is far enough south that Romans enjoy a mild climate. Farther north, the mountain range called the Alps runs from one edge of the boot shape to the other. The Alps protected the ancient Romans. Their rocky, snow-covered peaks kept out most invaders—but not *all*, as you will see.

Rome's Early Republic

For 250 years, Rome was ruled by kings. Some were strong and some were kind, but the last king was so mean and proud that the people drove him away (as you read in "Horatius at the Bridge," pages 56–57). To be sure that no bad king came to power again, the Romans invented a new form of government. They called it a *republic*, from the Latin words for "a thing of the people."

Every year the wealthy men of the Roman republic would select two leaders, called *consuls*. Every year a new pair of consuls was chosen, so no man was likely to grab all the power. In times of war, the consuls led the army. In times of peace, they ran the business of the city. To make decisions, both consuls had to agree. If one disagreed, he would say "Veto," which means "I forbid" in Latin.

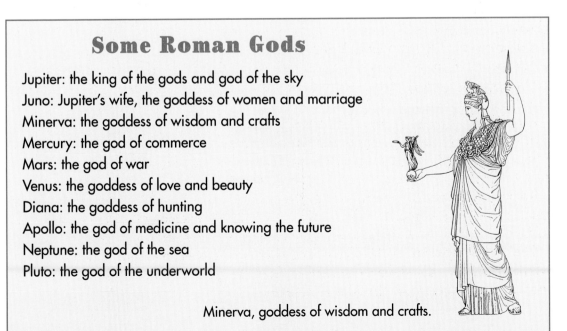

Some Roman Gods

Jupiter: the king of the gods and god of the sky
Juno: Jupiter's wife, the goddess of women and marriage
Minerva: the goddess of wisdom and crafts
Mercury: the god of commerce
Mars: the god of war
Venus: the goddess of love and beauty
Diana: the goddess of hunting
Apollo: the god of medicine and knowing the future
Neptune: the god of the sea
Pluto: the god of the underworld

Minerva, goddess of wisdom and crafts.

Roman senators.

The Romans had a *Senate*, which advised the consuls. The Senate was a group of as many as three hundred wealthy landowners. Once a man became a Roman senator, he held that position for life.

Who's Got Class?

Some people who lived in Rome were considered citizens, but some were not. Slaves and foreigners and, in the early times, people living in conquered lands were not considered citizens. Women were not considered citizens, no matter how smart or wealthy they were.

Among the citizens, there were two classes: the *patricians* [puh-TRISH-uns] and the *plebeians* [pluh-BEE-ans]. Patricians were wealthy men who owned a lot of land. They became consuls and senators. Plebeians were ordinary people who perhaps owned a little property but were still poor. The poorest in Rome were the slaves, who did hard work for both patricians and plebeians.

The plebeians wanted the power and riches of the patricians. As Rome conquered more lands, the patricians needed the plebeians more, since they fought in the army. Over time, the plebeians gained rights nearly equal to those of the patricians.

Rome and Its Provinces

Rome grew by taking over territory in every direction. Any area conquered by the Roman army became a province of Rome. Roman rulers assigned to each province governed the people and reported back to Rome. They collected taxes, either food or money, from the people in the provinces and sent them to Rome.

Roman soldiers.

Some of the conquered people became slaves. In other provinces, the Romans allowed people to follow their own customs and religions. They even let wealthy men from the provinces become Roman citizens. Those who did business in the provinces had to speak Latin, the language of Rome.

Latin Lives!

Some people call Latin a dead language because no one speaks or reads it in everyday life. Plenty of people study Latin, though, because it has played an important part in the history of many of the languages spoken around the world. In that way, Latin is far from a dead language.

Look at these Roman letters chiseled into stone and see how many letters in the Roman alphabet are the same as ours today. Can you find the name "Caesar" on the stone?

Latin was the language spoken and written in ancient Rome. As Rome conquered its provinces, Latin became the language spoken throughout the Roman Empire. Foreign merchants and local town rulers used Latin to communicate with the Roman soldiers, businessmen, and governors. Over centuries, the Latin language spread far, and words in Latin influenced the words spoken in the languages of all those regions.

Many languages spoken today are called Romance languages. Do you see the word "Roman" in that word? That is because all the Romance languages, including French, Spanish, Italian, and Portuguese, developed out of Latin.

How about English? Our language comes from German roots but contains many words from the Latin, such as "family" (*familia* in Latin) and "mother" (*mater* in Latin). Many other English words have a connection with Latin. "Library" comes from *liber*, the Latin word for "book." It's fun to find the Latin roots of English words in the dictionary. (Even "dictionary" comes from *dictio*, Latin for "word.")

Conquering Carthage

By 265 B.C., Rome had conquered most of the peninsula of Italy. Next the Romans decided to conquer lands that were farther away. To the north, that meant invading by land. But to the south, that meant invading by sea, and it meant facing the biggest threat to Roman power, the strong and wealthy city of Carthage. (Find Carthage on the map, page 88.)

Carthage was a city on the north coast of Africa, in the country we now call Tunisia. The city of Carthage began at just about the same time as Rome, and was founded by Phoenicians [fuh-NEE-shuns] who were seafarers and traders from the Middle East. By 265 B.C., Carthage controlled much of North Africa. The Carthaginians [car-thuh-JINee-uns] were great shipbuilders and sailors. One of the lands they had conquered was the island of Sicily.

Take a look at the map on page 88 to find Sicily. Which is closer: Italy or Carthage? Sicily is less than ten miles from Italy. Now you know why Rome considered Carthage a threat.

A war broke out between Carthage and Rome over who would control Sicily. Battles were fought at sea. Who do you think had the advantage? Not the Romans! They could fight a ferocious battle on land, but on the water, they were in big trouble.

But those Romans believed they were born to rule the world, so they weren't about to give up and go home. They found a wrecked Carthaginian warship and, with the help of Greek shipbuilders, made one hundred copies of it in sixty days.

Even with those ships, the Romans could not outsail their enemies. They could win

in hand-to-hand combat, though, so they added a new feature to their ships: a way to board enemy ships at sea.

Once the Romans learned to build ships, they began waging battles at sea, as shown in this drawing of a battle during the First Punic War.

When a Roman ship pulled alongside the enemy, the sailors lowered a drawbridge with a hook that attached to the deck of the enemy ship. Roman soldiers crossed the drawbridge and attacked the Carthaginians on board their own ships, wielding swords and spears and winning many battles.

After more than twenty years of struggle, Rome won its first war against Carthage, called the First Punic [PYOO-nick] War. The proud Carthaginians did not want to be conquered by the Romans. One man was so angry that he made his son promise to battle Rome for the rest of his life. That promise begins the next chapter in ancient Roman history.

Rome's wars against Carthage were called the Punic Wars because the Romans used the Latin word *Punicus* to mean a person from Carthage.

Hannibal Keeps His Promise

Hannibal was only nine years old when his father, angry over the Roman conquest of Carthage, took him to a temple. "Swear by the gods that you will be the enemy of Rome until the day you die!" he demanded. The young boy agreed, and from that day forward, his life was shaped by the promise. By the age of twenty-five, Hannibal had already led an army of Carthaginians across the Mediterranean and into Spain, capturing a city that was friendly with Rome. That's how the Second Punic War started.

When word arrived in Rome that Hannibal was attacking the city in Spain, the Senate sent soldiers out to find him. It took those soldiers a long time to reach Spain, and when they got there, Hannibal was nowhere to be found.

"He's headed east," everyone told them.

"East?" questioned the Romans. "Across the mighty Alps? Even if he were foolish enough to scale those icy slopes, his men would die trying."

Imagine leading thousands of soldiers and dozens of elephants along the narrow, icy paths of the Alps, as Hannibal did.

The Romans had no idea how courageous Hannibal was. He did lead his army across the Alps—and what an army it was. Hannibal started out with sixty thousand soldiers, marching all the way from Spain, through France (then called Gaul), across the Alps, and into Italy. Along with those men came forty massive beasts—animals that frightened the Romans, who had never seen them before. They were huge and heavy, much taller than a human, with big ears, thundering feet, and long trunks. Elephants!

Hannibal and his soldiers crossed the Alps on paths not much better than goat tracks. They marched across icy streams, up and down snow-covered slopes. Many soldiers and most of the elephants died, but that didn't stop Hannibal. He was devoted to his boyhood promise.

At last, he and his soldiers made it into Italy. They camped in the villages and countryside outside of Rome. They befriended villagers who hated Rome, and banded together to raid Roman villages. Hannibal stayed in Italy for more than sixteen years, tormenting the Romans but never actually capturing Rome. No matter what tactic they tried, the Romans could not defeat Hannibal.

The Romans finally decided that if they could not defeat Hannibal on their own soil, maybe they could defeat him on his. They sent a mighty army across the Mediterranean to Carthage. They thought that if Hannibal's own city were under siege, he would rush home to defend it.

The plan worked. Hannibal returned to Carthage, but he was too late. In 202 B.C., Rome defeated the Carthaginians again, ending the Second Punic War. The Romans demanded large sums of money, and they made the Carthaginians promise to keep a smaller fleet of ships.

But they still hadn't captured Hannibal. He lived in hiding for years, refusing Roman rule because of his boyhood promise. When it looked like Roman soldiers were going to capture him, Hannibal killed himself, choosing to die rather than to live under Rome.

The Final Defeat of Carthage

Rome and Carthage just wouldn't stop fighting. Fifty years later they fought the Third Punic War. Rome won this time and burned Carthage to the ground. The Carthaginians who survived were sold into slavery. Soldiers poured salt over the farmlands so crops would never grow again. With this victory, Rome extended its rule to North Africa, Spain, and the islands of Corsica, Sardinia, and Sicily.

All Roads Lead to Rome

This is one of the many roads that did lead to Rome.

Many roads were built to connect the city of Rome with its provinces. As soon as Rome conquered a new territory, soldiers and slaves would build roads from there to Rome.

Imagine building a road where there are only trees and rocks and dirt. And without trucks or bulldozers! The Romans wanted their roads as level and straight as possible. They dug tunnels through hills. They built bridges over rivers. Even today, more than two thousand years later, people still use the roads and bridges that the Romans built.

To this day, roads built two thousand years ago by the ancient Romans still traverse Italy and other countries in Europe.

Good roads and strong bridges helped Rome become powerful. The Romans had no cars, trucks, trains, or planes, yet they controlled an enormous area. You could travel on a Roman road in Great Britain or to the edge of the desert in North Africa. Good roads helped the Romans travel rapidly to the faraway provinces. If there was a foreign uprising, good roads and bridges meant that messages got to Rome more easily and Roman soldiers could reach the province more quickly to crush the rebellion.

Good roads and bridges also helped business. Romans could carry what they grew or made to the provinces to sell, and they could bring goods from the provinces back to Rome. We know that the Romans traded many things with their provinces, like pottery and wool, gold and silver, olive oil and wheat, copper, tin, and iron. The farther the Roman roads reached, the more materials could be brought back to Rome, making the city get richer all the time.

By 100 B.C., Rome had greatly expanded the territories it ruled. Tax money poured in from the provinces. Rich Romans did business with the conquered peoples. Thousands of foreign slaves worked on roads, bridges, and buildings. It sounds like a time of prosperity, but, in fact, it was a time of war and unhappiness. Then a man named Julius Caesar came on the scene, changing the course of Roman history forever.

Julius Caesar Shows the Pirates Who's Boss

Julius Caesar was born in 100 B.C., the son of a wealthy patrician who believed that the goddess Venus was one of his ancestors. In those days, if a rich young man wanted to make a name for himself, he would go off and fight in foreign lands. Julius Caesar did just that.

Roman ships carried gold from other territories back to Rome. Young Julius Caesar was assigned to protect the gold from pirates. He was captured and held prisoner. Rome paid a high ransom to make the pirates set him free. Later Caesar tracked down those pirates and killed them.

Julius Caesar became a great hero to the Romans. The consuls and Senate valued his leadership, and they sent him and many soldiers to fight in Gaul. Caesar conquered Gaul and led his soldiers into lands that are now part of Germany and Great Britain.

Pompey, Caesar's Rival

While Julius Caesar was off fighting in foreign lands, a man named Pompey rose in power. Like Caesar, Pompey was a spectacular military leader. He helped put an end to a huge slave rebellion. He led Roman soldiers into Sicily and Africa. He was put in charge of five hundred ships, assigned to control the whole Mediterranean Sea. In only forty days, Pompey managed to destroy thirteen hundred pirate ships and capture four hundred more!

At first, Pompey and Julius Caesar believed they could rule in Rome together. But Pompey grew jealous of Julius Caesar's power and popularity. While Caesar was fighting in Gaul, Pompey convinced some senators that Julius Caesar was a dangerous man who might try to take over Rome. The Senate declared Pompey "a protector of the state" and called Julius Caesar "a public enemy." They ordered Caesar to give up his leadership, disband his army, and come home to Rome.

Crossing the Rubicon

Can you imagine how Julius Caesar felt? If he obeyed the Senate's command, he lost all power. But if he chose not to obey their orders, what was he to do?

Roman soldiers salute their leader, Julius Caesar.

Caesar thought over his decision as he and his troops camped along the Rubicon River, on the border be-

tween Gaul and Italy. He and his soldiers had left Rome to conquer new territories. If they turned back and crossed the Rubicon, it would be like invading their own country. "The die is cast," Caesar said. "I have made my decision." He marched his army across the river and on to Rome. Ever since then, people have used the phrase "crossing the Rubicon" to mean making a decision from which you can never turn back.

Julius Caesar (about 100 B.C.–44 B.C.).

Soldiers fought against the approaching army, but Julius Caesar took control of the city and became ruler of the Roman republic. Later he got himself named dictator for life, governing the army and all the provinces. Elections continued, but only people chosen by Julius Caesar stayed in office. The consuls became less important. Rome's republic was coming to an end.

Caesar Meets Cleopatra

As you can imagine, once Julius Caesar seized power, Pompey decided to get out of Rome. He had turned the Senate against Caesar, after all. First he fled to Greece. Caesar's troops followed and defeated his army. From there he fled to Egypt, where he hoped the king, Ptolemy XII, would protect him. But Ptolemy's army met Pompey and killed him. Ptolemy wanted the powerful Julius Caesar on his side.

Caesar invaded Egypt anyway. There he met Ptolemy and his sister, Cleopatra.

Cleopatra of Egypt (69 B.C.–30 B.C.).

There was something about Cleopatra—her beauty, her power, the way she spoke her mind. Whatever it was, Julius Caesar fell in love with her. He ordered his army to overthrow her brother, making her the one and only ruler of Egypt. She was glad to have a way to unite her country with the powerful city of Rome.

Back home, the Romans got worried. What if their leader, Julius Caesar, married Cleopatra? What if he brought her home and made her queen of Rome? Had Caesar lost his mind? He had even ordered a gold statue of Cleopatra placed in a Roman temple! What would the gods think?

Julius Caesar stayed with Cleopatra in Egypt for a year. Then, when an uprising occurred in an eastern province, Caesar rushed his troops there and defeated the enemies. Back in Rome, Caesar celebrated his victory with a grand parade and a big sign that said, *"Veni, vidi, vici"* [WAY-nee, WEE-dee, WEE-kee]. Those are the words in Latin for "I came, I saw, I conquered." It was Caesar's way of saying, "I'm such a hero, winning that battle was not a problem."

Even though they were brother and sister, and even though Ptolemy XII was a teenager and Cleopatra was in her twenties, these two Egyptians were married. They were the king and queen of Egypt. What's more, they didn't get along very well. They kept fighting over who should be in charge of Egypt.

Pride Comes Before a Fall

Julius Caesar's behavior as an army general and a dictator scared many Romans. They didn't believe in letting one man rule the city and its territories. They didn't want Julius Caesar to be dictator for life, nor did they want Cleopatra as queen. They liked the old system of government, and they wanted their republic back. Some of the senators were so worried they plotted to kill Julius Caesar.

They planned the assassination for the Ides of March, which was the Romans' name for March 15. That day, in the year 44 B.C., as Julius Caesar walked out of the Senate, a

group of men jumped out from the shadows and stabbed him twenty-two times. Caesar tumbled down, right at the feet of a statue of Pompey. As he fell, he looked up and saw his old friend Brutus, who had helped plot his death. As he died, Julius Caesar said, *"Et tu, Brute?"* [et too broo-TAY]—Latin for "You too, Brutus?" That phrase has come down in history as Caesar's famous last words.

As Julius Caesar walked through the Roman Senate, Brutus and others attacked and murdered him.

All for Love—and Power

Those who killed Julius Caesar thought they had rescued their republic, but they were in for a big surprise. Many people, including soldiers in the army, did not support the senators' actions. They supported two men who had been close to Julius Caesar: Marc Antony, one of Caesar's best friends, and Octavian, Caesar's grandnephew and adopted son. Marc Antony and Octavian took control of Rome and divided the responsibilities for governing all its territories.

Octavian ruled the west. Marc Antony ruled the east and moved to Alexandria, the capital city of Egypt. There he met the famous Cleopatra. Like Caesar before him, Marc Antony fell in love with her. Soon they were married. Back in Rome, there was a problem. Marc Antony was already married to Octavian's sister! "How dare he?" the Romans cried. That was the end of Octavian's friendship with Marc Antony.

Octavian went to the Roman Senate and warned that Marc Antony planned to make Cleopatra queen of Rome. The senators had heard that story before, and they didn't like it any better the second time.

Marc Antony's army fought Octavian's navy near Greece, and Octavian won. Marc Antony went back to Egypt with Cleopatra. Soon, believing that he had lost all hope of

Our Calendar: A Gift from Rome

We have the Romans to thank for making up the calendar and the names for months we use today.

JANUARY—from Janus, the Roman god of entrances and exits

FEBRUARY—Latin for "the month for cleaning"

MARCH—from Mars, the Roman god of war

APRIL—from the Latin word *aperio*, which means "to open"

MAY—from Maia, the Roman goddess of spring

JUNE—from Juno, queen of the gods and the Roman goddess of marriage

JULY—from Julius Caesar, the Roman dictator

AUGUST—from Augustus Caesar, the Roman emperor

SEPTEMBER—from the number 7 in Latin

OCTOBER—from the number 8 in Latin

NOVEMBER—from the number 9 in Latin

DECEMBER—from the number 10 in Latin

achieving power, Marc Antony killed himself by falling on his sword.

Cleopatra still did not give up her quest to unite Egypt with Rome. Next she tried to make Octavian fall in love with her. But Octavian announced that he would capture Cleopatra, drag her back to Rome, and parade her through the streets like a slave. When she heard that, Cleopatra lifted an asp—a poisonous snake—to her breast, letting it bite her, and she died.

Octavian Becomes Augustus Caesar

Augustus Caesar, Rome's first emperor
(63 B.C.–A.D. 14).

When Octavian defeated Marc Antony in 31 B.C., he became the sole ruler of Rome. The senators welcomed him, and soon they gave him a new name of honor. They named Octavian *Augustus*, which was like calling him

Roman Waterworks

As Rome and its provinces grew, people in the cities needed more water than nearby streams and rivers could provide. Romans built *aqueducts,* which were stone troughs that carried water many miles, from a spring or river to the city where water was needed. The Romans built their aqueducts so well that you can still see some today. In France, cars now drive over the Pont du Gard [pohn dyoo GAR], which was built as an aqueduct by the Romans in 19 B.C.

Romans built the Pont du Gard (or bridge of Gard) in 19 B.C.
Cars still use the lowest of its three levels to cross the river.

With plenty of water brought into the cities, Romans could enjoy public fountains and baths. For them, taking a bath was something you did in the middle of town with a lot of your friends. How would you like that?

"Your Majesty." From 27 B.C. on, this great Roman leader was known as Augustus Caesar. Because of the power granted him by the Senate and the people, Augustus Caesar is considered Rome's first emperor. His name has stayed with us in another way as well, because the Senate decided to honor him by naming a month after him. Can you guess which month they named after Augustus Caesar?

Pax Romana

We often think of an emperor as someone who is cruel and selfish. Not so with Augustus Caesar. He made many decisions for the benefit of the people. He ruled for more than forty years and established peace and prosperity that lasted two hundred years. Historians call those two hundred years the *Pax Romana*, which means "Roman peace" in Latin.

Augustus made soldiers' lives better by increasing their pay and taking care of them when they retired. He created a strong police force in the city of Rome, which meant less crime and fewer riots. Life in the provinces changed, too. Augustus appointed governors in the provinces and found ways to tax more fairly. He made sure that the tax collectors didn't steal any money, and he insisted that tax money be spent to help the people, by building new roads, bridges, and public buildings.

No big wars upset the government. Cities and roadways were safer than ever. Trade increased, and both Rome and its provinces prospered. Everyone felt the benefits of the *Pax Romana*, but the Romans still worried about letting one man make so many decisions.

Augustus Caesar was also concerned with how people behaved toward each other. Family and marriage were important to him. He encouraged people to participate in religious festivals. He constructed temples and other great buildings. He bragged that he found Rome a city of brick and left it a city of marble. In this time of plenty, Rome was named the Eternal City, because it felt as if the good times might last forever. People still use that name for Rome today.

Downtown in the Roman Empire

Does your hometown have a downtown, a place where people gather and talk, shop and eat, and go to work?

The Roman Forum was the busy center of the city.

Rome did, too. Rome's downtown area was called the Forum. You can still visit the ruins of the Forum in the city of Rome today.

The busy Roman Forum.

Let's walk through the Forum and see what it's like to live in ancient Rome. Look, there's a merchant selling pottery, and another selling woven cloth. Mmm—I smell cinnamon. This shop must sell spices from Africa and the East. Here's a shop selling food. I see grapes and apples and olives.

There are dried fish hanging from the ceiling. Here's a big pot filled with wheat. You grind it yourself. Now I can smell the aroma of bread baking in an oven. Look, next door—there's the baker. He is pulling round brown loaves out of the stone oven.

Let's pass these shops and visit the temple, around the corner. Do you hear that man shouting in Latin? He is debating an issue on the steps of the courthouse. People are listening and answering him. They all have opinions on how the government should be run. There, in front of us, is the beautiful white marble temple to Saturn, a god of farming. I'll bet those two men in togas, carrying pitchers toward the temple, are bringing gifts of wine for the god.

Where's the Spaghetti?

As we stroll through the Forum, we might see a vendor cooking pieces of meat over an open fire and selling them to the men, women, and children passing by. Most Roman houses were built of wood, very close together, so ovens were considered fire hazards. Many Romans bought cooked food from vendors. Along with meat or fish, they might eat bread or cheese, onions or garlic, and a piece of fruit.

A Roman family with plenty of money could build a big, spacious house with enough room for an oven. These Romans often hosted big banquets. Slaves prepared enormous amounts of fancy food. Guests began arriving in the late afternoon. They wore fancy clothing, often pinned with jewelry. They usually took their shoes off as they entered a home. When they ate, they leaned back on couches near tables low to the ground. They ate with their fingers. Slaves stood nearby, ready to wipe the rich Romans' hands clean. Guests brought cloths to wrap leftovers and took them home for later.

Are you wondering what the Romans ate? Don't picture mounds of spaghetti covered with tomato sauce. Pasta and noodles were not made in Italy at that time, and the ancient Romans had never seen a tomato. They ate some things we still eat today, and many things we would never dream of eating. Take a look at this menu, which lists things that ancient Romans really did eat.

Menu from a Roman Banquet

Pig Udders

Stuffed Jellyfish

Flamingo

Roasted Parrot

Boiled Ostrich

Stuffed Dormice

Snails

Fig Wine

Dates Stuffed with Chopped Apples
and Spices

Roman Sports: Play at Your Own Risk

The ancient Romans loved sports. They seem to have preferred violent and bloody spectacles, like gladiators fighting to the death. From Greek architects, they learned to build *amphitheaters*, which were huge sports arenas with a field in the middle and seats raised all around it. One of the most famous Roman amphitheaters, the Colosseum, was so big that fifty thousand people could sit on its marble seats and watch athletic events. You can visit the remains of the Colosseum in modern-day Rome.

The Roman Colosseum
still stands today.

Crowds entered the Colosseum through any one of seventy-six doorways. Canvas awnings stretched above the seats, to shield spectators from the sun. The field was covered with sand, which would become so soaked with the blood of men and animals that slaves had to bring in new sand. Complicated stairways, and even mechanical elevators, brought people up to their seats and brought wild animals, caged in dens below, up to the field when an event was due to begin.

A typical day at the Colosseum might start out with a wild-animal fight. Roman officials paid lots of money for animals from far away. They bought polar bears, tigers, rhinoceroses, elephants, and leopards. Sometimes the sport was to make a ferocious animal fight a gladiator until one or the other died.

Gladiators were slaves or criminals who had been trained to fight. A gladiator who was an excellent fighter might win his freedom. Some fought animals, but more often two gladiators would fight each other to the death. Sometimes the spectators took a special liking to a gladiator. If they thought he was putting up a good fight, they might yell and point their thumbs up in the air, which meant "Let him live!" or they would point their thumbs down, meaning "Death to the loser!" We still use "thumbs up" or "thumbs down" to signal that we agree or disagree with someone or something.

This Roman patrician is signaling "thumbs down," to indicate that he believes the gladiator on the ground ought to lose.

Let's Go to the Races!

Romans also loved watching chariot races. Each racer stood in a chariot, holding the reins and driving a team of horses at top speed around a huge racetrack. In Rome, the main racetrack was called the Circus Maximus, which means "very big circle" in Latin. I'll bet you can figure out what English word comes from the Latin word *circus*!

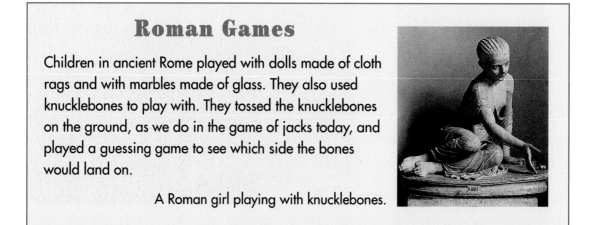

Roman Games

Children in ancient Rome played with dolls made of cloth rags and with marbles made of glass. They also used knucklebones to play with. They tossed the knucklebones on the ground, as we do in the game of jacks today, and played a guessing game to see which side the bones would land on.

A Roman girl playing with knucklebones.

Chariot races at Rome's
Circus Maximus.

The racecourse at the Circus Maximus was more than 650 yards long, longer than six football fields. Can you imagine the noise and excitement of all those chariots, pulled by snorting, stomping horses?

Pompeii: A City Frozen in Time

As you can see, we know a lot about the history of Rome and how the early Romans lived. How do we know so much? For one thing, the Romans did a good job of writing things down. For another thing, they built things well—statues and buildings, bridges and aqueducts—so we can study the remains of things from the days of ancient Rome.

We also have a volcano to thank for much that we know about ancient Rome. Thanks to Mount Vesuvius, a volcano that erupted one summer afternoon in A.D. 79, we know how people lived in Pompeii, about one hundred miles south of Rome.

Pompeii was a little town on the coast of Italy. Romans would go there to enjoy the sea breezes and the beautiful view of nearby Mount Vesuvius. Imagine their surprise the day when they felt the rumble, heard the blast, and looked out to see Mount Vesuvius erupting! The volcano spewed gas, stones, and hot lava all over Pompeii.

Mount Vesuvius, a volcano near the town
of Pompeii, erupted in A.D. 79.

Some lucky people escaped to tell the tale, but many in Pompeii were smothered by poisonous gases or buried under layers of hot ash. People considered the eruption of Vesuvius to be a punishment from the gods. They believed that the smoke, flames, and ashes were caused by Vulcan, the god of fire. They were afraid to return to Pompeii. It took many years before anyone returned to build a new city on the ruins.

A Firsthand Account of the Eruption
(written by a Roman named Pliny)

By now it was dawn, but the light was still dim and faint. The buildings around us were already tottering. We also saw the sea sucked away and apparently forced back by the earthquake. On the landward side a fearful black cloud was rent by forked and quivering bursts of flame, and parted to reveal great tongues of fire, like flashes of lightning magnified in size. Many besought the aid of the gods, but still more imagined there were no gods left, and that the universe was plunged into eternal darkness evermore.

Over time, people forgot about Pompeii. Then, in 1748, archaeologists began digging and discovered something astounding. The molten lava that had destroyed Pompeii had also preserved it. Hot ashes had hardened around people's bodies, preserving the very positions they were in when the volcano erupted. The bodies had long since rotted, but by pouring plaster into the holes in the hardened ash, archaeologists could make out the shapes of men, women, children, and even a dog. In some cases, they could even see the expression on a person's face. Inside the houses, they found impressions of a cake on the table, a half-eaten loaf of bread, an egg, a kettle on the fire.

This wall painting, which shows three actors wearing masks, was preserved in Pompeii after the volcano erupted.

Columns still stand from a house in Pompeii, destroyed by the eruption of Mount Vesuvius. See the volcano in the distance?

That hot lava preserved much more: shops, temples, a theater, paintings on the walls. Today you can visit the ancient city of Pompeii. In the paved streets, you can see the tracks made by the wheels of chariots. In the hallway of one house, you can see a sign, written almost two thousand years ago. The sign says CAVE CANEM—"Beware of the dog."

A Long Line of Emperors

Now that you have learned a little about what it was like to live in ancient Rome, let's go back to Augustus Caesar.

Augustus ruled a long while. When he died, millions of people across the empire felt sad. His stepson, Tiberius, became emperor next. Tiberius lived simply and saved lots of money for the empire. He was a good general and wise ruler, but the people did not like him. If they had known who was coming next, they would have appreciated Tiberius.

After Tiberius, Augustus Caesar's great-grandson became emperor. As a boy, he spent most of his time in army camps. The soldiers called him Caligula, which means "little boots" in Latin. Caligula hated his nickname, but it stuck.

What kind of emperor was Caligula? Here's a hint. When Caligula died, people ran through the streets cheering. Remember all that money Tiberius saved for Rome? Caligula spent it! He once spent more than one million dollars on a banquet!

Caligula thought the Romans should worship him as if he were a god. He dragged statues of Jupiter out of the temples and replaced them with statues of himself. He also appointed his horse a consul. You can imagine that these decisions did not go over well with the Romans. Finally, one of Caligula's own bodyguards killed him. One Roman historian joked that this was the day Caligula found out he *wasn't* a god.

Nero: Not a Hero

After Caligula, a man named Claudius became emperor. Both the people and the soldiers in the army liked Claudius. Under Claudius's rule, the Romans built more roads, aqueducts, and buildings. They also conquered more territory, to the north and to the east. Claudius did not reign long. His second wife poisoned him. Then she placed Nero, her son from another marriage, on the throne. That was a dark day for Rome.

Just as Caligula had done, Nero wasted public money on fancy parties. He built an enormous golden palace filled with precious jewels. He called it his Golden House and decorated it with a statue of himself, 120 feet tall! But Nero did worse than that. He tortured people and killed anyone who seemed a threat to his power. He even ordered his teacher, his mother, and his wife murdered.

Nero thought he was something special. He considered himself a brilliant actor and poet. Whenever he performed, the audiences were so scared of him they cheered.

In A.D. 64, a terrible fire burned down half of Rome. Some claimed Nero started it, just for a dramatic backdrop as he recited his poetry. "Nero fiddled while Rome burned," they

cried, meaning that Nero didn't care about how the people suffered.

We don't know the truth. We don't know how the fire started, and we don't know whether Nero played music or recited his poems while Rome burned. Nero blamed the fire on Christians living in Rome, and he began to kill and torture them.

Leaders in the Roman army hated Nero. When they named a new emperor, Nero knew he had lost control. He ordered a slave to stab him to death. As he died, Nero supposedly said, "What an artist the world is losing!"

Here's one artist's idea of what Nero looked like when he "fiddled while Rome burned."

Christians During the Days of Ancient Rome

Augustus Caesar became emperor of Rome in 27 B.C., or twenty-seven years before the birth of Jesus Christ. Rome burned during Nero's reign in A.D. 64, or sixty-four years after the birth of Jesus Christ. Between those dates, something big had happened. The man named Jesus had lived, died, and inspired a new religion. He lived in the area of the Middle East that we now call Israel. Jesus' ideas changed many people's minds about religion, but leaders of his time considered his ideas dangerous.

Jesus taught that there was one God. He said all people should love God more than anyone or anything else. He also said that people should love others as much as they love themselves. Jesus said that he was the son of God and that those who believed in him would live forever.

Jesus talked about a kingdom in heaven. Some people got excited, mistakenly thinking that Jesus planned to overthrow the Romans and set up a kingdom on earth. Jesus' popularity scared the leaders where he lived. They worked out a plan to kill Jesus by crucifying him, which means to kill by hanging on a cross.

Jesus' death did not stop his followers. They said that Jesus came back to life three days after his crucifixion. They also said that before Jesus went back up to heaven, he told them to invite the people they met to become followers of Jesus, too. They traveled all through the Roman Empire, preaching about Jesus. That was why Christians were in Rome during the reign of Nero.

Usually, Romans let the people in the provinces practice their own religions. But Christian beliefs presented a problem. Romans wanted all people to believe their emperors were gods, but the followers of Christ disagreed. They believed in only one God. They would worship only that God. They refused to worship any emperor.

Some Romans were willing to allow the Christians to have those beliefs, but other Romans, like Nero, were not. He ordered Christians jailed, tortured, and killed. Nero persecuted the Christians, which means that he was cruel and made them suffer, all because of what they believed.

The Beginning of the End for the Empire

For a hundred years after Nero, Rome was ruled by good emperors. The fifth good emperor named his son to take his place, but he wasted money and killed people for fun. The empire was struggling with other problems, too. A terrible disease called the plague had killed many people. With fewer people to buy and sell goods, Romans could not make enough money. Farmers went out of business, so there wasn't enough food. The government became poorer. The army became weaker.

At the same time, fierce warriors began attacking along the borders of the empire. At first, the Roman army fought successfully, but then the Romans began to fight among themselves. Invaders moved closer, and the Roman Empire began to shrink.

Constantine Sees a Burning Cross

In A.D. 310, a man named Constantine became emperor of Rome. He grew up worshiping the Roman gods and goddesses. On a night before leading his army to battle, though, Constantine said that he had a vision—something like a waking dream. A flaming cross appeared to him with the words "In this sign you will conquer."

In this engraving, Constantine sees a glowing cross in the sky, representing the vision that inspired him to become a Christian.

Constantine knew that the cross was a symbol for Jesus. He ordered his soldiers to paint crosses on their shields. When they won the battle, Constantine took it as a sign from the Christian God.

Constantine declared that all religions could be practiced in Rome, and he ordered that Christians should not be persecuted. He may have become a Christian himself, and he is known as the first Christian emperor. Christianity became the official religion of Rome.

Constantinople: A City Full of Art

During his reign, Constantine moved the capital of the empire from Rome to Byzantium, an ancient Greek town. The city became known as Constantinople, which means "Constantine's city" in Greek. Today it is named Istanbul, a city in the country of Turkey.

When you find Istanbul on the map, notice how the city sits right on the Bosporus Strait, which is a long, narrow water passage between the Black Sea and the Mediterranean Sea. The city was a connecting point between Europe and the western part of Asia, called Asia Minor. It had pleasant weather, good soil, and a safe harbor. Constantinople was a perfect center for trade.

Constantine divided his empire into two halves: the western half, called the Roman Empire, and the eastern half, called the Byzantine Empire, named after the old city of Byzantium. The people of the Byzantine Empire blended Roman traditions with Greek and Asian culture.

This is Hagia Sophia [HAY-ja so-FEE-a], the most famous building from the Byzantine Empire. It is in the city of Istanbul, Turkey, which is the modern name for Constantinople. Hagia Sophia was built as a Christian church. Fires and earthquakes damaged it, but the people of Constantinople rebuilt it. Its largest dome is 102 feet across and arches 180 feet above the floor. Later Hagia Sofia became a mosque, a holy building for Muslims. Today it is a museum.

The Byzantine Empire continued for another thousand years. Constantinople became one of Europe's most beautiful cities, its churches and palaces filled with art. It became especially famous for its *mosaics*, which are artworks made by arranging small colored tiles on walls or ceilings. You can see a Byzantine mosaic in the Visual Arts section of this book.

The Fall of the Roman Empire

It took a long time to build the Roman Empire, and the fall of the empire took a long time, too. Fierce warriors called Huns came from the north, attacking the Germanic tribes who lived north of Rome. The people in the Germanic tribes, scared of the Huns and eager for the safety and wealth of Rome, moved south through Italy. Slowly, they began to conquer other parts of the Roman Empire as well, moving into Britain, Spain, France, and North Africa.

Some of these tribes settled peacefully. They farmed, used the roads, and took control of the public buildings. When invaders moved peacefully into a province, the people did not bother to fight. They preferred the Germanic invaders to the Romans, who had demanded taxes and governed sternly.

Other tribes did not arrive so peacefully. In A.D. 410, after a two-year battle, the Visigoths marched into Rome. They stole, killed, and burned everything in sight. Romans hadn't seen anything like it since Hannibal, six hundred years before.

The days of Rome's glory were over. Historians name A.D. 476 as the date when the Roman Empire gasped its last breath. In that year, a German general forced the emperor to give up his power. That emperor was a sixteen-year-old boy named Romulus Augustulus.

Do you recognize that name? Oddly enough, the last emperor of Rome had the same name as the city's founder.

Roman History: A Timeline

753 B.C.   Legendary founding of Rome by Romulus

509 B.C.   Beginning of the Roman Republic

300s B.C.–200s B.C.   Rome expands throughout Italy and begins foreign conquests

100s B.C.   Rome conquers territories in Greece, Middle East, Spain, and North Africa

44 B.C.   Death of Julius Caesar and end of Roman Republic

27 B.C.   Augustus becomes emperor; beginning of Roman Empire

About A.D. 1   Birth of Jesus

A.D. 54   Nero becomes emperor

A.D. 64   Much of Rome destroyed by fire

A.D. 79   Mount Vesuvius erupts and destroys Pompeii

A.D. 310   Constantine becomes emperor

A.D. 394   Roman Empire makes Christianity the official religion

A.D. 395   Empire splits into Byzantine (Eastern) and Roman (Western) Empires

A.D. 410   Rome sacked by Visigoths

A.D. 476   Germanic invaders sack Rome; end of Roman (Western) Empire

A.D. 527   Justinian becomes emperor of Byzantine Empire

Justinian's Code: A Gift from the Byzantine Empire

Although the Roman Empire collapsed, the Byzantine Empire prospered. People built magnificent buildings and made beautiful art, which we still appreciate today. They also wrote important books about philosophy and law. We still use their ideas today as well.

Can you guess which person in this picture is the emperor Justinian? (He's the one in the middle.) This picture of him is one of the mosaics—paintings made of many little tiles—in a chapel in Ravenna, Italy. You can see another mosaic from Ravenna in the Visual Arts section of this book, on page 166.

A man named Justinian, who ruled the Byzantine Empire for almost forty years, from A.D. 527 to 565, began with the law of the Romans and organized it into ten books of law, called the Justinian Code. Some of the laws in the Justinian Code were:

1. A person is innocent until proved guilty.
2. Above all, the court should consider the rights of the individual.
3. No one should be punished for what he or she thinks.
4. When you are deciding on a punishment, you should consider the guilty person's age and experience.

These ideas, still regarded as important rules of law, were first written down by Justinian in the Byzantine Empire.

The Vikings: Raiders and Traders from the North

The Long, Dark Winter Night

The year is A.D. 753. You are a Viking child, and you live on a small farm in Norway. It is late at night, and the winter winds howl outside. You squat on a dirt floor by a smoky fire, trying to warm your stiff, cold hands. Your mother, brother, and two sisters sleep huddled near the wall on pillows stuffed with chicken feathers. You wonder where your father is. He is late getting back from hunting. You try not to worry.

Your stomach growls. There is not enough food. There's never enough food. An early frost last fall destroyed many of the vegetables. An ice storm in February killed the cow and two goats. Every night your family goes to sleep with empty bellies.

Did you use a Viking word today? Here are some words in English that began as Viking words: ugly, sky, happy, wrong, die, anger, husband, window.

Your mind wanders to the sea. Yes, that is where you would like to be: on a ship sailing swiftly away from this cold, this hunger, this long, dark winter night.

If you were a Viking child, you might live in cottages like these, with thin walls and roofs made of thatched straw.

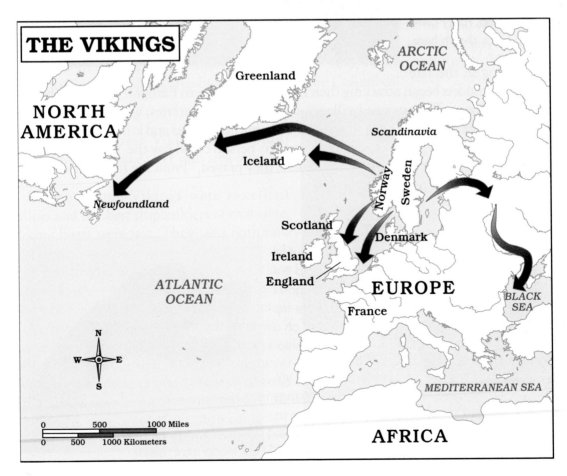

THE VIKINGS

by a team of dogs. In the water, they paddled kayaks, covered boats made from the skins of animals.

This Inuit boy, who lives in the Northwest Territories of Canada, stands beside his dog. He lives in a tepee and wears a coat made of animal hide, to keep himself warm. At his feet is the skull of a musk ox, with huge horns.

The Mound Builders

Imagine that you are a bird flying over part of what is now the state of Ohio. You gaze down and see something strange, something huge. What is it? It's a giant serpent coiling up a hillside! Then you realize that it's a snake-shaped mound of earth more than a thousand feet long. (That's longer than three football fields!)

This is a birds'-eye view of the snake-shaped mound found in Ohio, made by Native Americans almost two thousand years ago.

Who made this giant mound? It was made by Native Americans almost two thousand years ago. Today we call those people the Mound Builders. The mounds were burial places, like the pyramids of ancient Egypt.

About a hundred years ago, a farmer found mounds shaped like flat-topped pyramids all over his farm in Ohio. He called some archaeologists, scientists who study what people in the past left behind. The archaeologists dug carefully into the mounds and found things like seashells, pearls, and shark's teeth. But there is no ocean in Ohio. How did these things get into the mounds?

Archaeologists think the Mound Builders must have traded for the seashells, pearls, and shark's teeth. Perhaps they traveled toward the ocean and brought the unusual items back to their homes.

Cliff Dwellers: The Anasazi

At about the same time that the Vikings were crossing the Atlantic to North America, the Anasazi people lived in what is now the southwestern United States. The Anasazi lived where the states of Utah, Arizona, New Mexico, and Colorado meet. (Can you find that place on a map?) But they lived there long before there were any states.

Today we can see the cliff dwellings built a thousand years ago by the Anasazi people. They are now part of the Mesa Verde National Park in Colorado.

Another Indian tribe gave the Anasazi their name, which means "ancient other people." We don't know what they called themselves. The Anasazi made their homes out of hard, dry rock. An overhanging cliff served as a roof. About a thousand years ago, hundreds of Anasazi people lived in the many rooms of these cliff dwellings. They almost look like apartment buildings, don't they?

Many Anasazi homes included an underground room with a fireplace in the middle. You can imagine the people, on a cold desert night, sitting in a circle around the fire, telling stories or praying for their crops to grow well.

What happened to the people who lived in these cliff dwellings? We don't know for sure. We do know that the Anasazi lived in the same area for hundreds of years, building their homes out of hard rock, planting their crops, and making beautiful pottery and baskets. Then, about seven hundred years ago, they disappeared, leaving their cliff dwellings behind. Some historians think they were attacked by another tribe. Others think their crops failed, perhaps because of drought, a long time with no rain.

The Pueblo People

Today the Native Americans called the Pueblos are related to the Anasazi of long ago. The Pueblos call the Anasazi the Ancient Ones.

Back in the 1500s, Spanish explorers first came upon these Native Americans who built their homes out of bricks of *adobe* [uh-DOE-bee], a mixture of clay, sand, and straw. Some adobe buildings were several stories high. The Spanish called these Indians Pueblos, since *pueblo* is the Spanish word for "town."

Early Explorers in North America

A "New World" for Europeans

In fourteen hundred and ninety-two, Columbus sailed the ocean blue.

And what did he find? He found what was, for Europeans, a "new world." He landed on an island in the Caribbean Sea that he named San Salvador. He met the Native Americans living there, the Taino [tie-EE-no] people, and he mistakenly called them Indians. Do you remember why? It was because he thought he had landed on islands near Asia, which Europeans then called the Indies.

EUROPEANS EXPLORE A NEW WORLD

Hudson Bay

Canada

ROCKY MOUNTAINS

Great Lakes

Grand Canyon

United States

APPALACHIANS

Colorado R.

Mississippi R.

GULF STREAM

ATLANTIC OCEAN

Rio Grande

St. Augustine

Florida

San Salvador

Gulf of Mexico

Mexico

Cuba

Puerto Rico

PACIFIC OCEAN

Caribbean Sea

0   400   800 Miles
0   400   800 Kilometers

SOUTH AMERICA

Explorers from Europe were eager to find a new world and new ocean passages. Many were driven by the desire to get rich. Some explorers were careless and cruel in the way they treated the people who were already living in these new lands. The Spanish conquistadors, Cortés and Pizarro, conquered the Aztecs and destroyed the Inca civilization. Was it all for gold and silver?

Why is this country called America instead of Columbia? Columbus thought he had reached Asia. Soon other explorers realized they were finding lands new to the Europeans. Around 1500, an Italian named Amerigo Vespucci [ah-MARE-ee-go ves-POO-chee] explored the coast of what we now call South America. A mapmaker used Vespucci's descriptions to make a map of the new continent. He called the continent to the south America, after Vespucci's first name. Soon people began to use that name to refer to both continents in the New World.

A Fountain of Youth?

King Ferdinand and Queen Isabella of Spain paid for Columbus to make four voyages to the New World. In all of these voyages, Columbus never landed on the continent of North America, though he did visit many islands in the Caribbean Sea, including Puerto Rico and Cuba. Ferdinand and Isabella wanted to claim ownership of the new lands being discovered, even though Native Americans were already living there. The king named one of his men, Juan Ponce de León [hwahn PON-suh deh leh-OWN], the governor of Puerto Rico.

Ponce de León found gold in Puerto Rico. It made him rich, but he kept exploring. Some say he believed he could find a "Fountain of Youth" in the West Indies—one drink of its water would keep you young forever. Of course, he never found a Fountain of Youth. What did he find?

Ponce de León thought he had landed on another island. He landed at Eastertime, which he and his fellow Spaniards called *Pascua Florida*. They called the land Florida, which means "full of flowers," and we still call it that today.

A few years later Ponce de León returned to Florida, this time with soldiers and horses, to conquer the land. He was sure he would find cities of gold even greater than the Aztec city that Cortés had conquered. But the Indians were waiting for him. They had seen their people captured or killed by explorers. They shot poisoned arrows at the soldiers. One of the arrows hit Ponce de León in his leg. The Spaniards sailed back to Cuba, where Ponce de León died.

In Search of the Cities of Gold

Back in Europe, everyone was buzzing with stories about seven cities of gold. "The people eat off gold plates with gold knives and forks. The streets are paved with gold!"

Many men set off, seeking the legendary Seven Cities of Cíbola [SEE-bow-lah]. One was Francisco Vásquez de Coronado [co-ro-NAH-doe]. The king of Spain had made Coronado governor of Spanish territories in Mexico. Coronado kept hearing that the golden cities lay somewhere to the north, in the area that is now Arizona and New Mexico.

Coronado and about three hundred followers were led by Native American guides to the town that they called Cíbola. They expected to find riches, but, as Coronado wrote back to Spain, "The Seven Cities are seven little villages." He found Native American pueblos—"very good houses, three and four and five stories high"—but no gold. So Coronado sent explorers in different directions to continue the search for gold.

Coronado led soldiers from Mexico north into the territory we now call Arizona and New Mexico, looking for cities of gold.

The Grand Canyon is about a mile deep, more than two hundred miles long, and in some places eighteen miles wide from one edge to the other.

One group traveled for many days. Then they came to a river canyon so wide and deep they could not cross. They had found what we now call the Grand Canyon. The sight of it must have taken their breath away. For days, Coronado's men searched for a way to get

down to the river, but the canyon walls were too steep and dangerous, so they had to give up.

Coronado's men may not have found gold, but they did find one of North America's natural wonders: the Grand Canyon.

Another band of Coronado's men marched past a city of pueblo buildings, where they met friendly Native Americans who grew maize, beans, melons, and chickens. Then they came to a big river, which they named Nuestra Señora, which means "Our Lady," in honor of the Virgin Mary. Today we call that river the Rio Grande, which means "big river." Can you find it on a map? It forms the boundary between Texas and Mexico.

Spanish Missions

Coronado marched as far as today's state of Kansas, but eventually, the Spanish gave up their search for gold. They still moved into the lands where Native Americans lived, but they did so because they wanted to teach their religion, Christianity, to the Indians. Priests built churches and schools, called *missions*, near Indian villages. They taught

classes and held worship services, wanting the Indians to become Christians.

In this drawing, the Spanish settlers and some of the Native Americans are following the missionaries and bowing down in prayer.

The missionaries thought they were doing good, but they made some Native Americans angry. These Indians did not want to give up their own religion. The missionaries did not know it, but they also brought disease from Europe. Many Indians got sick and died. There were as many as one hundred pueblo villages in the Southwest when Coronado first began to explore, in 1540. By 1700, only eighteen pueblo villages were left.

Up North

At the same time that the Spanish were exploring the southwestern part of our country, others were exploring the North.

King Henry VII of England paid for the voyages that John Cabot made to North America.

In 1497, not long after Columbus made his first voyage, John Cabot and his crew of only eighteen men bravely sailed a ship across the Atlantic. Cabot was an Italian sailor, but the English paid his way. Like Columbus, Cabot thought he had reached Asia, but he had really landed on what is now called Newfoundland in Canada. (As you can find out on page 115 in this book, Viking sailors had visited this part of North America, but they did not stay.) Because of Cabot's voyage, the English later claimed that they owned the whole North American continent.

> One of Cabot's sailors wrote that in the waters off Newfoundland there were "fish swarming so thick" that the boat couldn't sail. They were in the waters now called the Grand Banks, one of the best places in the world for catching fish, such as cod, haddock, herring, and mackerel.

Seeking a Northwest Passage

Look at a world map or globe, and you can see it's a long way from Newfoundland to Asia. The Europeans wanted to find a quick route to Asia. They enjoyed many things from Asia, like tea, perfumes, spices, and silk. Trading companies and governments wanted to bring those goods to Europe faster, but unknown lands kept getting in the way.

People thought there must be a *strait*, a water passage, through the North American continent that would lead to Asia. They called this hoped-for shortcut the Northwest Passage.

If you have a globe to look at, see whether you think the Europeans could find a Northwest Passage to Asia. What sort of waters would they go through if they did? Frigid, icy cold! A ship would have to pass through the Arctic Ocean, not far from the North Pole. Even in summer, these waters are clogged with ice—but the explorers didn't know that.

The Sad Story of Henry Hudson

An Englishman named Henry Hudson tried four times to find the Northwest Passage. He died trying.

First, in 1607, he tried sailing north from England. If you look at a globe, you can see what he was trying to do. He understood that the earth was round, and he thought he could sail across the North Pole. He didn't understand that solid ice always covers the Arctic Ocean. "I hoped to have a clear sea," Hudson wrote of this first journey, but "that proved impossible due to the ice surrounding us."

Hudson tried again in 1608. He sailed northeast, and again found icebergs and freezing weather. He turned his boat around and tried sailing northwest. When his crew realized that they weren't heading home, they rebelled against Hudson, saying they wouldn't work unless they sailed to England. And so, home they went.

In 1609, Henry Hudson sailed west. This time he was working for a group of businessmen called the Dutch East India Company. On this trip, he reached North America and claimed land for Holland.

Hudson saw many Native Americans. One man who sailed with him wrote in his journal, "They are well dressed in loose deer skins, and brought green tobacco which they gave us in exchange for knives and beads." The Indians also gave the sailors bread made of maize.

Hudson sailed past "a very good piece of ground and a cliff close by of white-green color . . . on the side of the river called *Manna-hata*." It was the island we now call Manhattan (the center of New York City today). Next Hudson sailed up a river that still bears his name. You'll find the Hudson River on a map of the state of New York.

In 1610, Henry Hudson tried once more to find a shortcut from Europe to Asia. He sailed a ship called *Discovery* into a wide expanse of water in the northern part of Canada. Today it is named after him: Hudson Bay.

On the map, Hudson Bay looks like a big open body of water. But in many places, the

People who come from the Netherlands are called Dutch. Another name for this country is Holland.

water gets too shallow for sailing. In many other places, it is frozen solid almost all year long. Once again Henry Hudson had sailed into icy waters, just as winter was coming.

Angry at their leader for forcing them through a winter without enough food and water, Henry Hudson's crew rebelled. They took over the ship *Discovery* and left Hudson, his son, and a few others adrift in a rowboat. Henry Hudson was never seen again.

Hudson and his crew spent the winter on board the *Discovery*, frozen in the ice. They ran short of food and water. Some of the crew got sick. Some died. The sailors blamed

Canada Today

In land area, Canada is the largest nation in the Western Hemisphere and the second largest nation in the world. Only Russia is bigger.

Canada stretches from the Atlantic Ocean in the east to the Pacific Ocean and Alaska in the west, and from its long boundary with the United States in the south all the way up to the Arctic Ocean. While the United States is divided into states, Canada is divided into provinces. (See the map on page 79.)

The province of Québec used to be called New France. People in Québec speak French, while people in other provinces speak English. Farmers in Manitoba, Saskatchewan, and Alberta grow so much that these provinces have been nicknamed "the food basket of the world."

In the west, Canada's Rocky Mountains connect with the Rocky Mountains of the United States and stretch all the way north through the Yukon Territory, where Canada meets Alaska. The biggest river in western Canada is the Yukon River, which starts in the Rockies and flows through Alaska into the Bering Sea.

The farther north you go in Canada, the colder it gets. Above the Arctic Circle, snow covers the land, and the waters stay frozen almost all year long. Only a few trappers and fishermen live in the forests around Hudson Bay. More than eight out of every ten Canadians live in the south, near the border with the United States. All of Canada's big cities, like Québec, Montréal, Toronto, and Vancouver, are found in the south. Ottawa, in the province of Ontario, is the capital of Canada.

Henry Hudson for caring more about finding the Northwest Passage than about keeping his crew safe and healthy.

When the ice began to melt, the crew rebelled. They forced Hudson, his son, and a few crew members loyal to Hudson to get into a small boat with no oars. Then they left them behind and sailed the *Discovery* back to England. No one ever heard from Henry Hudson again.

Fur Trade in New France

A man from France named Samuel de Champlain [shawm-PLAIN] made many voyages across the Atlantic Ocean, getting to know the land that is now Canada. Champlain sailed down the river we call the St. Lawrence. He met Native Americans who shared a stew of moose, beaver, and seal blubber. He met others who ran foot races to celebrate when they won a battle.

Champlain was looking for furs, not gold. People in Europe paid plenty for the soft pelts of bears, beavers, and foxes. He came upon a place where the river turned and the land jutted into the water. He called that place Kebec, after an Indian word for "narrows in a river." In 1608, he built a trading post there. Over the years, the trading post grew into a town, and the town grew into one of Canada's biggest cities: Québec.

Samuel de Champlain established a trading post, with fences and gardens, at a site on the river's edge. He named the place Kebec. Today we call it Québec, the capital of one of Canada's provinces.

After that, Champlain sailed along the coast of Newfoundland and traveled back and forth to France. He spent one winter with the Huron Indians. He liked their bread of cornmeal and red beans and their roasted ears of corn. The Hurons told him stories of the big lakes that we now call the Great Lakes. Champlain visited three of the five Great Lakes—Lake Ontario, Lake Erie, and Lake Huron, but not Lake Superior or Lake Michigan. He hoped that one of them might lead to Asia, but he finally realized there was no Northwest Passage.

Samuel de Champlain always came home to Québec. He brought his wife from France to live with him there, even though not many European women lived in the new settlements. Champlain is often called "the Father of New France." The region he settled is now called French Canada.

English Colonies in North America

Thirteen Colonies

July 4, 1776.

Why is that date important? It's the birthday of the United States of America. It's the day on which American leaders signed the Declaration of Independence—the day America said, "We will no longer be ruled by England. We will be our own country."

Before 1776, America was not its own nation but a cluster of English colonies. After the American Revolution, thirteen of those colonies became the first states in the United States (which is why our flag has thirteen stripes).

A colony is a place that is owned and ruled by another country. In the 1600s, many European countries had claimed parts of the world as colonies. Spain had colonies in the West Indies and in Central and South America. The Netherlands and Portugal had colonies in Brazil. France had colonies in North America and the West Indies.

Take a look at the map on the next page. It shows that in 1750, Great Britain had thirteen colonies in North America:

- the New England colonies: Massachusetts, New Hampshire, Connecticut, and Rhode Island, founded mainly by Puritans
- the Middle Atlantic colonies: New York, New Jersey, Delaware, and Pennsylvania, started by the English and the Dutch
- the Southern colonies: Virginia, Maryland, North and South Carolina, and Georgia, which made their wealth from growing tobacco, rice, a blue dye called indigo, and (later on) cotton

---

People often use "English" and "British" to mean about the same thing. A long time ago, the country called England took over the neighboring lands of Scotland and Wales. The English used the name "Great Britain" to refer to their own country and the lands they had taken over.

The first English colonists crossed the Atlantic Ocean on creaky wooden ships that pitched and rolled. The trip took months. When they finally landed, they found no houses, no churches, no schools, no shops. Just deep, dark forests. Native Americans made their homes in and around these forests, hunting the animals, fishing in the streams, grow-

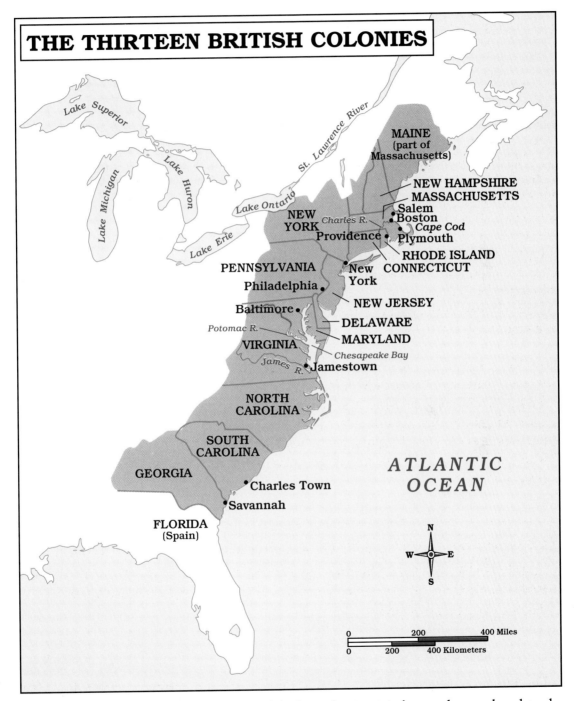

THE THIRTEEN BRITISH COLONIES

Lake Superior

Lake Michigan

Lake Huron

Lake Ontario

Lake Erie

St. Lawrence River

MAINE
(part of
Massachusetts)

NEW HAMPSHIRE

MASSACHUSETTS

Salem

Charles R.

Boston

Cape Cod

NEW
YORK

Providence

Plymouth

RHODE ISLAND

CONNECTICUT

PENNSYLVANIA

New
York

Philadelphia

NEW JERSEY

Baltimore

DELAWARE

Potomac R.

MARYLAND

VIRGINIA

Chesapeake Bay

James R.

Jamestown

NORTH
CAROLINA

SOUTH
CAROLINA

GEORGIA

Charles Town

Savannah

FLORIDA
(Spain)

ATLANTIC
OCEAN

N

W   E

S

| 0 | 200 | 400 Miles |
| 0 | 200 | 400 Kilometers |

ing corn, raising their families. Sometimes the colonists tried to understand and trade with the Indians. But more often they saw them as "savages" and fought them for the land.

The colonists worked hard to clear land and build homes in the New World. Most of the tools and materials they used came with them on sailing ships from Europe.

The colonists chopped down trees and mowed the fields. They hammered and sawed. They worked, prayed, and fought, but all too often they were sick, hungry, and cold. Many died. But many more kept coming, with many different dreams and desires.

Jamestown: Dreaming Big

Gold, silver, jewels, silk, fine wine—don't those sound like treasures fit for a king? They are what King James I of England hoped to find in the New World. In 1607, King James and many other English people were sure that great treasures awaited them in America. They heard stories about Spanish explorers who found jewels and gold scattered on the ground. As Spain grew rich and powerful, the leaders in England asked, "Why not us? We want our share of the New World!"

So the king of England wrote *charters*, which gave permission to settle in parts of North America. One charter went to a group of businessmen called the Virginia Company. They were willing to pay for a voyage to the New World. They hoped to get much richer in return.

Smith Lays Down the Law

"He who does not work shall not eat!" shouted Captain John Smith. He glared angrily at the men, who scowled back at him. A hardened soldier, Smith meant business. It was the bitterly cold January of 1608, and the colony of Jamestown faced disaster.

Captain John Smith of the Jamestown Colony.

Only a year before, the mission had begun with high hopes. The Virginia Company had prepared three ships for the voyage: the *Susan Constant*, the *Discovery*, and the *Godspeed*, with 144 men and boys aboard. From the start, things did not work out as planned. Strong winds forced them back toward London. It took six weeks before the winds changed and the ships could sail away from England.

Once they were on their way, many of the men must have thought those winds were trying to tell them something. Rough seas tossed the little boats. Supplies of food and water ran low. The men grew hungry, tired, and afraid. Some considered mutiny, when a crew rebels against the ship's captain.

By May 1607, when they finally saw land, just over a hundred sea-weary men stepped ashore. Forty of their crewmates had died on the way.

They found no gold or jewels. "We could find nothing worth the speaking of," wrote one of the men, "but fair meadows and goodly tall trees." They also found fresh water, plenty of oysters, and strawberries "four times bigger and better than ours in England."

They sailed up a river, which they named the James, in honor of the king. Looking for a place to start a colony, they chose a grassy peninsula and called their settlement Jamestown. The spot they picked seemed green, pleasant, and easy to defend.

The Jamestown Colony, founded in Virginia in 1607 and named for King James I of England.

But it turned out to be a terrible place. It was hard to build on the swampy ground. The stale, dirty water made the men ill. Mosquitoes buzzed all around, and they carried the deadly disease called malaria. Many Jamestown colonists did not survive to see the fall.

Winter came, and still they found no gold. They stored no food; they built no strong shelters. Men were dying of hunger and pneumonia. That's when John Smith took charge, thinking, "There is treasure here, but it's not gold. We've got to concentrate on fish and timber and fur. We must make the Indians fear us or they'll attack. We can't afford to waste time looking for gold."

In the cold and miserable January of 1608, when John Smith took charge of the Jamestown colony, only 38 of the original 144 colonists who had set sail from England remained alive. Smith put them to work. They chopped trees and dug wells. They drove posts into the ground and built forts. Many of the colonists were "gentlemen adventurers," used to having servants. Many had never used an ax in their lives. They complained about having to chop and dig and carry. Smith sternly replied, "He who does not work shall not eat!"

The men grumbled, but they worked. They built forts, fished, and combed the forest for nuts and berries. They had some good luck, too. "It pleased God to move the Indians to bring us corn, when we rather expected they would destroy us," wrote John Smith. He got to know some of the Powhatan [POW-uh-tun] Indians around Jamestown. He traded blankets and tools for food. He gratefully accepted the gift of corn, which would get his hungry men through the winter.

The Powhatans and the English

Relations between the English and the Native Americans were never simple. Sometimes they traded, and at other times they fought. The ruler of the Indians near Jamestown was named Wahunsonacock, though he was honored by the title of "Powhatan." He ruled over thousands of Indians, called the Powhatan people.

You probably know the story of Powhatan's favorite daughter, Matoaka, but you know her by her nickname, Pocahontas, which means "playful." According to John Smith, Pocahontas saved his life. Smith wrote how he was captured by the Powhatan Indians:

Their clubs were raised, and in another moment I should have been dead, when Pocahontas, the King's dearest daughter, a child of ten years old, . . . darted forward, and taking my head in her arms, laid her own upon it, and thus prevented my death.

Here is an illustration from a book written by John Smith, telling the story of how Pocahontas saved him from death. Do you see the Indian chief Powhatan and his daughter, Pocahontas? They are the two large figures on the right. Do you see John Smith? He is lying down, about to be beaten.

King Powhatan comands C. Smith to be slain daughter Pokahontas beggs his life his than

Smith wrote that Pocahontas risked "the beating out of her own brains to save mine." Is that what happened? Some historians think not, but the story has been told like this ever since. Smith said that the Powhatan Indians treated him "with exceeding great courtesy." He also wrote that if in that first winter the Indians "had not fed us, we [would have] starved."

How did the Powhatan people feel about the English? They were both curious and suspicious. They admired English tools, metal, and swords, and wanted to trade for them. But they did not trust these people who dressed so strangely, talked differently, and built their forts on lands where the Indians had once hunted freely. Sometimes the Indians and colonists managed to live in peace. More often they fought, unable to find a way to live together.

The "Indian Princess" in London

When Pocahontas was seventeen years old, she was kidnapped by Englishmen. They wanted to trade her for prisoners held by Indians, but instead she went to live among the colonists. She joined their Christian religion and took a new name, Rebecca. When an Englishman named John Rolfe proposed, she agreed to marry him. They were married in the church at Jamestown. Soon they had a baby boy, and the family set sail for a visit to England. The English were delighted by "Lady Rebecca, the Indian princess."

Sadly, Pocahontas did not live long. In England, she became ill and died. She was only twenty-two, far from her homeland. She never knew whether her people and the colonists could ever make peace, but her marriage, in 1614, marked the beginning of eight years of friendly relations between the English and the Powhatan people. Those eight years are called the Peace of Pocahontas.

The Starving Time

In the fall of 1609, John Smith was hurt by an explosion of gunpowder. His wounds were so bad that he was sent back to England, never to return.

That winter the colonists suffered even worse than before. There were no gifts of corn from the Indians. In fact, the colonists were so afraid of Indian attacks that they stayed locked inside their fort. Soon hunger and disease began to gnaw at them. By winter's end, they had eaten every horse, dog, cat, and rat they could find. Nearly all of the settlers died during this awful winter, called the Starving Time. There had been about five hundred of them when the winter began. Only sixty survived to see the spring.

A Cash Crop

If they couldn't find gold, what else could the colonists do? Some Englishmen said they should plant mulberry trees to feed silkworms and start producing silk in Jamestown. That didn't work. Some merchants said, "Try planting grapes to make fine wines." That didn't work, either.

Then in 1614, the colonists found an answer: tobacco. The Indians smoked tobacco in their peace pipes. John Rolfe, the colonist who married Pocahontas, brought premium tobacco from the Caribbean. Europeans enjoyed it, and the Jamestown colonists were happy to grow all they wanted. Soon the colonists were growing tobacco up and down the riverbanks and even in the streets of Jamestown!

King James warned against tobacco. He said smoking was "hateful to the nose, harmful to the brain, [and] dangerous to the lungs." But many people enjoyed smoking it, and many people depended on growing and selling it to make money. Tobacco became the most important crop raised and sold by the settlers of Jamestown.

Ladies and Laws

One spring afternoon in 1619, the first shipload of women sailed into the Chesapeake Bay. For 120 pounds of tobacco, a man could pay a lady's travel expenses and make her his wife. It may not seem very romantic, but it meant big changes for Jamestown. Now the colonists could raise families in the New World.

In 1619, Jamestown took another huge step forward. The Virginia Company sent a governor from England. The new governor told the colonists to choose men to represent them and help make laws. Why was this important? Virginia was a colony, ruled from a faraway nation, England. But now the colony would begin to make its own rules. Early on, Virginians got used to governing themselves.

The Arrival of the Africans

The year 1619 was important for another reason. For the first time, Dutch ships came to the Virginia coast, carrying not just cocoa or linen but African people, brought to work in the fields.

The first Africans to arrive in Jamestown were not brought as slaves. Instead, just like some poor Englishmen, they were *indentured servants*. They worked for a landowner as if they were slaves, but after a few years they gained their freedom. Soon some of these first Africans came to own their own land and farms.

Soon, though, the white colonists decided that the Africans brought to Virginia should not be given their freedom, no matter how long they worked. By 1661, slavery was legal in Virginia. Africans who stepped onto the shores of the Chesapeake Bay were likely doomed to a lifetime of slavery.

This drawing, from about 1730, shows a Virginia landowner, puffing on his pipe, with two slaves working hard in his tobacco fields. Tobacco was packed in large wooden barrels like these and shipped back to England for sale.

The Pilgrims at Plymouth

In September 1620, 102 passengers crowded aboard a small ship called the *Mayflower*, starting from Plymouth, England, setting off for the New World. They feared the vast ocean, but these men and women were eager to leave their troubles behind them. These travelers, called Pilgrims, had not had an easy life. A pilgrim is a person who goes on a journey, usually for religious reasons. The Pilgrims on the *Mayflower* had already made one hard journey, leaving their homes in England and sailing to Holland in 1608. They left because they did not agree with the Church of England. They thought that its leaders had forgotten the simple faith that Jesus taught. They wanted to separate from the Church of England and worship in simpler ways.

The *Mayflower* may have looked like this under sail.

But choosing to worship more simply was not a simple matter. As King James saw it, to challenge the Church of England was to challenge the king himself. He would not put up with any "separatists"—his word for people who wanted to separate from the Church of England. He ordered that they be hunted down and punished. Some were thrown into jail, their homes destroyed, their businesses threatened.

But Holland was known for letting people worship as they wanted to. That is why, with heavy hearts, the Pilgrims fled to Holland in 1608. But Holland did not feel like home. The Pilgrims began to fear for their safety. They decided to leave Holland and start an even more difficult voyage, this time to America.

As the Pilgrims gathered in Plymouth, England, more people joined the voyage. They did not share the Pilgrims' religion, so they were called "strangers." In September 1620, 102 people set sail on the *Mayflower*, headed for Virginia, planning to settle just north of Jamestown.

The Mayflower Compact

The winds howled. The seas swelled so high that one wave swept a sailor right off the deck. He grabbed a line from the topsail and swung himself back on board. Meanwhile, the Pilgrims huddled below, praying that God might deliver them from the fury of the sea.

The Pilgrims had intended to go to Virginia, but the *Mayflower* sailed farther north, and they landed on the coast of what is now Massachusetts.

After sixty-six days, the *Mayflower* landed at Cape Cod, in today's Massachusetts, much farther north than Virginia. It was late November. Temperatures were dropping, and snow was in the air. The captain of the *Mayflower* declared this would be home for the Pilgrims. When they landed, one man wrote that "they fell upon their knees and blessed the God of Heaven, who had brought them over the vast and furious ocean . . . and again set their feet on the firm and stable earth."

The Pilgrims needed to take care of a problem that had come up while at sea, however. During the crossing, some of the "strangers" said they would not follow any rules or listen to any Pilgrim leaders. The Pilgrims believed they needed an agreement among all the people in this new land as to how they would govern themselves and what laws should be made.

On board the *Mayflower*, Pilgrims and "strangers" sign the Mayflower Compact.

Before they left the *Mayflower*, Pilgrims and strangers gathered around a massive wooden table in the captain's quarters. There they signed their names to an agreement, which was called the Mayflower Compact. In it, they agreed to "combine ourselves together into a civil Body Politick" (a group of people agreeing to work together) and to create "just and equal laws" for the colony. Every man signed the Mayflower Compact before stepping ashore. The Mayflower Compact shows that the colonists were concerned about "the general good" and were willing to work together to make laws that were fair for all.

A "Wild and Savage" Land

Imagine stepping onto the shore of this strange new land, a land that William Bradford, a leader among the Pilgrims, described as "wild and savage." Behind you lies the ocean. Before you looms the forest, thick and dark. What might be lurking behind those trees?

But there is no time to worry. Winter is upon you. The damp smell of snow is in the air. Where will you build? What will you do first? How will you survive? *Will* you survive?

This was the reality the Pilgrims faced in November 1620. Scouts from the *Mayflower* rowed out to search the rocky coast. They found some land, partly cleared by Indians and named "Plymouth" by John Smith years before. They had sailed from Plymouth, England, so it seemed right that they should make a new home in Plymouth, America. The land was fed by a stream and sat on top of a small hill, which would make it easy to defend.

The Pilgrims had not even begun to build houses when the first snow fell. In December, January, and February, they struggled to build their homes, trudging back and forth to the *Mayflower* through frigid ocean water several times a day. Many caught colds that turned to pneumonia. They had no warm homes to shelter them, no hot meals to eat. Less than half the Pilgrims lived to see the spring. Still, the Pilgrims of Plymouth, like the settlers of Jamestown, survived—partly through courage and good leadership, but even more through the friendship of the Wampanoag Indians.

The Pilgrims and the Wampanoags

Imagine you are a Pilgrim child, one of the lucky ones who made it through that first winter. It's a blustery March day and the leaves have not yet returned to the trees. You're hungry, but there's little to eat. Sometimes you see faces in the forest. They look, then dart away. What are they thinking? What are they planning? Will they attack?

Then you hear a deep voice: "Welcome, Englishmen!" A man dressed in deerskin walks boldly into your camp. You can hardly believe your ears. An Indian speaking English!

Everyone gathers round. The man says his name is Samoset. He says he knows another who speaks English even better. Your governor gives him presents, and Samoset promises to return.

Days later he comes back, and he brings more Indians with him. He introduces you to Tisquantum, who speaks English very well. Over time, Tisquantum teaches you and the other Pilgrims how to plant corn, pumpkins, and beans. He shows you good places to fish. He guides you through the lands around Plymouth. He introduces your leaders to Massasoit, chief of the Wampanoag tribe. Soon the Wampanoags and the Pilgrims sign a treaty of peace and friendship that will last for many years.

Squanto's Story

The Pilgrims took to calling Tisquantum by the name of Squanto. Years before they arrived, Squanto had been kidnapped by traders. He was taken first to Spain and then to England, where he learned to speak English. A London merchant helped him back to America on an English fishing ship, but on his return he found that all his people had been killed by chicken pox, which some historians think was brought by the English settlers. Squanto found a home with Massasoit and the Wampanoag people nearby. He was a good friend and a great help to the Pilgrims.

Peace and Plenty: Thanksgiving

During the spring and summer of 1621, the Pilgrims built homes near the ocean shore. Following Squanto's advice, they raised good crops. With William Bradford as their new governor, the Pilgrims decided to celebrate with a harvest festival. They invited their Wampanoag friends to a three-day celebration. Bradford sent fishermen and hunters to bring back food. Massasoit, with ninety of his men, hunted in the forest and brought five deer. For three days, the Indians and Pilgrims feasted on goose, duck, turkey, venison, cod, bass, stewed pumpkin, corn bread, wild onions, custard, and fruit tarts. The English danced jigs and sang the Twenty-third Psalm. The Indians chanted hymns and danced in ways that made the stone necklaces bounce on their chests. For these three days in the fall of 1621, they gathered in peace and friendship. We remember this gathering as the first Thanksgiving.

One artist's concept of the first Thanksgiving. What do you see in this picture that reminds you of Thanksgiving at your house?

Massachusetts Bay: The Puritans

The Pilgrims soon had company on the shores of the land they called New England. Another group of English colonists, called the Puritans, began coming in large numbers. The Puritans were deeply religious, well educated, and highly skilled. They were tailors, cobblers, weavers, and blacksmiths, lawyers, and teachers. Like the Pilgrims, they were unhappy with the Church of England. They wanted to "purify" it and bring it closer to their sense of the Bible. While the Pilgrims wanted the freedom to worship in their own way, the Puritans wanted to change the Church of England.

Of course, that did not please the English kings. When King James died in 1625, his son became the new king, Charles I—which was bad news for the Puritans. He had them thrown into jail, kept them from their jobs, and made life miserable for them.

The Puritan leaders decided to make a church in the New World. King Charles chartered the Massachusetts Bay Company, giving them the right to establish a colony in New England. He was happy to see the Puritans go.

By the end of the summer in 1630, about a thousand Puritans had arrived in New England. They were led by John Winthrop, a wealthy lawyer. Governor Winthrop told the Puritans that they must set an example for all the world to see. "We must consider that we shall be as a City upon a Hill," he said. "The eyes of all people are on us."

In the next ten years, the Puritans did more than build a single "City upon a Hill." With twenty thousand more Puritans arriving in the Massachusetts Bay Colony between 1630 and 1640, they built *lots* of towns and cities. Salem came first. Then came Boston, well placed on a bay and bordered by a river. Boston became the capital of the Massachusetts Bay Colony.

As the ambitious Puritans kept spreading, they established three new colonies: Connecticut, Rhode Island, and New Hampshire.

People of the Book

Most of all, the Puritans cared about their faith, based on a close and careful reading of the Bible. Most Puritans could read, and they were determined to keep it that way. One of the first things the Massachusetts Bay Colony did was to pass a law requiring parents to teach their children to read. This law was copied in Connecticut, Rhode Island, and New Hampshire.

Then the Massachusetts Bay Colony passed another important law. Every town with at least fifty families was to open a "grammar school" to teach reading, Latin, and Greek, "to instruct youth so far as they may be fitted for the university." A whole system of "public schools," schools supported by the towns, sprang up in Massachusetts. Students were not forced to attend, but the towns were required to provide the schools. There was nothing like it back in England. Now, here in New England, not just the children of wealthy parents but *any* child could hope for an education. That is what public education is all about—and it began with that law, passed by the Puritans. The Puritans wanted to educate new ministers and lawmakers, too, so they founded Harvard College, still one of the most respected universities in the world.

Roger Williams and Rhode Island

Like most people in their time, the Puritans thought of themselves as people who were following the truth, and they thought there could be only one truth. This caused problems for people who had different beliefs.

One such person was Roger Williams, a Puritan minister who had come to Massachusetts Bay in 1631, just a year after John Winthrop arrived with the original one thousand settlers. Williams was a kind and thoughtful man, but in Massachusetts Bay his thoughts got him in trouble.

For one thing, Roger Williams said that the king of England had no right to grant the settlers of Massachusetts Bay a charter because the land belonged to the Indians. Williams also said that kings had no right to decide the religion of their subjects, and that individuals should be free to decide their own religious beliefs.

These bold ideas worried John Winthrop, the governor of the Massachusetts Bay Colony. First the Puritans just warned Williams that he needed to change his beliefs, but when he wouldn't, they banished him from Massachusetts Bay, which meant he had to leave the colony and never come back. The Puritan leaders planned to send Roger Williams back to England. But Williams, even though he was old and sick, slipped out of Boston and traveled south. He found shelter with the Narragansett Indians, who helped him make it through the winter.

When Roger Williams was made to leave the Massachusetts Bay Colony, he traveled south, to the area we now call Rhode Island. Narragansett Indians made friends with him and helped him survive the winter.

Williams bought some of the land around the beautiful Narragansett Bay from the Indians. He called the land Providence, which was another word for "God." Providence became the capital of Rhode Island.

Williams was determined to start a colony based on the idea that government should not tell the people how to worship. He believed in *the separation of church and state*, which became one of the most important ideas upon which our country was founded.

Williams practiced religious toleration, accepting people of all religions, even atheists, who didn't believe in God. While the Puritans and Pilgrims were rejecting Quakers and Jews and Catholics, Roger Williams welcomed them to Providence, Rhode Island.

The *separation of church and state* refers to the separation of *religion* and *government*. It means that governments should not tell people what to believe about religion.

Anne Hutchinson

The Puritans could hardly believe their ears. Who was this woman, a mother of fourteen children, who dared to tell the Puritan ministers what to think? Didn't she know that she should remain quiet and obedient, like a good Puritan wife?

Anne Hutchinson, who came to Massachusetts Bay with her family in 1634, was certainly not a meek and mild Puritan wife. She was brilliant, and she loved to teach. She held weekly meetings in her home, and more and more people, both men and women, came to hear her discuss the Bible and the teachings of the church.

Like Roger Williams, Anne Hutchinson was saying bold and daring things that worried most Puritan leaders. For example, she said that God communicated with people directly, and not through church officials. She also said that most of the ministers in Massachusetts Bay did not teach the Bible properly.

The stern Puritan ministers mistrusted Anne Hutchinson.

In 1637, the Puritan leaders put Anne Hutchinson on trial. Governor Winthrop said she was "troubling the peace of the commonwealth" with her strange ideas. Anne Hutchinson told her judges, "If you do condemn me for speaking what in my conscience I know to be truth, I must commit myself to the Lord." In the end, the Puritans announced, "Mrs. Hutchinson is deluded [or fooled] by the devil!" And they banished her from the colony.

She and her family went to Rhode Island, which had become the colony for "dissenters"—people who did not agree with the official religion, whether that of the Church of England or the Puritans.

One People's Prosperity, Another's Peril

More and more people, most of them Puritans, left England to come to Massachusetts Bay. They spread out and settled in what are now the states of Connecticut and New Hampshire. They tended small farms. They chopped trees to sell lumber. They caught plenty of fish to sell. And they began a new industry, shipbuilding. The timber from New England forests supplied busy shipyards.

As the New Englanders built more towns and farms, they took over more of the land where the Indians had long hunted, fished, and farmed. Fighting broke out often between the colonists and the Native Americans. The Indians attacked colonists and burned their homes. The colonists struck back fiercely, attacking even the friendly Narragansett Indians in Rhode Island.

New England bustled with busy ports and shipyards. But down south, Virginia and other colonies relied more on agriculture, growing crops such as tobacco and rice.

But the Indians suffered even more because of the diseases that came to the New World from Europe. Native Americans had never been exposed to smallpox, chicken pox, or measles. In seventy-five years, from 1600 to 1675, the Native American population in New England fell from 100,000 to 10,000. Most of those deaths came from disease.

Refuge for Other Religions: Maryland and Pennsylvania

Soon other English colonies stretched between New England and Virginia. Like Massachusetts Bay, Pennsylvania and Maryland were started by people seeking religious freedom. First let's learn how Pennsylvania became a refuge, or safe place, for Quakers, who were being treated badly in England at the time.

Their real name was the Society of Friends, but the English called them Quakers because the Friends appeared to rock or "quake" when they prayed. Quakers didn't believe in churches or religious ceremonies. They thought war was wrong and refused to fight. They believed loyalty to anyone but God was wrong, so they would not give their loyalty to the king.

Quakers believed God spoke to each individual and guided him or her through an "inner light" in his or her soul. They said that people did not need to listen to priests or ministers, or even study the Bible. Instead, they simply needed to sit quietly and learn to be guided by the inner light. In God's eyes, the Quakers said, all people are equal. And so they would not bow to dukes or lords or other members of the upper classes in England.

William Penn, a wealthy and well-educated gentleman, and the son of a famous British naval hero, joined the Society of Friends when he was young. His father wanted him to stay in the Church of England, but Penn clung to his beliefs, even though he was thrown in jail for holding them.

After his father died, William Penn went to see King Charles II. The king had borrowed money from William's father, and now Penn wanted to be paid back. For years, Penn had dreamed of starting a "holy experiment," a Quaker colony in North America. He asked the king to pay him back with land instead of money.

The king gave Penn *29 million* acres, an area larger than England itself. Penn wanted to name it Sylvania, which means "woods." The king suggested that William honor his father by calling the land Pennsylvania, "Penn's woods."

When Quakers said they believed that all men and women are equal in God's eyes, they included Native Americans and Africans. The Quakers were among the first people to say that slavery was wrong.

William Penn wasted no time. He printed brochures urging people, "Come to Pennsylvania where brotherly love will guide us all." Pennsylvania welcomed not just Quakers but people of all religions, including Jews and Catholics. By 1682, there were four thousand colonists in Pennsylvania. By 1700, there were eighteen thousand! People came from Germany, Holland, Scotland, and other countries.

William Penn.

For the capital of the colony, Penn chose a site on the Delaware River and named it Philadelphia, which means "city of brotherly love." Penn helped plan the city. He laid out the streets in an orderly crisscross pattern. Philadelphia quickly grew into a busy port town, one of the colonies' most important cities.

In 1776 (when the colonies declared their independence from Britain), the southeastern part of Pennsylvania became the state of Delaware.

A Refuge for Catholics

To find out how the colony of Maryland got started, we have to look back to England. In the early 1600s, a wealthy nobleman, Sir George Calvert, shocked the English by becoming Catholic. Calvert began thinking about starting a colony in America that would welcome Catholics. He had been forced to give up an important government job because of his religion, but Charles I still liked him and gave him a colony in America, stretching from the Potomac River to what is now Philadelphia.

How does this picture show that a colonist's kitchen was different from kitchens today? What looks familiar?

George Calvert died soon after the king granted him a charter. But his son Cecil [SESS-ul] Calvert carried on with his father's plans to start the new colony and sent his brother to be the first governor. They named the new colony Maryland after the king's wife, Queen Henrietta Maria, and also for Mary, the mother of Jesus.

In 1634, while Puritans were settling in Massachusetts Bay, 250 colonists landed in Maryland. This time the settlers arrived in March, with plenty of time to plant crops and prepare for winter. They traded with friendly Indians. They started growing tobacco. Maryland got off to a good start and kept growing.

> George Calvert held the title of Lord Baltimore. His son Cecil was the second Lord Baltimore. And now you know where Maryland's busy port city, Baltimore, got its name.

New Netherland

By 1700, British North America had grown into a bustling, rowdy place. Up and down the Atlantic seaboard, colonists of many different religions and backgrounds made their homes. Most of these colonists came from England. But the area we now call New York, which started out as New Netherland, belonged to the Dutch.

You might remember that Henry Hudson, sailing for the Dutch East India Company, had claimed this area for Holland. Find Holland (which is also called the Netherlands) on a map of Europe. It's a tiny country, but it was also a powerful country with a strong navy and many colonies around the world.

The Dutch wanted to turn New Netherland into a fur trading post. But first they needed more land, so in 1626 they bought a neighboring island from the local Manhate Indians. Legend says that the Dutch bought the island for a bunch of beads worth twenty-four dollars. You might think, "What a bargain," especially since the island they bought is the one we now call Manhattan, the heart of today's New York City.

A New Amsterdam street in the 1600s.

Soon windmills were going up everywhere as Dutch colonists built the port town of New Amsterdam on the tip of Manhattan Island. They planned to grow rich by shipping furs from this location. French, Germans, Swedes, and Finns came to settle in the colony, as did black people from Brazil. Jews from Spain and Portugal made a home with the Dutch as well.

When you walked down the streets of New Amsterdam, you could hear more than a dozen different languages—much as you can in New York City today!

But the Dutch seemed more interested in their colonies in India and South America. They failed to set up a good government in New Netherland. Everybody fought and argued. No one could make the colony work. The British decided to take advantage of the confusion. In 1664, English ships sailed into New Amsterdam, demanding that the Dutch surrender the colony to King Charles II. Then Charles II gave it as a gift to his brother, the Duke of York, who changed its name to his own: New York. That land now forms part of New York and New Jersey today.

Charles's Carolina

Names often tell who was important in the past. Consider the names of the colonies south of Virginia that we now call North and South Carolina. Where do you think the name "Carolina" came from? From "Carolus," Latin for "Charles," since Charles II was the king of England.

King Charles granted a charter for one big colony between Virginia and Florida, to be called Carolina. The colony had a fine harbor, which was named—you'll never guess—Charles Town. In time, this town became Charleston, which grew to be one of the busiest ports in the colonies.

With a charter that granted total religious freedom, Carolina attracted people from all over. In the 1680s, settlers spilled out of the older colonies into Carolina. Puritan New Englanders, land-hungry Virginians, English and French dissenters, Scots, and many colonists from the West Indies poured into Carolina.

Many African American slaves worked in rice fields in South Carolina and Georgia.

Carolina had two big cash crops: rice and indigo, which makes a fine blue dye. These crops grew on large farms and required lots of heavy labor. At first, indentured servants—Europeans, Africans, and Native Americans—all worked together on the Carolina farms. But farmers began to rely on slaves from Africa, and soon there were more slaves than freemen in the colony.

In the early 1700s, Carolina split into two colonies, North and South Carolina. Then the king of England took back the region farthest south for a new colony. He called it Georgia. Guess what this king's name was? Yes, indeed—George. King George II, to be exact.

A Debtor's Tale

Imagine this. The year is 1730. Your family is living in a small, dark room of a run-down building in a dirty section of London. Rats scurry beneath a rickety wooden table.

Your parents work hard, but somehow they can't pay their bills. You and your little brother beg for food each day. Then one day an English constable (a police officer) drags your father off to jail because he can't pay his debts. Your father is thrown into debtors' prison, where he will stay for a long time. Now you've lost your father's income. How will your family ever survive?

Today anyone who thinks about these debtors' prisons can see that they were a terrible idea. Back then, only a few people saw the problem. James Edward Oglethorpe wanted to give debtors a second chance. He went to King George II and said, "Don't send debtors to prison. Give them a chance to do something useful. Send them to the New World, and let them settle a colony there."

The king agreed. He liked the idea of sending more English people to the land that bordered Florida. Florida was owned by Britain's rival, Spain. King George II thought, "If I can get colonists to settle there, they will keep out the Spaniards."

So in 1732, James Oglethorpe set off for Georgia with 120 colonists. As it turned out, most of them were *not* debtors. Oglethorpe found that most debtors preferred to remain in England, even in prison, rather than face the dangers of the New World.

Oglethorpe and his colonists settled between two rivers, in the area we now call Savannah. For the next few years, Oglethorpe paid for more and more people to come and settle in Georgia. The colonists in Georgia made friends with the Creek Indians, who hated the Spanish. Together the colonists and the Creeks drove the Spaniards back to Florida, but they did not take Florida from the Spanish, which is what the English wanted them to do.

By 1743, James Oglethorpe had run up so much debt from his efforts that he had to go back to England to be put on trial! Would Oglethorpe himself be sent to debtors' prison? No, the jury let him go. But James Oglethorpe was fed up. He returned the charter to King George II and told the king, ever so politely, to run the colony himself.

The Slave Trade

Today everyone knows that slavery is wrong. No one should take away any person's freedom (except when a person has been convicted of a crime). No human being can own another person the way you can own a piece of furniture. But in the 1600s and 1700s, many believed differently, and nobody tried very hard to stop slavery. Slavery had been around for so long that many people took it for granted.

There have been slaves just about as long as there has been civilization. Slaves built the pyramids in ancient Egypt and the Great Wall in ancient China. There were many slaves in ancient Greece and Rome. The Aztecs enslaved the people they conquered. In Africa, too, when people fought wars, the victors often enslaved the conquered people. The victorious chieftain would then sell the slaves to Arab traders.

So, when European traders started buying African slaves from West African chieftains, they were not starting something new. Between the 1580s and the early 1800s, European traders transported *10 million* slaves to European colonies in North and South America. More than nine out of ten of these slaves went to Central and South America, including Caribbean islands with big sugar plantations. About half a million slaves came to North America.

The growing demand for slaves in the colonies led to a horrible expansion of the business of buying and selling human beings. Europeans took goods such as guns and cloth to Africa and traded them for slaves. The captains of slave ships clamped chains onto the wrists and ankles of hundreds of Africans and crammed them into tightly packed quarters below deck. And so began the Middle Passage, the nightmare of crossing the Atlantic from Africa to America. Many Africans died before they reached America.

Those who survived faced a life of hard work with little hope of freedom. They could not own property. They could not marry. They could be sold at any point. Children could be taken from their parents and sold to a new master hundreds of miles away.

With overseers watching, male and female slaves worked together to hoe the fields.

The southern colonies, such as Virginia and the Carolinas, came to rely more and more on slaves to work on the plantations. Most slaves worked as field hands, growing tobacco, rice, and indigo. Others worked as craftsmen and house servants.

But don't think that there were slaves only in the Southern colonies. It's true that in the 1800s the South came to depend on slaves, while the North came to oppose slavery. But back in the 1600s, there were slaves in almost every colony. Most came from Africa, but some were American Indians.

You might be thinking, "How horrible! Why didn't anybody do anything?" A few people tried, but only a few. The Quakers in Pennsylvania wanted slavery to end. But the sad truth is, when our country was first founded, not many people thought slavery was wrong.

III.

Visual Arts

INTRODUCTION

For third graders, as in earlier years, the primary experience of art should come by *doing:* drawing, painting, cutting and pasting, working with clay and other materials. A few such activities are suggested here, but many more can be developed to complement your child's discovery of image and light, shape and color.

No book can offer the experience of actually viewing works of art in person by visiting museums and galleries. This chapter suggests how to introduce concepts and vocabulary to third graders, helping them talk about what they see, what the artist decided, and how it affects them. By looking closely at these works of art, both classic masterpieces and fine folk and ethnic artwork, you help enlarge your child's mental museum of our culture's finest works.

Suggested Resources

Mary Ann Kohl and Kim Solga, *Discovering Great Artists: Hands-On Art for Children in the Styles of the Great Masters* (Bright Ideas for Learning, 1997). Introduces artists and their work by inviting children to make their own masterpieces in similar styles.

Mike Venezia, Getting to Know the Great Artists series, including *Pieter Breughel, Mary Cassatt, Rembrandt* (Children's Press). Venezia combines offbeat humor and funny drawings with color reproductions of the artists' own works.

Caught in the Light

Think about waking up on a bright sunny day. As the sunlight pours through the windows of your room, it makes every detail stand out and every color seem brighter. You feel bright and alive inside, ready to face the day.

Now think about waking up on a dark and cloudy morning. Your room looks gray and blurred. Don't you wish you could pull the covers over your head and go back to bed?

Light can affect the way you feel. It can lift your spirits and make you feel happy. Without light, you can feel sad and dreary. The way that artists use light in their paintings can affect your emotions as well.

The Milkmaid.

Let's look at the painting called *The Milkmaid* by the Dutch artist Jan Vermeer [YON fair-MEER]. Vermeer has made this milkmaid's kitchen feel warm and bright and pleasant to be in. Sunlight pours through the window. It brightens the woman and all the objects in the room. It makes the metal lantern shine and highlights the rim of the pitcher.

Of course, there is no real sunlight in this painting. Vermeer has made you think that there is. By carefully studying how different surfaces reflect light, he painted what you would expect to see in a sunny room. The light seems to reflect off shiny objects. Even the white wall and the wood of the foot warmer on the floor seem to shine. He also made sure that some things in the painting were quite dark. The sharp contrast between dark and light makes the bright things look even brighter.

Look at the way Vermeer has used color. He knew that the colors we see depend on how much light is falling on them. He makes us think that sunlight is coming in through the window by making the white of the milkmaid's hat, the yellow of her dress, and the blue of her apron brightest on the side close to the window. The back of her skirt and the bottom of her apron are darker, because the light does not reach them. Compare the bright wall behind the milkmaid to the dark wall under the window.

Now let's look at the way another artist uses light. Look at the painting called *Ruby Green Singing* by the American artist James Chapin. This painting is full of light. But unlike Vermeer, Chapin decided not to show the source of the light. In *Ruby Green Singing*, where do you think the light is coming from? Is it sunlight? How are the dark and light colors in this painting different from the dark and light colors in *The Milkmaid*?

Ruby Green Singing.

Like the milkmaid in Vermeer's painting, Ruby Green is the only person in this painting. Her upturned face is framed by her dark hair and the shadows beneath her chin. Look at the flashes of light in Ruby Green's eyes and on her teeth. The title tells us that Ruby Green is singing. What kind of songs do you think she is singing? Why?

Out of the Shadows

Have you ever been surprised by a flash of lightning in a dark, stormy sky? The man standing in the center of the next painting looks as though the same thing has just happened to him!

Belshazzar's Feast.

Belshazzar's Feast was painted by the Dutch artist Rembrandt van Rijn [REM-brant fahn RINE]. The painting tells a story from the Bible. While King Belshazzar was giving a great feast, a

Rembrandt experimented with light to see how it affected people's facial expressions. Try this. Stand in front of a mirror in a well-lit room. Try moving your eyes, eyebrows, and mouth to show several different expressions—fear, anger, surprise. Now darken the room, then shine a flashlight on your face from the side, then above, then below. Do your expressions look different?

hand suddenly appeared and wrote a message on the wall, predicting that the king would be overthrown. Belshazzar could not read the message, but he was astonished by that hand. This painting makes you see how he was surprised.

Rembrandt was a master at showing sharp differences between light and shadow. You can clearly see the profile of King Belshazzar, but you have to strain to see the shapes in the dark shadows. You can see all the details of Belshazzar's robe, but little of the clothes on the bearded man behind him. Rembrandt has used the contrast between dark and light to make the scene look more exciting.

Rembrandt applied dabs of white paint to indicate reflections from the light. There are glints of light on the metal surfaces, silky fabrics, and sparkling jewels. Can you find the strands of pearls, the crown, and the plate of grapes, that Rembrandt has highlighted as well?

A Wall Filled with Light

Let's take an imaginary trip to the beautiful city of Ravenna, in Italy, to visit the church called San Vitale, where we can see world-famous *mosaics*. A mosaic is made from thousands of tiny pieces of colored glass, jewels, and precious metals, fitted together like a puzzle.

The empress Theodora and her court, a mosaic from Ravenna.

Mosaics cover the walls of San Vitale. The mosaic you see here shows the empress Theodora and her

Make Your Own Mosaic

You will need a pencil, a piece of cardboard, glue, and construction paper of many colors. Cut the paper into tiny squares. Decide what picture you want your mosaic to show, and draw it on the cardboard. Keep the design simple. One by one, glue the paper squares to the cardboard, fitting them next to one another to make the design.

court. In the World History section of this book, you can read about Theodora's husband, the emperor Justinian, who ruled the Byzantine Empire. This mosaic is a good example of Byzantine art.

Many great works of art were created when the Byzantine Empire was strongest (from about A.D. 400 to 1400). Since Christianity was so important, much of this art was made for churches. This mosaic honors the empress Theodora because she and her husband built many new Christian churches.

The mosaic in San Vitale looks as if it is filled with light. Much of the background is made of gold, which catches and reflects the light coming through windows or from candles. Byzantine artists used gold to remind people of heaven. Imagine how it would feel

to be in a room full of mosaics shimmering with all the colors of the rainbow!

Can you tell which figure is Theodora in the mosaic? She is the tallest figure, carrying a golden cup. What else makes her more noticeable than the others?

Here is a close-up of part of Theodora's face, so you can see the tiles that make up the mosaic.

If you actually visited San Vitale, you would see that this mosaic is quite large. The figures are almost life-size. Just think how many tiny squares it took to make Theodora!

Filling a Space

Circles, triangles, and squares are plane figures. Spheres, pyramids, and cubes are solid figures. A painter starts with a flat plane—a wall, a piece of paper or cloth—and paints shapes that are supposed to look solid. An artist begins in two dimensions—height and width—and creates something that looks like it has three dimensions: height, width, and depth. How does a painter make something that looks round, or thick, or deep, or far away?

The Gleaners.

Try this experiment. Look out a window. Some of the things you see are farther away than others. Those things appear smaller, and may be partially blocked from your view by other things that are closer to you. You can't see the trees behind your neighbor's house as clearly as you can see the tree in your own yard. The trees far away are not as clear, and their colors are not as bright. They seem smaller, even though you know that they are as big as the tree closer up.

What you are seeing can be divided into three parts:

- the foreground (those things closest to you, like your tree)
- the background (those things farthest from you, like the trees in back of the house)
- the middle ground (those things between the foreground and the background, like the house)

Many paintings also have a foreground, background, and middle ground. For example, let's look at a farm scene called *The Gleaners,* painted by the French artist Jean-François Millet [mee-YAY]. The central figures in the painting are three women who are gleaning, or gathering what is left in a field after the harvest.

Millet makes you focus on the women by placing them in the foreground, larger and more brightly colored than anything else in the painting. While their faces are not visible, you can see the detail of their clothes and the stalks they hold in their hands. In back of them, in the middle ground, you see a wagon, several large stacks of grain, and many people. There is hardly any detail in these shapes, and the colors are much more pale. They seem little more than dabs of paint. The buildings and trees far in the background are even smaller. They seem out of focus, so pale they seem to fade away.

Now let's look at a painting called *Peasant Wedding,* which gives us a view of a room filled with people. These are peasants, poor farm people like the women in *The Gleaners.*

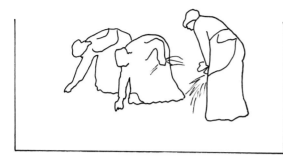

These figures are in the foreground.

This wagon and stacks of grain are in the middle ground.

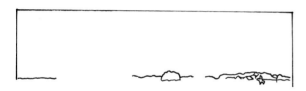

These buildings and trees, and a person on a horse, are in the background.

Peasant Wedding.

Have you ever heard of a wedding in a barn? When the artist, Pieter Brueghel [BROY-gul], was painting in northern Europe, peasant families would hold weddings in barns.

Brueghel has kept the picture from looking too crowded by placing people in the foreground, middle ground, and background. What happens to the size of the faces and bodies of the people as you look down the table? Can you see the people waiting to enter the room? Did Brueghel paint them with the same amount of detail as the people in the front?

Brueghel used the brightest colors in the foreground. The colors in the background almost blend with the walls. The bride, seated in front of the dark green cloth, has pale skin. The hat hanging above her head makes her stand out. To what are the guests paying the most attention?

Speaking of Space

Now let's look at the painting called *The Interior of the Pantheon*. The Pantheon is a real building in Rome, built by a Roman emperor in the second century A.D., with a huge domed ceiling and a window through which you can see the sky.

This painting, created by an Italian artist named Giovanni Panini [jo-VAH-nee pa-NEE-nee], shows the Pantheon in the eighteenth century, when Panini was alive. Imagine standing in the middle of this room and looking up. You would feel very small. Look how small the artist made the figures in this painting, to convey that sense of the space.

The vertical lines of the columns lead your eyes upward to the huge curved roof. There the panels in the dome become smaller and their lines fade into the shadows, the closer they are to the top. The floor is divided into rectangles, and your eye follows the lines of those rectangles to the doorway. There, in the distant background, you see tiny figures walking out through enormous gates.

The Interior of the Pantheon.

Panini has used lines and shapes, color and shadow, to make a two-dimensional painting look like a three-dimensional scene, so high that you see the clouds in the sky, so wide that you see sunlight spreading and many people inside, and so deep that you see far, far away through the gates of the building.

Design

What have we been looking at in these paintings? Light and shadow, bright colors and dark colors, shapes and lines, a sense of space. All these different elements work together in every painting. We use the word "design" to refer to the way the artist made the elements of a piece of art work together. Let's look at some more artworks and think about their design.

First let's look at *The Horse Fair*. The artist who painted it spent a year and a half attending horse sales, studying the animals, and making sketches. During the entire time, the artist wore a disguise—because she was a woman.

The Horse Fair.

Her name was Rosa Bonheur [baw-NUR]. In the 1800s, when Bonheur lived, only men went to the horse market. But Bonheur wanted to go. She got permission from the head of police and dressed as a man, so no one told her to leave.

Let's look at the way she uses light in *The Horse Fair*. Where do you look first? Most people look first at the light-colored horses and the white shirts of the men near them. Do you see how Bonheur has made those horses and men seem to form a ring? As your eyes look at them, they move in a circle. You can almost feel all the motion in the painting.

Now let's look at all the diagonal lines, made by the legs of the horses and the bodies of the men. Can you see the push and pull? The zigzag lines of some of the horses' legs make them alive and moving.

The Horse Fair is said to be the largest animal painting ever done, more than sixteen feet long and eight feet high—large enough to cover a wall! The painting makes such a strong impression not only because it is big but also because the artist's design includes so much movement and energy.

Using Line to Design

When you decide to draw a picture, what do you do? You begin by drawing lines. Even a painter designs by using lines.

Let's look at how the artist uses lines in the next painting, called *The Bath*, painted by the American artist Mary Cassatt [cah-SAHT] about a hundred years ago. In *The Bath*, we see more than just a woman washing a child. We can also sense the tenderness of mother and child. How does Cassatt show this? Look at the way the mother cradles her child on her lap. Look at how closely their heads are drawn together.

Cassatt uses lines to show the connection between the woman and her child. The lines of the mother's sleeve lead your eyes to the basin. Your eyes follow the curve of the basin, then they move back up to see the body of the child. Then your eyes look again at the heads of the two figures. Your eyes have traveled in a circle, which is part of the artist's design in this painting.

The Bath.

Cassatt has used light in her painting, too. Look at the little girl's legs. One side is darker than the other. Look at the glints of light in the hair of both mother and child. Whenever you notice lines and light in a painting, you are noticing the artist's design.

Lines, Shapes, and Colors Move

Now let's look at the design of a very useful object.

To save time and money, early Americans made the most out of what they had. They saved their worn-out clothing and cut the cloth into pieces, arranged them in a design, and sewed them together into a warm bedcover called a *quilt*. Often all the women in a town would turn their sewing work into a party, called a quilting bee. Making art meant fun for everyone.

Let's look at a quilt made around 1850 by a woman named Margie Gorrect, who lived in Pennsylvania. The design in this quilt is called Double Irish Chain in Christmas Colors. This design is made by repeating a shape over and over in a regular pattern. The shapes inside the lines of red and green squares are *symmetrical*. A shape is symmetrical when you can fold it in half (maybe just in your imagination) and the halves match perfectly. What about the entire quilt? Is its design symmetrical?

Double Irish Chain Quilt.

The design of this quilt makes your eyes travel from square to square, along all the straight lines. Your eyes also travel because of the artist's choice of colors. Red and green are *complementary* colors. When complementary colors are placed side by side, they appear more vivid.

Willow Oak Quilt.

Now let's look at another quilt. Its pattern is called Willow Oak. We don't know who made it. We do know that she cut many copies of the same shapes out of blue fabric and stitched them in a regular pattern onto a white piece of fabric. How many different shapes do you see?

To answer that question, you probably counted the blue shapes. But there are white shapes in this design, too. The blue shapes are the *figures*. The white shapes are the *ground*. An artist pays attention to both the figures and the ground in creating a design.

There's another element of design that adds beauty to these quilts, something you can't feel from a picture in a book. The quilt artist created a lovely texture. If you could run your hands over these quilts, you would feel the stitches. Even they form part of the design.

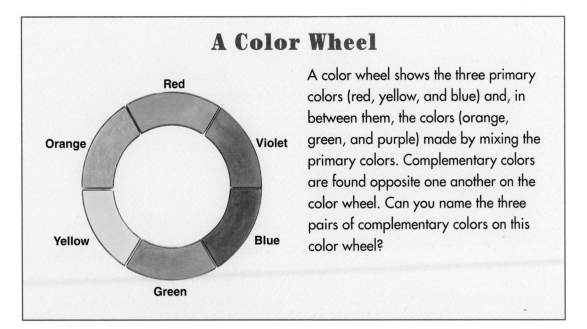

A Color Wheel

Red

Orange

Violet

Yellow

Blue

Green

A color wheel shows the three primary colors (red, yellow, and blue) and, in between them, the colors (orange, green, and purple) made by mixing the primary colors. Complementary colors are found opposite one another on the color wheel. Can you name the three pairs of complementary colors on this color wheel?

Drawing with Scissors

For years, the French artist Henri Matisse [on-REE ma-TEECE] painted bright, colorful pictures. He became too ill to stand at an easel. He started cutting out paper figures and gluing them onto a ground. Matisse said he was "drawing with scissors." He made *collages*, works of art made of pictures and papers pasted together in a design.

One of Matisse's collages is called *Icarus*, after a Greek myth. Icarus's father, Daedalus, made wings out of wax and feathers. They fastened the wings and began to soar, but Icarus—against his father's warnings—flew too close to the sun. The wax in his wings melted, and he fell into the sea.

Icarus.

Which part of this story do you think Matisse's collage tells? The arms and shoulders of the figure are curved like wings, but he does not seem to be flying. It looks as though gravity is pulling his body down. His right leg hangs a bit below the blue background. What do you think Matisse meant by this? Do you think the blue is the sky or the sea?

Did you notice the bright yellow shapes? They could be feathers or stars. Their sharp straight lines contrast with the curves of the figure. They seem to be moving right off the page. And what about that tiny red oval? In his design, Matisse chose to show Icarus's heart instead of his face. It's interesting to consider why.

Have you seen books created by Eric Carle or Ezra Jack Keats? Both of them create collages. Why don't you choose one of your favorite stories and make a collage to illustrate it?

A Very Formal Room

An African American artist named Horace Pippin painted *Victorian Interior*. He taught himself and never went to art school. His paintings, like the quilts, belong to a category of art called *folk art*. Folk art is the art of everyday life, created by people who did not study art in school. Pippin liked to say, "My heart tells my mind what to draw."

Victorian Interior.

This painting does not seem to have a lot of depth—it looks quite flat. Its design is not exactly symmetrical, but it does have balance. The shapes on one side are similar in size to the shapes on the other.

Pippin made many design decisions as he used lines and colors. What makes the rug look so lively and bright? Is it made of complementary colors? Are there more straight or curved lines in the room? How many circles and ovals? How many rectangles and squares? How many shapes are painted red? Notice how the delicate lines of the white lace doilies break up the heavy, solid furniture.

Picturing an Idea

In the American History section of this book, you can read about the Quakers, who came to America looking for religious freedom. They settled in Pennsylvania and hoped to live in peace. Let's look at a painting by a Quaker artist named Edward Hicks. In this

painting, he was trying to express a very important idea from the Bible. But before we talk about the idea, let's look carefully at the painting.

The Peaceable Kingdom.

Do you see anything unusual? All those animals together in one place! What about the little children with the animals? And who are the people in the background?

This painting is called *The Peaceable Kingdom*. The artist was probably remembering these lines from the Bible as he designed it: "The wolf shall dwell with the lamb, and the leopard shall lie down with the kid; and the calf and the young lion and the fatling [or young, fattened animal] together; and a little child shall lead them." These lines describe a perfect world of peace, which is what the Quakers hoped their new home in America would be. How does the painting express this idea of a peaceful world?

This painting is very three-dimensional. Hicks painted two scenes in one painting. The children and the animals are painted in the foreground. We can see each shape clearly because of the way Hicks placed dark shapes next to light ones.

The Native Americans and the Quakers are painted in the background, much smaller to show that they are far away. None of them are looking out from the painting. They just look at each other, busy with their meeting. What do you think they are saying to each other? What do you think the foreground scene has to do with the background scene? Are they both about living in peace? Edward Hicks thought living in peace was so important that he created more than fifty paintings to convey that idea.

Can You Feel It?

What is your first reaction when you look at this painting created by the Norwegian artist Edvard Munch [moonk]? Most people look first at the face of the figure in the foreground. Many people find the wavy lines and the colors in the background strange. Did you expect a red sky?

The artist called this painting *The Scream*. Munch explained that one day he was walking with some friends when suddenly all of nature seemed to cry out. He put his hands to his ears to close out the scream.

The Scream.

Munch belonged to a group of artists called the Expressionists. Expressionist artists tried to show their innermost feelings in their art. Munch had a lot of sadness in his life. Can you see it expressed in his work?

Look at the pale hands and skull-like head of the central figure. How would you describe his expression? Fear? Terror? Surprise? His body seems unable to bear the emotion. It seems wavy, as though it might collapse. Only the bridge seems straight and solid in the midst of all that is swirling around. We see these contrasts because of decisions the artist made in his design.

A Quilt That Tells a Story

Tar Beach.

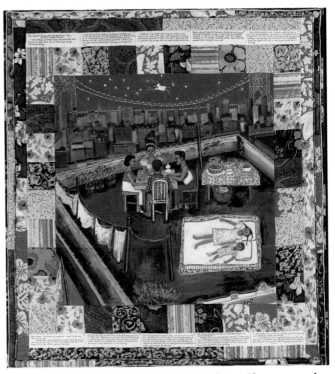

Faith Ringgold, an African American artist, makes quilts that tell stories. This one, called *Tar Beach*, was made in 1988. It tells the story of a girl named Cassie Lightfoot, who lay on the tar-covered rooftop of her building (her "tar beach") and imagined herself flying over the city. Do you see Cassie lying on the rooftop? Do you see Cassie flying? If you read "The People Could Fly," elsewhere in this book, then you know another story in which flying refers to the feeling of being free.

This quilt may seem more complicated than the others in this chapter, but Faith Ringgold used the same process of cutting pieces of cloth and stitching them together. She created a frame of fabric squares all around the quilt. There are other frames in the quilt's design as well. One is formed by the lines and colors that outline the rooftop. Another is formed by the colored fabric on which Cassie and her brother are lying. Ringgold also sewed in ten fabric blocks, five at the top and five at the bottom, with words that tell Cassie's story. These blocks are stitched in between bright print fabric squares and rectangles.

Faith Ringgold wrote and illustrated a picture book called *Tar Beach* (Crown Publishers, 1991), which tells the story of Cassie Lightfoot.

Over and Under with Wool and Thread

A Ganado rug.

Here is an image of a beautiful rug that was woven by hand by Navajo Indians. It is called a Ganado rug [ga-NAW-do], named for a place in Arizona. Ganado rugs have a red background and a dark border around a design of diamonds in black, white, and gray.

We don't know the name of the woman who wove this rug. She probably raised sheep. She sheared the sheep, washed the wool, combed it, then spun it into thread. She probably gathered plants to make dyes to color the threads she used for weaving.

A rug like this is woven on a loom. A loom is a large wooden frame that holds lots of threads strung up and down in the same direction. The weaver laces more threads in and out of the threads on the loom, pulling them tight to make a piece of cloth. The weaver makes sure that the threads stay tight by pressing them down with a wide-toothed comb. She thinks about the design that she is making and chooses the color of her next thread with that design in mind.

Just like a painting, this work of art has strong lines and colors that are important in its design. You can divide this rug in half two ways: down or across. The pattern is symmetrical either way. The weaver had to match the pattern from side to side and from top to bottom. She kept track of everything in her head—there were no written instructions for her to follow.

Part of a
Native American sandpainting.

Have you ever woven anything? Maybe you have made a paper place mat by weaving strips of colored paper. Maybe you have made a pot holder by weaving colored loops on a frame. Many pieces of cloth are made by weaving. If you look very hard at the clothes you are wearing, you might be able to see the threads that were woven together to make them.

A Navajo woman weaving on a loom.

A Painting Made Without Brushes or Paint

Have you ever played with sand on the beach, poking your finger in it to draw or letting handfuls of it dribble onto a flat surface? Can you imagine creating a beautiful work of art on the ground, using handfuls of sand? That is exactly how this painting was made. The artist took sand and let it flow between his thumb and forefinger to make a sandpainting. Every line and shape has been made with sand.

Are you surprised by the different colors? How many do you see? Sandpainting artists make colors by mixing ground-up stones with sand. Sometimes they add flower petals, charcoal, or flower pollen for color.

Some Navajo sandpaintings are as small as this book. Some are large, up to twenty feet across. What you see here is only part of a much larger sandpainting. Sandpaintings are more than just beautiful pictures to the Native Americans who make them. The paintings use symbols of nature and the gods. They often recall ancient stories. They are created as part of special ceremonies, and often they are created one day and destroyed the next.

See if you can find some of the special symbols in this sandpainting: cactus, feathers, rainbows. In the Navajo tradition, female holy people have square or rectangular heads, and male holy people have round heads. Which do you see?

IV.

Music

INTRODUCTION

In music as in art, third graders will benefit from learning by *doing*. Singing, playing rhythm and musical instruments, even counting to the beat or dancing to rhythm, sharpen a child's sense of how music works and what goes into its creation. In this chapter, we continue to teach musical notation, so that as children grow, they learn to read music for themselves, and become more sensitive to the choices made by composers.

This chapter introduces some vocabulary and concepts that you can use to talk about music with your child. You can also help your third grader learn about the lives of composers, the times in which they lived, and the stories that inspired their music. No talk or text, though, can substitute for a live performance. We encourage you to share good music with your children by attending concerts, tuning in to performances on radio or television, and playing good music at home.

Suggested Resources

The Core Music Collection, Third Grade. A six-CD set with works of music discussed here as well as other works. For more information, call the Core Knowledge Foundation at 888-876-2220.

Music for Little People. This company produces a good selection of recorded music for children, both contemporary and classical, along with books and videos on music and composers. Write P.O. Box 757, Greenland, NH 03840, or call 800-409-2457.

Amy L. Cohn, ed., *From Sea to Shining Sea: A Treasury of American Folklore and Folk Songs* (Scholastic, 1993). Music and lyrics for many American favorites, with read-aloud folktales and illustrations by award-winning artists.

Elements of Music

Have you ever whistled a tune, just making it up as you go? Or sat on the sidewalk and hummed just for fun? Maybe you found a phrase that was fun to say, then you said it over and over until it sounded like music. If you have, then you have been a composer. You have created music.

What if you liked your musical creation so well that you wanted to share it with your friends? You could sing it for them and teach them to sing along. But what if you wanted to share it with a friend who had moved to another city? Sure, you could call and sing it long-distance, or you could tape-record it and send the tape by mail. But you could also write the music down. That way your friend could read the music.

Just as you are learning how to write and read the words you say, musicians learn to write and read music. You can, too. It's like learning a code. Different symbols tell you when to sing high or low, whether to play your instrument loudly or softly, and what kind of beat the music has. Let's learn some of those symbols.

Reading and Writing Musical Notes

Each sound in a piece of music is represented by a musical *note*. Notes are written on a *staff*, which looks like five lines running across the page. Here are the notes, on a staff, of a song you probably know.

A note sits high or low on the staff, depending on its *pitch*. When you sing, you make some sounds that are low and some that are high, don't you? When you talk about how low or how high you can sing, you are talking about the pitch of the notes you are singing.

Musical notes take their names from the first seven letters of the alphabet: A B C D E F G. When you get to G, you start all over again with A.

Try this. Instead of speaking those seven letters of the alphabet, sing them. Start low with A and go a little higher with each letter you sing. After you sing G, go a little higher and start with A again. That's the way letters name the notes in music.

Going backward is not so easy. Can you say the alphabet backward from G to A? Starting up high with G, go a little lower with each note. It's not much of a melody, but it's a start.

Now it's time to match the lines with the letters. On a musical staff, each note sits either on a line or on a space between lines, starting low and moving up.

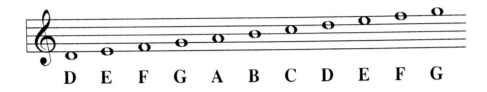

D   E   F   G   A   B   C   D   E   F   G

Here's one way to remember where the notes come on the staff. See the fancy swirling symbol on the left side of each staff? That is called a *treble clef*. It's a fun shape to draw. Try it.

When you draw a treble clef on the five lines of the staff, it always curls around the second line. The note that sits on that line is always G. In fact, sometimes the treble clef is called the G clef. If you remember that G is on the line where the clef swirls, you can figure out all the other notes around it.

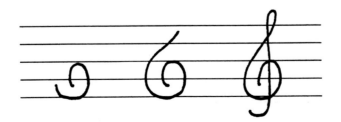

What happens if the song you are composing has a note lower than E? It's simple. The next note down, D, sits just below the lowest line. The next note down, C, gets drawn with a short line through it.

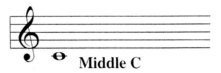

Middle C

This note looks different from all the others. We call it middle C. To find this note on the piano, you play the key that's right in the middle of the keyboard.

Reading and Writing Rhythm

Sometimes you sing a song slowly. Sometimes you sing it fast. The same song sounds different, depending upon the rhythm you give it. Rhythm is the way you keep time as you make music. To write down rhythm, musicians use another set of symbols.

Remember that piece of music you saw at the beginning of this chapter? Let's look at it again. See all those circles with tails? Each of them represents a note. Some circles are filled in and others are empty. That is one way musicians represent the rhythm of the notes.

The notes with empty circles and tails are called *half notes*. They last longer than the notes with filled-in circles and tails, which are called *quarter notes*.

Every piece of music has a *beat*. You have to listen carefully to find it. Pick a song that you know how to sing and see if you can clap to the beat. The beat stays steady, like a ticking clock.

When you march around the room, one-two, one-two, you are following a steady beat. If you start to skip or run, you aren't following that beat anymore. No matter if it moves fast or slow, most music has a steady beat.

Let's try an example. Let's sing the first line of "Yankee Doodle," clapping out a steady beat. Clap for every beat, even if you don't sing for each time you clap.

Yan -	kee	Doo -	dle	went	to	town,		
clap	*clap*	*clap*	*clap*	*clap*	*clap*	*clap*		
A -	rid -	ing	on	his	po-		ny	
clap	*clap*	*clap*	*clap*	*clap*	*clap*	*clap*	*clap*	*clap*

Did you notice any time that you clapped without singing a new sound? It happened when you sang the two syllables of the word "pony," didn't it?

If we want to use musical notes to write the rhythm of this part of "Yankee Doodle," it would look like this:

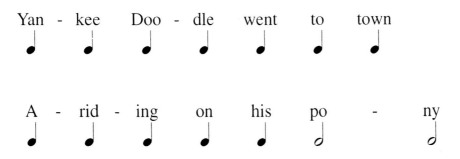

Let's put those notes on the treble clef where they belong.

Now you can sing the song and point to the notes as you sing them.

Maybe you want your music to go faster. Then it's time to learn about another note, called the *eighth note*. It looks something like a quarter note with a wing on the tail. Sometimes eighth notes get joined together when they're written. Each eighth note lasts half the time of a quarter note.

Or maybe you want to hold a note even longer. Then you would write a *whole note*, which looks like an empty circle with no tail at all. A whole note lasts the same length of time as four quarter notes.

Keeping Time

What if we were going to put all the notes for all the verses of "Yankee Doodle" onto the treble clef? That would be a lot of notes, all in a row. To make it easier to read so many notes, musicians divide the music into *measures*. They show each measure by drawing a line down through the staff. The line is called a *bar line*. They draw two thick lines, or a double bar line, to end a piece of music.

Let's use bar lines to divide the first part of "Yankee Doodle" into measures.

Every measure in a piece of music has the same number of beats. In "Yankee Doodle," every quarter note gets one beat. So how many beats per measure are in "Yankee Doodle"? How do you find that out? Try clapping again as you sing. This time, notice how many times you clap between the bar lines. What's your answer? Four? That means there are four beats per measure in "Yankee Doodle."

There's another way to find the answer to that question. Musicians write down numbers called the *time signature* to tell about the rhythm of a piece of music.

The time signature is always made of two numbers. The top number tells how many beats are in each measure. The bottom number tells what kind of note equals one beat as you count the rhythm. Since "Yankee Doodle" has four beats per measure, and each of those beats equals a quarter note, the time signature for "Yankee Doodle" is $\frac{4}{4}$. You read it "four-four," but you know it means "four beats per measure, and one beat equals a quarter note." Look at the very first piece of music you saw in this chapter, on page 184. See the time signature?

$\frac{4}{4}$ is just one time signature. There are many more. What would the time signature be if you saw $\frac{3}{4}$ written on the staff? Three beats to the measure, and one beat equals a quarter note. Can you count out that rhythm? One-two-three, one-two-three. It feels like a swing. Sway up and back as you count: up-two-three, back-two-three, up-two-three, back-two-three.

Many songs have a $\frac{3}{4}$ rhythm. Remember "My Bonnie Lies Over the Ocean"? Clap along and see if you feel the rhythm divide into three. "My BON-nie lies O-ver the O-cean, My BON-nie lies O-ver the SEA."

Rests

Music is made of silences as well as sounds. Musicians use symbols called *rests* to show when and for how long the singer or instrumentalist should be silent—and rest!

Look at this musical notation and see how many things it tells you. The treble clef tells the pitch of every note on the staff's lines and spaces. The time signature says that each measure has three beats and that a quarter note equals one beat. The quarter and half notes tell you how long to hold the sounds. The bar lines divide the music in equal measures.

What's that squiggly sign at the end? That's a rest. It's a quarter rest, which lasts the same amount of time as a quarter note. It tells the musician to keep quiet and rest during that beat.

Rests have different rhythms, too, just as notes do. Here's a chart of the most common notes and rests, paired to show you which ones last the same number of beats.

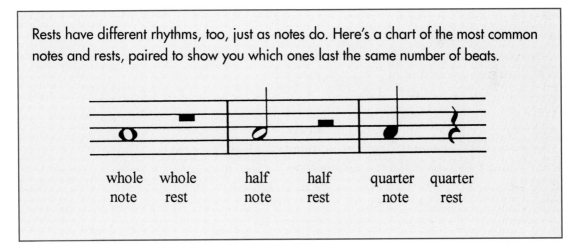

| whole note | whole rest | half note | half rest | quarter note | quarter rest |

Loud and Soft

You could sing "Yankee Doodle" in a whisper or at the top of your lungs. Musicians have special ways to write down how loud the music should sound. They use words borrowed from Italian, the language spoken in the country of Italy. When the music should be quiet, musicians say it should be "piano" [PYAH-no]. When the music should be loud, they say it should be "forte" [FOR-tay].

In Italian, you can add "-issimo" [EES-see-mo] to a word to emphasize its meaning. In music, "pianissimo" [pyah-NEES-see-mo] means "very soft," and "fortissimo" [for-TEES-see-mo] means "very loud." Sometimes a composer might write the whole word in the music, but abbreviations do just as well.

p = piano (quiet)   **f** = forte (loud)
pp = pianissimo (very quiet)   **ff** = fortissimo (very loud)

Now you have learned everything you need in order to read the piece of music with which this chapter began, on page 184. Have you guessed what it is? It's the first two bars of "Yankee Doodle"! You have learned about notes and their pitch and rhythm, about the treble clef, time signatures, rests, and measures. Turn back to that page and point to the notes as you sing along. Congratulations! Now you're reading music.

Let's Join the Orchestra

Let's pretend you're going to join an orchestra. Look at all the instruments you could play: *strings, brass, woodwinds,* or *percussion.*

Triangle

Bass Drum   Kettle Drum   Snare Drum   Xylophone

Percussion Family

Percussion and Strings

Maybe you want to bang on a drum and help keep the beat. Then join the *percussion* section of the orchestra! You might get to shake a tambourine or ring the bells or tap on the cymbals, because all those noisemaking instruments are in the percussion family.

Maybe you would rather make the beautiful singing sound of a *stringed instrument,* like the violin, the viola, the cello, or the big bass viol. Usually, musicians use bows to play stringed instruments, but sometimes they pluck the strings. What stringed instrument is played that way? Did you think of a guitar? A banjo?

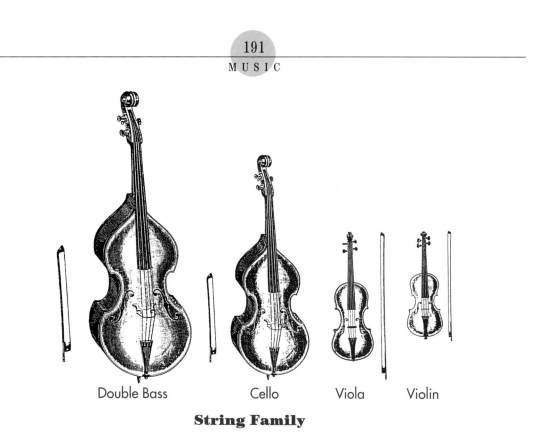

String Family

The Brass Family

Maybe you would rather toot on a horn. Then you will join the *brass* section of the orchestra. You have quite a few brass instruments to choose from: trumpet, trombone, French horn, and tuba.

Why do you think these are all called "brass" instruments? It's because they are all differently shaped tubes made of the metal brass. Each one is played by blowing into a cup-

Brass Family

shaped mouthpiece at one end. The shape and design of the tube takes that burst of air from the horn player's mouth and turns it into sound. Some horns have keys that the musician can press, opening and closing valves to change the sound. Another horn has a tube that slides in and out to change the sound. Do you know which one that is? The trombone.

Here is Louis Armstrong, a famous jazz musician. Which brass instrument is he playing?

Long ago, horns weren't made with valves or fancy shapes. They were just long metal tubes with a mouthpiece at one end and a big opening at the other. The sound that each horn made depended on the length of the horn, so it took many horns to play a whole melody.

The French horn is shaped like a circle. When the player blows into the mouthpiece, the air goes around and around. French horn players change the shape of their mouths as they play in order to change the sound they are making. The Austrian composer Wolfgang Amadeus Mozart [VULF-gahng ah-mah-DAY-us MOAT-zart] wrote four different

Famous for Its Trumpets

The story of William Tell is told in the Literature section of this book. The Italian composer Gioacchino Rossini [jwa-KEE-no ro-SEE-nee] liked the story so well he wrote an opera about it. An opera is like a play in which the actors sing rather than speak. Usually, an opera opens with an *overture*, played by the orchestra. The overture of Rossini's opera *William Tell* is a well-known piece of music. If you listen to a recording of it, you may find that you already know the tune. You will also hear how Rossini planned the music to include first one solo trumpet, then more, and more!

pieces in which the star instrument is the French horn. If you can listen to Mozart's Horn Concertos, you will hear the sound of a French horn playing alone. Once you recognize its sound, see if you can hear it even when it's playing with the other instruments of the orchestra.

The tuba is the largest horn in the brass family. It's big and heavy, and the sounds it makes are big and low, deep and round. Once in a great while the tuba plays the melody, but most of the time it keeps the rhythm in the background with an *oom-pa, oom-pa*.

The Woodwind Family

Do you like to whistle? Maybe you would like to join the *woodwind* section of our orchestra. You could play the flute or the piccolo, the clarinet or the oboe, the English horn or the bassoon. They are all woodwinds.

Have you ever blown across the top of an empty glass bottle? Try it. You position your lips on the rim of the bottle, just so, and the wind from your mouth makes a breathy, hollow sound.

Now fill that same bottle one-third full with water. Blow across it again. What happens? Your empty bottle instrument changes pitch.

Musicians who play the flute hold their mouths the same way you did. They blow over a hole on the top of their instruments. Just as your breath vibrated through the bottle and made a pleasant sound, theirs does, too. Flute players also press keys with their fingers to change pitch as they are playing. A piccolo works the same way, but it is smaller than a flute. (In fact, the word "piccolo" means "little" in Italian.) A piccolo's sound is higher in pitch than a flute's.

The other woodwinds are played differently from the flute and the piccolo. They are also called reed instruments, because the mouthpieces of these instruments use "reeds." A reed is a flat, flexible piece of wood (or other material) that vibrates when you blow on it.

To understand better how a reed works, you can make your own outdoors. Maybe you have done this before. Put a long, wide blade of grass flat between your thumbs and blow

A Dreamy Flute Song

Do you know what a faun is? It's a creature that comes from ancient Greek mythology, half-man and half-goat. The French composer Claude Debussy [clode deb-yoo-SEE] wrote a piece of music called *Prelude to the Afternoon of a Faun*. Maybe he was trying to write music that would carry us back to ancient times, when myths seemed real. Debussy made the flute an important instrument in his piece. He knew that even the ancient Greeks played music on simple flutes.

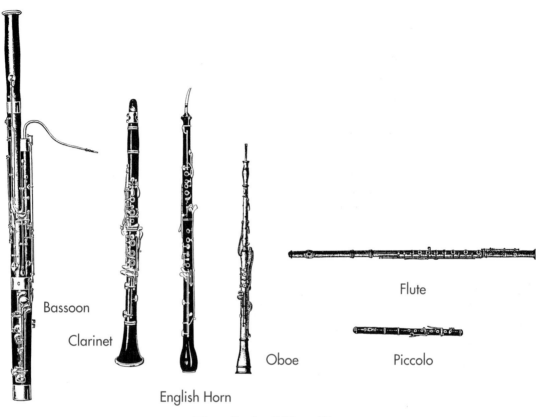

Bassoon

Clarinet

English Horn

Oboe

Flute

Piccolo

Woodwind Family

on it. If you do it just right, you'll get a buzz or a squawk. The sound comes when your breath makes the blade of grass vibrate. A reed in an instrument works like that blade of grass. The breath of the musician makes it vibrate, and that makes music.

Each of these woodwinds has a sound all its own. The oboe can sound sad. The bassoon can sound clownish. The clarinet is the best known of the woodwinds. Clarinetists play in orchestras, bands, and jazz groups. Sometimes people call the clarinet a "licorice stick." Look at the picture—can you guess why?

You can get to know the sound of the clarinet by listening to *Rhapsody in Blue* by the American composer George Gershwin. The piece starts with a solo performance, one clarinet playing a swinging, swooping melody.

All Together Now

Now you have four families of instruments to choose from: the strings, the percussion, the brass, and the woodwinds. Which will you play? Or would you rather stand in the middle and conduct the orchestra?

Composers and Their Music

One way to learn about music is to learn about different great composers like Mozart, Vivaldi, Bach, and Beethoven. Knowing something about the lives of composers can help you hear new things in their music.

Musical Connections

Do you remember, earlier in this book, the two stories from *A Thousand and One Nights* (pp. 21–28)? They were said to have been told by Scheherazade, the beautiful queen of Persia, who made up stories, night after night, to save her life.

A Russian composer named Nikolai Rimsky-Korsakov [NEE-ko-lie RIM-skee-KOR-sa-koff] was so enchanted by these stories that he wrote a *suite* (or a collection) of pieces of music called *Scheherazade*.

Rimsky-Korsakov's *Scheherazade* suite has four *movements*, which is a word used to name the parts within a larger piece of music. In each movement, we hear the voice of the storyteller as a melody played by a solo violin. Whenever we hear that theme, we think of Scheherazade spinning one of her fantastic tales.

As a young man, Rimsky-Korsakov served in the Russian navy and went to sea. He probably used those memories to compose the first movement of his suite, called "The Sea and Sinbad's Ship." At the very beginning, we hear a forceful theme that suggests the sultan demanding another tale. The solo violin answers, as if the clever queen has begun to tell her tale. Next we hear a rocking and swelling rhythm, played by the strings. You can practically feel the waves! The music goes on and on, just like the sea, as Sinbad's ship sails over it.

Tchaikovsky: Music That Brings Strong Feeling

Peter Ilyich Tchaikovsky [IHL-yich chy-KOFF-skee] was born in Russia in 1840. Even in his childhood, he had deep, tender feelings. After an evening of listening to a musical performance, he had trouble going to sleep. "This music! This music!" he told his parents. "It's here in my head and won't let me sleep!" Many things made him cry.

One day Tchaikovsky's music teacher gave him a short piece of music. "Write variations on this piece," his teacher said. He expected Tchaikovsky to write ten or twelve

Down in the Valley
(American folk song)

Down in the valley, valley so low,
Hang your head over, hear the wind blow.
Hear the wind blow, love, hear the wind blow,
Hang your head over, hear the wind blow.

Roses love sunshine, violets love dew,
Angels in heaven know I love you.
Know I love you, dear, know I love you.
Angels in heaven know I love you.

Write me a letter, send it by mail,
Send it in care of Birmingham jail.
Birmingham jail, love, Birmingham jail.
Send it in care of Birmingham jail.

Polly Wolly Doodle
(American folk song)

Oh, I went down South for to see my Sal,
Sing polly wolly doodle all the day.
My Sal she is a spunky gal,
Sing polly wolly doodle all the day.

Chorus:
Fare thee well, fare thee well, fare thee well my fairy fay,
For I'm going to Louisiana for to see my Susianna,
Singing polly wolly doodle all the day.

Simple Gifts
(Shaker song)

'Tis a gift to be simple, 'tis a gift to be free,
'Tis a gift to come down to where we ought to be,
And when we find ourselves in the place just right,
'Twill be in the valley of love and delight.
When true simplicity is gained,
To bow and to bend we won't be ashamed.
To turn, turn will be our delight
'Til by turning, turning we come 'round right.

This Little Light
(African American spiritual)

This little light of mine, I'm gonna let it shine.
This little light of mine, I'm gonna let it shine.
This little light of mine, I'm gonna let it shine,
Let it shine, let it shine, let it shine!

He's Got the Whole World in His Hands
(African American spiritual)

He's got the whole world in His hands,
He's got the whole world in His hands,
He's got the whole world in His hands,
He's got the whole world in His hands.

He's got you and me, brother, in His hands,
He's got you and me, sister, in His hands,
He's got you and me, brother, in His hands,
He's got the whole world in His hands.

My Bonnie
(Scottish folk song)

My bonnie lies over the ocean.
My bonnie lies over the sea.
My bonnie lies over the ocean.
Oh, bring back my bonnie to me.

Bring back, bring back,
Oh, bring back my bonnie to me, to me.
Bring back, bring back,
Oh, bring back my bonnie to me.

The Sidewalks of New York
(by Charles B. Lawlor and James W. Blake, 1894)

East side, west side, all around the town.
The tots play "ring a rosie," "London Bridge is falling down."
Boys and girls together,
Me and Mamie Rorke.
We trip the light fantastic
On the sidewalks of New York.

The Man on the Flying Trapeze
(words by George Leybourne,
music by Alfred Lee, 1868)

He flies through the air with the
    greatest of ease,
The daring young man on the flying
    trapeze.
His movements are graceful, all girls
    he does please,
and my love he has purloined away.

In the Good Old Summertime
(by George Evans, 1902)

In the good old summertime,
In the good old summertime,
Strolling through the shady lanes,
With your baby mine.
You hold her hand and she holds yours,
And that's a very good sign
That she's your tootsy-wootsy in
The good old summertime.

A Bicycle Built for Two

(by Harry Dacre, 1892)

Daisy, Daisy, give me your answer, do,
I'm half-crazy all for the love of you.
It won't be a stylish marriage,
I can't afford a carriage.
But you'll look sweet
On the seat
Of a bicycle built for two.

You're a Grand Old Flag
(by George M. Cohan, 1906)

You're a grand old flag, you're a high-flying
   flag,
And forever in peace may you wave.
You're the emblem of the land I love,
The home of the free and the brave.
Every heart beats true under red, white and
   blue
Where there's never a boast or brag,
Should auld acquaintance be forgot,
Keep your eye on the grand old flag.

America
(old English tune; words by Samuel Francis Smith)

My country, 'tis of thee,
Sweet land of liberty,
Of thee I sing.
Land where my fathers died,
Land of the pilgrims' pride,
From every mountainside,
Let freedom ring.

V.

Mathematics

MY CALENDAR
OCTOBER

SUN	MON	TUE	WED	THU	FRI	SAT
2	3	4	5	6	7	8
	10	11	12	13	14	15
16	17	18	19	20	21	22
23	24	25	26	27	28	29
30	31					

INTRODUCTION

Success in learning math comes through practice, practice, practice: steady practice, thoughtful practice, and practice with a variety of problems. Encourage your child to approach problems from different angles. Psychologists who have studied how math is learned explain that ability gained through practice is *not* different from mathematical understanding. Indeed, practice is the prerequisite for more advanced problem solving.

Some well-meaning people fear that practice in mathematics—memorizing arithmetic facts or doing timed work sheets, for example—constitutes joyless, soul-killing drudgery for children. Nothing could be further from the truth. It is not practice but anxiety that kills the joy in mathematics. One effective way to practice with your child is to have him or her talk out loud while doing problems, explaining computational steps along the way. Your child's mental process becomes visible to you, and you can correct misunderstandings as they happen.

The best math programs incorporate the principle of incremental review: once a concept or skill is introduced, it is practiced again and again through exercises of gradually increasing difficulty. One result of this approach is that a child's arithmetic skills become automatic. Only when children achieve automatic command of basic facts—when they can tell you instantly what 9 plus 8 equals, for example—are their minds prepared to tackle more challenging problems. Math learning programs that offer both incremental review and varied opportunities for problem solving get the best results.

This chapter presents a brief outline of the math skills and concepts that should be part of a good third-grade education. We emphasize, however, that this outline *does not constitute a complete math program*, since it does not include as many practice problems as a child ought to do while learning this material. To learn math thoroughly at the third-grade level, children need to be shown these concepts and then encouraged to practice, practice, practice.

Suggested Resources

Jean Kerr Stenmark, Virginia Thompson, and Ruth Cossey, *Family Math* (University of California, Berkeley). This book offers plenty of activities for parents to do with children up to age twelve, to supplement (but not replace) math instruction. To order, call 510-642-1910.

Saxon Publishers produces a series of rigorous math workbooks that can be used to complement your child's math work in this book. *Math 3* offers practice problems in most of the areas covered in this chapter. Write, phone, or visit their website for further description of the books and some sample chapters: Saxon Publishers, Inc., 2450 John Saxon Blvd., Norman, OK 73071; 800-284-7019; www.saxonpub.com.

Multiplication—Part One

Multiplication Words

In the equation $2 \times 5 = 10$, 2 and 5 are *factors*, and 10 is the *product*. You can multiply factors in any order without changing the product.

$$2 \times 5 = 10 \qquad 5 \times 2 = 10$$

Multiplying Vertically

$4 \times 5 = 20$ can also be written

$$\begin{array}{r} 5 \\ \times\, 4 \\ \hline 20 \end{array}$$

You read both as "four times five equals twenty." Notice that when you read a vertical multiplication problem, you begin with the number next to the multiplication sign and read up.

Showing Multiplication

You can make a "picture" of a multiplication problem using graph paper. For example, you can show 3×5 by a rectangle with 3 rows and 5 columns.

If you count the squares by the rows, you have

$$5 + 5 + 5, \text{ which is } 3 \times 5$$

If you count the squares by the columns, you have

$$3 + 3 + 3 + 3 + 3, \text{ which is } 5 \times 3$$

Either way, there are 15 squares in all.
You can also show 3×5 by a rectangle with 5 rows and 3 columns.

Now have some fun making at least three other multiplication facts into graph-paper pictures like 3×5. Try 3×4 or 4×5. What about 5×5?

Multiplication is a quick way of doing repeated addition. It's good to practice writing multiplication as repeated addition, and repeated addition as multiplication. For example, 4×5 can also be written $5 + 5 + 5 + 5$. And $3 + 3 + 3 + 3 + 3 + 3$ can also be written 6×3.

The Multiplication Table

As a second grader, you learned the multiplication tables up to 5. Here are the rest of the multiplication tables.

6 as a factor	7 as a factor	8 as a factor	9 as a factor
$0 \times 6 = 0$	$0 \times 7 = 0$	$0 \times 8 = 0$	$0 \times 9 = 0$
$1 \times 6 = 6$	$1 \times 7 = 7$	$1 \times 8 = 8$	$1 \times 9 = 9$
$2 \times 6 = 12$	$2 \times 7 = 14$	$2 \times 8 = 16$	$2 \times 9 = 18$
$3 \times 6 = 18$	$3 \times 7 = 21$	$3 \times 8 = 24$	$3 \times 9 = 27$
$4 \times 6 = 24$	$4 \times 7 = 28$	$4 \times 8 = 32$	$4 \times 9 = 36$
$5 \times 6 = 30$	$5 \times 7 = 35$	$5 \times 8 = 40$	$5 \times 9 = 45$
$6 \times 6 = 36$	$6 \times 7 = 42$	$6 \times 8 = 48$	$6 \times 9 = 54$
$7 \times 6 = 42$	$7 \times 7 = 49$	$7 \times 8 = 56$	$7 \times 9 = 63$
$8 \times 6 = 48$	$8 \times 7 = 56$	$8 \times 8 = 64$	$8 \times 9 = 72$
$9 \times 6 = 54$	$9 \times 7 = 63$	$9 \times 8 = 72$	$9 \times 9 = 81$

Only the sixteen multiplication facts that are red are actually new. The others you already know. For example, if you know $9 \times 5 = 45$, then you know $5 \times 9 = 45$. Learn these facts so that you can say them easily. Also be able to give any product quickly, without making any mistakes.

Remember that you can skip-count to get to the next fact in a table.

$8 \times 6 = 48$, so 9×6 is 6 more, or 54.

$7 \times 7 = 49$, so 8×7 is 7 more, or 56.

When you know all the multiplication facts well, practice filling in a table with all of them.

MATHEMATICS

x	0	1	2	3	4	5	6	7	8	9
0										
1										
2										
3						15				
4										
5								35		
6								42		
7										
8										
9										

Square Numbers and Square Roots

How many squares are there in each of these grids?

To find out, you can add the number of squares in each row.

$3 + 3 + 3 = 9$ $4 + 4 + 4 + 4 = 16$ $5 + 5 + 5 + 5 + 5 = 25$

Or you can multiply the number of rows by the number of columns.

$3 \times 3 = 9$ $4 \times 4 = 16$ $5 \times 5 = 25$

The numbers 9, 16, and 25 are called *square numbers*. A square number is the product of any number multiplied by itself. The number 3 is called a *square root* of 9, because 3 multiplied by itself equals 9. The number 4 is called a square root of 16, because 4 multiplied by itself equals 16.

You can do square root problems in the other direction, too. What is a square root of 25? In other words, what number multiplied by itself equals 25? (The answer can be found in the grids on the previous page.)

The sign for square root looks like this: $\sqrt{}$. For example, $\sqrt{9} = 3$ and $\sqrt{16} = 4$.

Find the square numbers:

1. $7 \times 7 =$ _____

2. $9 \times 9 =$ _____

3. $10 \times 10 =$ _____

Find the square roots:

1. $\sqrt{64} =$ _____

2. $\sqrt{36} =$ _____

3. $\sqrt{100} =$ _____

Extra and interesting: If you fill in the square numbers on the practice table on page 215, what sort of line will the square numbers make on the table?

Parentheses, Multiplying Three Numbers

The symbols ( ) are parentheses. In math, you do what is inside parentheses *first*.

You add (2 + 3) + 5 like this:

(2 + 3) + 5 =

5   + 5 = 10

You add 2 + (3 + 5) like this:

2 + (3 + 5) =

2 +   8   = 10

Notice that whether you put 2 + 3 in the parentheses or 3 + 5 in the parentheses, the sum is the same. No matter how you group the numbers you are adding, the sum stays the same.

You can also multiply three or more numbers using parentheses.

Multiply (3 × 2) × 4 like this:

(3 × 2) × 4 =

6   × 4 = 24

Multiply 3 × (2 × 4) like this:

3 × (2 × 4) =

3 ×   8   = 24

Notice that the product is the same both times. No matter how you group factors, the product is the same.

Division—Part One

Operations

Addition, subtraction, and multiplication are called *operations*. They are three of the four operations of arithmetic. The fourth operation is *division*.

You already know that subtraction is the inverse of addition. We also say that addition and subtraction are inverse operations. The inverse operation of multiplication is division. Let's see how division works.

An Example of Division

Peter has 18 stamps. He wants to divide them into groups of 3. How many groups will he have?

$$18 \div 3 = 6$$

This is a division problem, because you need to divide the 18 stamps into groups of 3 to solve it. How many groups of 3 are there in 18? There are 6 threes in 18. So Peter will have 6 groups of stamps. We write this division problem: $18 \div 3 = 6$. We read it: "Eighteen divided by three equals six." The sign $\div$ means "divided by" and shows that you are dividing.

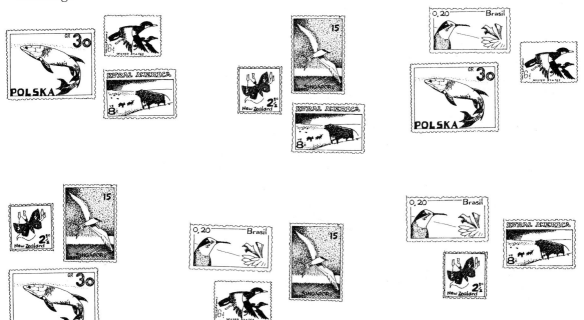

Solving Division Problems

Division and multiplication are *inverse operations*. Sometimes the easiest way to solve a division problem is to think of a multiplication problem. Here is an example. What is $30 \div 6$? You want to know how many 6's there are in 30. **Think:** What times 6 equals 30? $5 \times 6 = 30$. So $30 \div 6 = $ **5.** In the picture below, the 30 spools of thread are divided into 5 groups, with 6 spools in each group.

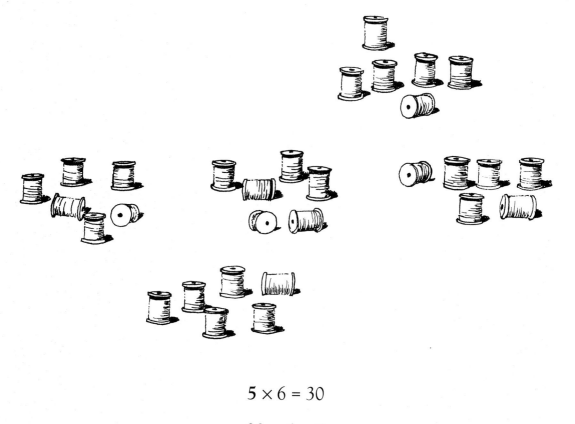

$$5 \times 6 = 30$$

$$30 \div 6 = \mathbf{5}$$

Here is another example. What is $54 \div 9$? You want to know how many nines there are in 54. **Think:** What times 9 equals 54? $6 \times 9 = 54$. So $54 \div 9 = $ **6.**

Division Words

The answer to a division problem is called the *quotient*. The number you are dividing is called the *dividend*. The number you are dividing by is called the *divisor*.

Learn to use these words to describe the numbers in a division problem. For example, in 12 ÷ 4 = 3, 12 is the dividend, 4 is the divisor, and 3 is the quotient.

There are two ways to write division. You can write it like this:

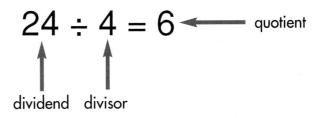

or like this:

$$6 \longleftarrow \text{quotient}$$
$$\text{divisor} \longrightarrow 4 \overline{)\ 24} \longleftarrow \text{dividend}$$

Notice that the answer, the 6, goes over the ones' place. Learn to write division in both ways. For example:

$$8 \div 2 = 4 \quad \text{is the same as} \quad 2\overline{)8}^{\,4}$$

$$8\overline{)\ 56}^{\,7} \quad \text{is the same as} \quad 56 \div 8 = 7$$

Division Facts

Learn the basic division facts. These facts will help you solve any division problem. You can use the multiplication facts you already know to find the quotient of each division fact. We'll talk more about this later. Here are the division facts with 2, 3, 4, and 5 as divisors.

2 as a divisor	3 as a divisor	4 as a divisor	5 as a divisor
0 ÷ 2 = 0	0 ÷ 3 = 0	0 ÷ 4 = 0	0 ÷ 5 = 0
2 ÷ 2 = 1	3 ÷ 3 = 1	4 ÷ 4 = 1	5 ÷ 5 = 1
4 ÷ 2 = 2	6 ÷ 3 = 2	8 ÷ 4 = 2	10 ÷ 5 = 2
6 ÷ 2 = 3	9 ÷ 3 = 3	12 ÷ 4 = 3	15 ÷ 5 = 3
8 ÷ 2 = 4	12 ÷ 3 = 4	16 ÷ 4 = 4	20 ÷ 5 = 4
10 ÷ 2 = 5	15 ÷ 3 = 5	20 ÷ 4 = 5	25 ÷ 5 = 5
12 ÷ 2 = 6	18 ÷ 3 = 6	24 ÷ 4 = 6	30 ÷ 5 = 6
14 ÷ 2 = 7	21 ÷ 3 = 7	28 ÷ 4 = 7	35 ÷ 5 = 7
16 ÷ 2 = 8	24 ÷ 3 = 8	32 ÷ 4 = 8	40 ÷ 5 = 8
18 ÷ 2 = 9	27 ÷ 3 = 9	36 ÷ 4 = 9	45 ÷ 5 = 9

Learn to find the quotient of each division fact quickly, without making any mistakes. Here are the division facts with 6, 7, 8, and 9 as divisors.

6 as a divisor	7 as a divisor	8 as a divisor	9 as a divisor
0 ÷ 6 = 0	0 ÷ 7 = 0	0 ÷ 8 = 0	0 ÷ 9 = 0
6 ÷ 6 = 1	7 ÷ 7 = 1	8 ÷ 8 = 1	9 ÷ 9 = 1
12 ÷ 6 = 2	14 ÷ 7 = 2	16 ÷ 8 = 2	18 ÷ 9 = 2
18 ÷ 6 = 3	21 ÷ 7 = 3	24 ÷ 8 = 3	27 ÷ 9 = 3
24 ÷ 6 = 4	28 ÷ 7 = 4	32 ÷ 8 = 4	36 ÷ 9 = 4
30 ÷ 6 = 5	35 ÷ 7 = 5	40 ÷ 8 = 5	45 ÷ 9 = 5
36 ÷ 6 = 6	42 ÷ 7 = 6	48 ÷ 8 = 6	54 ÷ 9 = 6
42 ÷ 6 = 7	49 ÷ 7 = 7	56 ÷ 8 = 7	63 ÷ 9 = 7
48 ÷ 6 = 8	56 ÷ 7 = 8	64 ÷ 8 = 8	72 ÷ 9 = 8
54 ÷ 6 = 9	63 ÷ 7 = 9	72 ÷ 8 = 9	81 ÷ 9 = 9

Division Rules for 0 and 1

Here are some rules for dividing with 0 and 1.

Rules for 0

1. 0 divided by any number (except 0) equals 0.

$$0 \div 8 = 0 \qquad 0 \div 5 = 0$$

2. You cannot divide by 0.

$$5 \div 0 \text{ is an impossible problem.}$$

Rules for 1

1. Any number (except 0) divided by itself equals 1.

$$8 \div 8 = 1 \qquad 6 \div 6 = 1$$

2. Any number divided by 1 equals that number.

$$5 \div 1 = 5 \qquad 7 \div 1 = 7$$

These rules can help you learn the division facts. For example, the last rule makes it easy to learn all the division facts that have 1 as a divisor: $0 \div 1 = 0$; $1 \div 1 = 1$; $2 \div 1 = 2$; $3 \div 1 = 3$; $4 \div 1 = 4$; $5 \div 1 = 5$; and so on.

Division Word Problems

Here are two kinds of division problems. Learn to solve both kinds.

1. Margaret has 35 green peppers. She wants to put 5 into each basket. How many baskets does she need?

You want to know how many groups of 5 there are in 35. You write $35 \div 5 = 7$. She needs 7 baskets. (What other way can you write $35 \div 5$?)

2. Mrs. Fletcher has 27 roses. She wants to divide them equally into 3 vases. How many roses should she put into each vase?

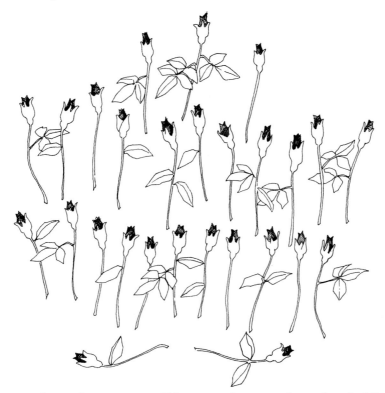

You want to know how many will be in each group if you divide 27 into 3 groups. You write 27 ÷ 3 = 9. She should put 9 roses into each vase.

Sometimes you want to know how many groups. Sometimes you want to know how many are in each group. You solve both kinds of problems in the same way.

Picturing Multiplication and Division Facts

As you've just read, multiplication and division are inverse operations. For example, the inverse of multiplying by 9 is dividing by 9. The inverse of $7 \times 9 = 63$ is $63 \div 9 = 7$. Here is a picture of how this works.

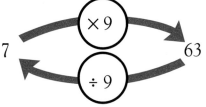

Here is another example. The inverse of $48 \div 6 = 8$ is $8 \times 6 = 48$.

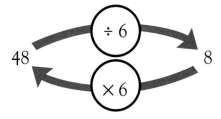

Learn to draw pictures like these to show inverse multiplication and division facts. When you can do this, you can find inverse multiplication and division facts.

Picturing Multiplication and Division Facts with Blank Spaces

Learn to fill in the blanks in pictures like these:

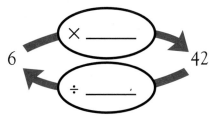

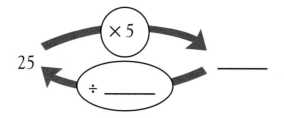

You should also be able to do the same thing with equations that have blank spaces.

$$\text{\_\_\_\_\_} \times 5 = 40$$

Think: What times 5 equals 40? 8. So $8 \times 5 = 40$.

Try these:

1. _____ $\times 8 = 56$ 3. $63 \div$ _____ $= 9$ 5. $3 \times$ _____ $= 24$

2. _____ $\div 8 = 9$ 4. $4 \times$ _____ $= 28$ 6. $12 \div$ _____ $= 2$

Division and Fractions

When something is divided into 3 equal parts, each part is one-third, written as a fraction: $\frac{1}{3}$.

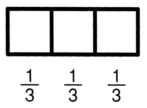

If you want to find $\frac{1}{3}$ of 24, you divide it into 3 equal parts. To divide 24 into 3 equal parts, you divide by 3.

$$24 \div 3 = 8$$

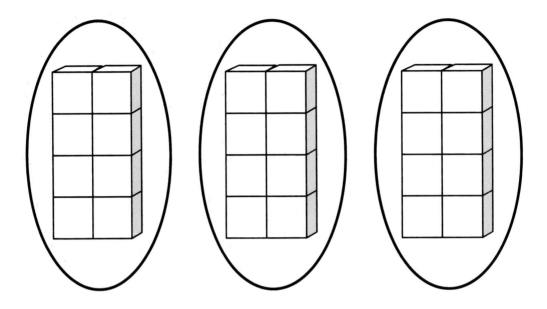

In the same way, if you want to find one-fourth (or $\frac{1}{4}$) of 36, you divide 36 by 4. $36 \div 4 = 9$, so $\frac{1}{4}$ of 36 equals 9.

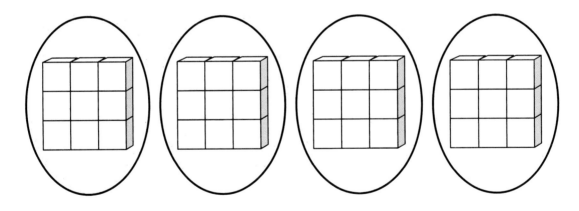

Using the division facts, learn to find the fractions $\frac{1}{2}, \frac{1}{3}, \frac{1}{4}, \frac{1}{5}, \frac{1}{6}, \frac{1}{7}, \frac{1}{8}$, and $\frac{1}{9}$ of different numbers.

Numbers Through Hundred Thousands

Thousands

We have been learning how to build and recognize numbers. You can count to 100. Now let's count by hundreds, like this: 100, 200, 300, 400, 500, 600, 700, 800, 900. What comes next? 1,000. Remember that 10 hundreds are the same as 1,000.

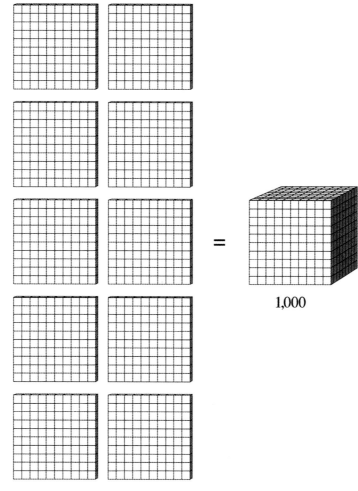

1,000

Ten hundreds

The number 1,000 has four digits. The place of a digit in a number affects its value. Let's look at the place values in the four-digit number 2,453.

thousands,	hundreds	tens	ones
2,	4	5	3

The 2 in the thousands' place is   2,000.
The 4 in the hundreds' place is   400.
The 5 in the tens' place is   50.
The 3 in the ones' place is   3.

You read 2,453 as "two thousand, four hundred fifty-three."

Make a place-value chart and practice putting four-digit numbers in it. 1,965 would look like this:

thousands,	hundreds	tens	ones
1,	9	6	5

Reading and Writing Four-Digit Numbers

In digits, the thousands are written 1,000, 2,000, 3,000, 4,000, 5,000, 6,000, 7,000, 8,000, 9,000. In words, the thousands are written one thousand, two thousand, three thousand, four thousand, five thousand, six thousand, seven thousand, eight thousand, nine thousand.

Learn to read any four-digit number, beginning with the thousands' place. For example, 8,329 is read "eight thousand, three hundred twenty-nine." How would you read 5,791? How would you read 2,015?

Learn to write any four-digit number in digits or in words. For example, in digits, two thousand, seven hundred thirty-three is written 2,733. In words, 6,364 is written "six thousand, three hundred sixty-four." Notice that you always put a comma between the thousands' place and the hundreds' place. This comma makes it easier to read large numbers.

If we were to fill in the place-value chart with some numbers we have learned so far, it would look like this:

thousands	,	hundreds	tens	ones
				1
			1	0
		1	0	0
1	,	0	0	0

The place-value chart can show numbers so big we couldn't fit the whole chart on the page. For now, let's learn these two new place values.

Ten Thousands and Hundred Thousands

The next two place values we will learn are the ten thousands' place and the hundred thousands' place.

hundred thousands	ten thousands	thousands	,	hundreds	tens	ones
2	6	7	,	3	5	3

The 2 in the hundred thousands' place is   200,000.
The 6 in the ten thousands' place is   60,000.
The 7 in the thousands' place is   7,000.
The 3 in the hundreds' place is   300.
The 5 in the tens' place is   50.
The 3 in the ones' place is   3.

You read 267,353 as "two hundred sixty-seven thousand, three hundred fifty-three."
Learn to read and write five- and six-digit numbers. For example, you read 864,374 as "eight hundred sixty-four thousand, three hundred seventy-four."
You write six hundred thousand, eighty-four in digits as 600,084. You write 450,057 in words as "four hundred fifty thousand, fifty-seven."
Get the picture? Now write down a few numbers above 100,000 and say them out loud.

Expanded Form

We say that 287 is in standard form, but the expanded form of 287 is 200 + 80 + 7. Learn to write numbers with places in the thousands in expanded form.

4,325 in expanded form is 4,000 + 300 + 20 + 5.

50,802 in expanded form is 50,000 + 800 + 2.

72,981 in expanded form is 70,000 + 2,000 + 900 + 80 + 1.

Practice writing many large numbers like these in expanded form. Also practice writing numbers that are in expanded form in standard form. In standard form, 700,000 + 5,000 + 600 + 7 is 705,607.

Counting with Thousands

You count from a thousand to the next thousand by counting all 999 numbers in between. From 1,000 to 2,000, the numbers are 1,001, 1,002, 1,003, . . . 1,999, 2,000. (The three dots (. . .) mean "and so on.")

It takes too long to count from any one thousand to the next. Practice counting in short stretches. Count from 4,994 until you reach the next thousand: 4,994, 4,995, 4,996, 4,997, 4,998, 4,999, 5,000. Or count backward from 56,003 like this: 56,003, 56,002, 56,001, 56,000. Can you count forward from 7,899 to the next thousand and backward from 23,010 to the nearest thousand?

Counting forward is the same as adding 1 each time. Learn to add 1 quickly in your head to numbers, like this:

$$3,999 + 1 = 4,000 \qquad 62,099 + 1 = 62,100 \qquad 124,999 + 1 = 125,000$$

Counting backward is the same as subtracting 1 each time. Learn to subtract 1 quickly in your head from numbers, like this:

$$3,000 - 1 = 2,999 \qquad 94,260 - 1 = 94,259 \qquad 300,000 - 1 = 299,999$$

Also practice writing the numbers that come before and after a number. Here are the numbers that come before and after 76,609.

before   after

76,608 ←——— 76,609 ———→ 76,610

Skip-Counting with Thousands

Learn to continue a line of numbers either forward or backward, counting by tens, fives, evens, or odds. Here are some examples.

counting by tens: forward — 7,210, 7,220, 7,230, 7,240

backward — 7,210, 7,200, 7,190, 7,180

counting by odds: forward — 23,995, 23,997, 23,999, 24,001

backward — 23,995, 23,993, 23,991, 23,989

counting by fives: forward — 8,005, 8,010, 8,015, 8,020

backward — 8,005, 8,000, 7,995, 7,990

> Pick numbers in the thousands to practice skip-counting by fives and tens and by either evens or odds. Practice going both forward and backward from that number.

Rounding Numbers

Sometimes it is easier to say *about* how much something is instead of *exactly* how much it is. For instance, you might say that the night sky looks as if it contains "about 100,000 stars," not "128,347 stars." This is called *rounding numbers*. You round a number to show about how large it is. You can round a number to the nearest ten, hundred, thousand, or hundred thousand.

To round a number to the nearest ten, you make it into the ten that is closest. Take the number 23, for example. 23 is between 20 and 30. It is closer to 20. So 23 rounded to the nearest ten is 20.

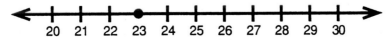

The number 27 is also between 20 and 30, but it is closer to 30. So 27 rounded to the nearest ten is 30.

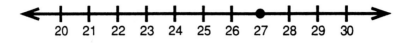

There is a rule you need to learn about rounding. When a number is exactly between two numbers, you round up to the greater number. For example, take 25, which is exactly between 20 and 30. You round 25 up to 30.

You round to the nearest hundred or thousand in the same way. Round 362 to the nearest hundred. 362 is between 300 and 400. It is closer to 400, so 362 rounded to the nearest hundred is 400. Round 8,257 to the nearest thousand. 8,257 is between 8,000 and 9,000. It is closer to 8,000. So 8,257 rounded to the nearest thousand is 8,000.

You do not always round numbers to the highest place value. 7,048 rounded to the nearest ten is 7,050. 6,152 rounded to the nearest hundred is 6,200.

Comparing and Ordering Thousands

When you compare two numbers to see which is greater, always compare the digits in the largest place value first. That means you start from the left. Then compare the number in the next largest place value, and so on. As soon as you find that a number is greater in a place value, the entire number must be greater. Of course, any number that has thousands is greater than any number that just has hundreds. For example, 1,002 > 998. In the same way, 100,002 > 99,998.

Let's look at an example that will help you see how to figure out whether <, >, or = belongs between two large numbers. Our numbers are 4,827 and 4,900. If you think of them arranged by place values, you can set them up like this:

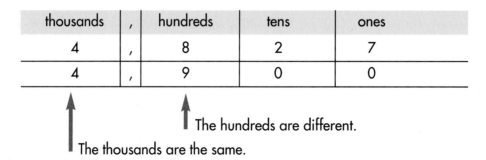

thousands	,	hundreds	tens	ones
4	,	8	2	7
4	,	9	0	0

The hundreds are different.

The thousands are the same.

First compare the thousands' place. 4,000 = 4,000. The thousands are the same. So far the numbers seem equal. Then compare the hundreds' place. 800 < 900. So 4,827 < 4,900.

Now compare 53,505 and 53,089.

ten thousands	thousands	,	hundreds	tens	ones
5	3	,	5	0	5
5	3	,	0	8	9

Remember that you can order numbers from least to greatest. To order 4,567; 5,892; 3,853; 5,889 from least to greatest, you would write: 3,853; 4,567; 5,889; 5,892.

You can also order numbers from greatest to least. These six numbers are ordered from greatest to least: 58,694; 58,599; 46,822; 46,083; 1,003; 99.

Order these numbers from least to greatest: 65, 96; 4,560; 4,575; 4,556; 45,765; 79,243; 67,221. Now find numbers all over your house, at least six of them, and order them from greatest to least. (Hint: Appliance serial numbers are fun. So are grocery store product code numbers.)

Working with Numbers

Equations and Inequalities

Remember that a number statement that uses an equals sign is an *equation*. 5 + 4 = 9 and 221 = 221 are both equations.

A number statement that uses the signs > or < is called an *inequality*. An inequality shows in what way numbers are *not* equal. 4,827 < 4,900 and 1,002 > 997 are both inequalities, saying that 4,827 is less than 4,900 and that 1,002 is greater than 997.

Ordinal Numbers Through One-Hundredth

Ordinal numbers give the place of something in an order. For example, June is the *sixth* month of the year. "Sixth" is an ordinal number.

You may already know some ordinal numbers, like "first" and "tenth" and "thirty-first." The ordinal numbers continue in the same way to one-hundredth: thirty-first, thirty-second, thirty-third, thirty-fourth, thirty-fifth, thirty-sixth, thirty-seventh, thirty-eighth, thirty-ninth, fortieth, forty-first, . . . , ninety-ninth, one-hundredth.

You don't always have to write ordinal numbers out; sometimes they can be abbreviated. Here's a chart that gives you a few examples of the ways to abbreviate them:

Ordinal Number	Abbreviation	Ordinal Number	Abbreviation
first	1st	thirty-first	31st
second	2nd	thirty-second	32nd
third	3rd	thirty-third	33rd
fourth	4th	thirty-fourth	34th

All the ordinals that end in "-th" are abbreviated in the same way as "fourth" and "thirty-fourth." For example, "sixty-fifth" is 65th. "Eighty-ninth" is 89th.

Using Number Lines

A *number line* shows numbers in order. A number line has arrows because the numbers on the line keep going on forever.

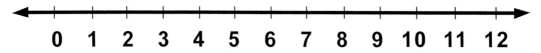

A number line can show the larger numbers you've been learning about.

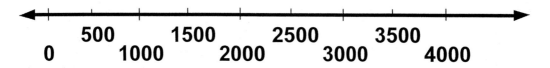

And a number line can show negative numbers. Negative numbers are the numbers to the left of zero on a number line.

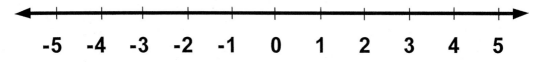

Positive numbers are the numbers to the right of zero on the number line. Zero is neither positive nor negative. You can write positive numbers with or without a + sign: +2 = 2 ("positive two equals two"). You *must* write a negative sign with a negative number: −2 = negative 2.

Addition and Subtraction

Column Addition

Learn to add four or more numbers in a column. Here is an example. Begin by adding the ones column down.

Add the ones.
Regroup if necessary.

Add the tens.

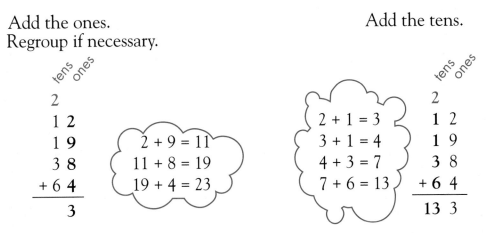

To do column addition, you often need to add combinations like $11 + 8 = 19$ or $19 + 4 = 23$ in your head. You also often have to regroup more than 1 ten. 23 ones is the same as 2 tens, 3 ones.

When you do a math problem, you should always check your work. To check column addition, you add up from the bottom. Here's a check of the problem we just did.

Add the ones.

Add the tens.

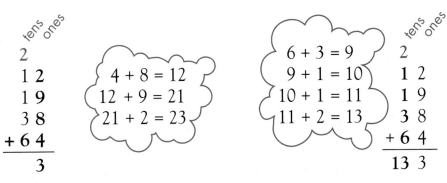

Mental Addition

Remember that you can use parentheses to group addends in different ways without changing the sum.

$$(8 + 2) + 3 = 13 \qquad\qquad 8 + (2 + 3) = 13$$

You can also add numbers in a different order without changing the sum.

$$2 + 3 = 5 \qquad\qquad 3 + 2 = 5$$

So, when you are adding many numbers together, you can group them, and then add them, in the easiest way. To find the sum of $8 + 6 + 2 + 9 + 4$ easily, group the pairs of numbers that add to 10, like this:

$$8 + 6 + 2 + 9 + 4 = (8 + 2) + (6 + 4) + 9$$
$$= \quad 10 \quad + \quad 10 \quad + 9$$
$$= \quad 29$$

When you are adding two-digit numbers in your head, look for two numbers that make an even ten. To add $28 + 35 + 12$ easily, group the numbers like this:

$$28 + 35 + 12 = (28 + 12) + 35$$
$$= \quad 40 \quad + 35$$
$$= \quad 75$$

More Mental Addition Techniques

Here is another method to help you add numbers in your head. When you are adding a number that ends in 9, you can make it an even ten, and then subtract 1 from the final sum. For example, to add 37 and 29, you can think $29 = 30 - 1$.

Think: $37 + 29 = 37 + 30 - 1 = 67 - 1 = 66$

You can make an addend an even hundred and then subtract in the same way. To add 253 and 198, you can think 198 = 200 − 2.

Think: 253 + 198 = 253 + 200 − 2 = 453 − 2 = 451

When you are adding in your head, it is often easier to add a number in two parts. To find the sum of 84 and 28, you can think: 84 + 16 makes an even hundred. So make 28 into 16 + 12.

Think: 84 + 28 = 84 + 16 + 12 = 100 + 12 = 112

Here is another example.

Think: 365 + 411 = 365 + 400 + 11 = 765 + 11 = 776

Practice doing many mental addition problems, using these methods whenever they will help you.

Estimating Sums and Differences

To "estimate" means to come quickly to an answer that is close to right. When you do not need to know an answer exactly, you can estimate to find out quickly what the approximate answer is. You can estimate the sums of two-digit numbers by rounding each number to the nearest ten, then adding. Here is an example.

rounds to

$$
\begin{array}{r}
29 \\
+ 45 \\
\hline
\end{array}
\qquad\longrightarrow\qquad
\begin{array}{r}
30 \\
+ 50 \\
\hline
80
\end{array}
$$

29 + 45 is about 80.

You can estimate the differences of two-digit numbers in the same way.

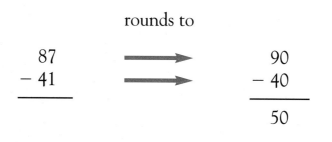

rounds to

$$
\begin{array}{r} 87 \\ -\ 41 \\ \hline \end{array}
\qquad
\begin{array}{r} 90 \\ -\ 40 \\ \hline 50 \end{array}
$$

87 − 41 is about 50.

You can estimate the sums and differences of three-digit numbers by rounding to the nearest hundred, then adding or subtracting.

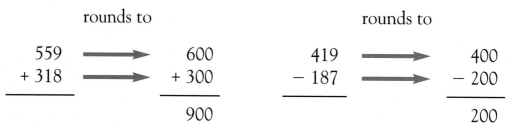

rounds to   rounds to

$$
\begin{array}{r} 559 \\ +\ 318 \\ \hline \end{array}
\qquad
\begin{array}{r} 600 \\ +\ 300 \\ \hline 900 \end{array}
\qquad
\begin{array}{r} 419 \\ -\ 187 \\ \hline \end{array}
\qquad
\begin{array}{r} 400 \\ -\ 200 \\ \hline 200 \end{array}
$$

Practice adding and subtracting by estimating. Since you can add and subtract very quickly when you estimate, you can also use estimation as a quick way to check an answer. But estimation can only tell you if your answer is *about* right; it is not a sure way to check.

More Than One Operation

Sometimes you have to do more than one operation in a problem. For example, sometimes you have to both add and multiply. When there is more than one operation, always do the operation inside the parentheses first. Here is an example.

$$7 \times (12 - 8) = 7 \times 4 = 28$$

Practice doing many problems with different kinds of operations. Here are some more examples.

1. (10 + 2) − (6 + 2) =   2. (43 − 38) × (5 + 3) =

    12   −   8   = 4   5   ×   8   = 40

3. $(9 \times 4) + (6 \times 5) =$

    36   +   30   = 66

4. $(36 \div 6) \div (4 - 1) =$

    6   ÷   3   = 2

Practice writing >, <, or = in problems like these, which use more than one operation.

$8 \times 6 < 82 - 31$ $63 \div 9 > 3 \times 2$ $21 + 11 = 4 \times 8$

Remember that $8 \times 6 < 82 - 31$ and $63 \div 9 > 3 \times 2$ are inequalities. $21 + 11 = 4 \times 8$ is an equation.

Mental Subtraction

Here is a method to help you subtract numbers in your head. When you are subtracting a number that ends in 9, you can subtract an even ten instead, and then add 1.

For example, to take 19 away from 54, you can think: subtracting 19 is the same as subtracting 20, then adding 1.

Think: $54 - 19 = 54 - 20 + 1 = 34 + 1 = 35$

You can make a number you are subtracting an even hundred in the same way. For example, to subtract 198 from 426, you can think: subtracting 198 is the same as subtracting 200, then adding 2.

Think: $426 - 198 = 426 - 200 + 2 = 226 + 2 = 228$

When you are subtracting in your head, it is often easier to subtract a number by first taking away part of the number, then taking away the rest. For example, to subtract 23 from 48, you can first subtract 20, then subtract 3 more.

Think: $48 - 23 = (48 - 20) - 3 = 28 - 3 = 25$

To solve $125 - 29 =$ _____, you can think: $125 - 25$ makes an even hundred. So think of taking away 29 as first taking away 25, then taking away 4 more.

Think: $125 - 29 = (125 - 25) - 4 = 100 - 4 = 96$

Practice doing many mental subtraction problems, using these methods whenever they will help you.

Sums and Differences of Four-Digit Numbers

Adding with Thousands

Sometimes when you add, you need to regroup hundreds as thousands. When you add vertically, always work from right to left. Let's find the sum of 2,635 and 3,728. To find this sum, add the ones, then the tens, then the hundreds, then the thousands.

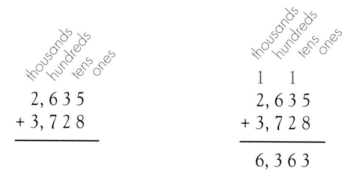

$$
\begin{array}{r}
2,635 \\
+\ 3,728 \\
\hline
\end{array}
\qquad
\begin{array}{r}
\ \ 1\ \ \ 1 \\
2,635 \\
+\ 3,728 \\
\hline
6,363
\end{array}
$$

In the same way you have learned to regroup ones as tens, regroup when necessary as you move to the left. In this problem, you do not need to regroup tens as hundreds, but you do need to regroup hundreds as thousands. 6 hundreds plus 7 hundreds equals 13 hundreds. You regroup 13 hundreds as 1 thousand, 3 hundreds. Then you add the thousands. The sum equals 6,363.

$$
\begin{array}{r}
5,627 \\
7,482 \\
38 \\
+\quad 975 \\
\hline
\end{array}
\qquad
\begin{array}{r}
12,\ 2\ 2 \\
5,627 \\
7,482 \\
38 \\
+\quad 975 \\
\hline
14,122
\end{array}
$$

Practice finding sums with three or more addends, as well as with two addends. Sometimes when you are adding four-digit numbers, you need to regroup thousands as ten thousands. You write 14 thousands as 1 ten thousand, 4 thousands.

You often have to add numbers together that have a different number of digits. Given a problem like 3,584 + 723 + 19 + 250, practice writing the numbers in columns and then adding them. Make sure to keep the numbers in the correct place-value column.

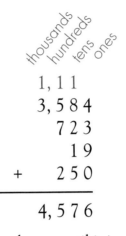

In general, practice doing addition in columns until it is easy for you and you are very good at regrouping. With three addends, add up to check. With only two addends, rewrite the addends in a different order, and add up. Also practice estimating, to see if the sum is about right.

To estimate the sum of four-digit numbers, round to the nearest thousand.

rounds to

$$
\begin{array}{r}
5,334 \\
+ 2,926 \\
\hline
\end{array}
\qquad\longrightarrow\qquad
\begin{array}{r}
5,000 \\
+ 3,000 \\
\hline
8,000
\end{array}
$$

5,334 + 2,926 is about 5,000 + 3,000, which equals 8,000. So you know that the sum of 5,334 and 2,926 should be *about* 8,000. When you actually add the two numbers, what do you get? Is it near 8,000?

Subtraction: Regrouping More Than Once

Sometimes when you subtract, you need to regroup more than once. When you subtract vertically, work from right to left.

Since you cannot take 9 from 4, regroup.	Subtract the ones.	Since you cannot take 8 tens from 1 ten, regroup again.	Subtract the tens. Subtract the hundreds.

$$
\begin{array}{r}
5\ 2\ 4 \\
-\ 3\ 8\ 9 \\
\hline
\end{array}
\qquad
\begin{array}{r}
1\ 14 \\
5\ \cancel{2}\ \cancel{4} \\
-\ 3\ 8\ 9 \\
\hline
5
\end{array}
\qquad
\begin{array}{r}
11 \\
4\ \cancel{1}14 \\
\cancel{5}\ \cancel{2}\ \cancel{4} \\
-\ 3\ 8\ 9 \\
\hline
3\ 5
\end{array}
\qquad
\begin{array}{r}
11 \\
4\ 114 \\
\cancel{5}\ \cancel{2}\ \cancel{4} \\
-\ 3\ 8\ 9 \\
\hline
1\ 3\ 5
\end{array}
$$

The difference is 135.

Make up subtraction problems in which you have to regroup more than once, and practice them many times.

Subtracting Across Zeros

Sometimes when you need to regroup, there is a zero in the next place. Then you need to regroup in a different way. Here is an example. Find the difference of 304 and 187.

$$
\begin{array}{r}
3\ 0\ 4 \\
-\ 1\ 8\ 7 \\
\hline
\end{array}
$$

Subtract the ones. Since you cannot take 7 from 4, you need to regroup. But there are no tens to regroup. Change 3 hundreds to 2 hundreds and 10 tens. The 1 in front of the 0 in the tens column indicates a ten in that column. Now change the 10 tens to 9 tens and 10 ones.

$$
\begin{array}{r}
9 \\
2\ 1\cancel{0}\ 14 \\
\cancel{3}\ \cancel{0}\ 4 \\
-\ 1\ 8\ 7 \\
\hline
1\ 1\ 7
\end{array}
\qquad \text{OR} \qquad
\begin{array}{r}
29\ 14 \\
\cancel{3}\ \cancel{0}\ 4 \\
-\ 1\ 8\ 7 \\
\hline
1\ 1\ 7
\end{array}
$$

You can also think: Change 30 tens to 29 tens and 10 ones, adding those to the 4 in the ones' place.

Let's see how this process works when you have to subtract across several zeros. When subtracting four-digit numbers, first subtract the ones, then the tens, then the hundreds, then the thousands.

$$
\begin{array}{r}
4,000 \\
-\ 2,896 \\
\hline
\end{array}
$$

Think: You need an extra ten for the ones' place. Change 400 tens to 399 tens and add the extra ten to the ones' place. Then subtract the ones, the tens, the hundreds, and the thousands, column by column.

$$
\begin{array}{r}
3\ \ 9\ 9\ 10 \\
4,\ \cancel{0}\ \cancel{0}\ \cancel{0} \\
-\ 2,\ 8\ 9\ 6 \\
\hline
\end{array}
\qquad\qquad
\begin{array}{r}
3\ \ 9\ 9\ 10 \\
4,\ \cancel{0}\ \cancel{0}\ \cancel{0} \\
-\ 2,\ 8\ 9\ 6 \\
\hline
1,\ 1\ 0\ 4
\end{array}
$$

Four-Digit Subtraction

Practice subtracting with four-digit numbers until you can do it easily, especially across zeros. Practice writing a subtraction problem in columns and then subtracting. Here is an example. Find the difference of 3,037 and 1,682.

$$
\begin{array}{r}
3,0\ 3\ 7 \\
-\ 1,6\ 8\ 2 \\
\hline
\end{array}
\quad
\begin{array}{r}
3,0\ 3\ 7 \\
-\ 1,6\ 8\ 2 \\
\hline
5
\end{array}
\quad
\begin{array}{r}
2\ \ 9\ 13 \\
3,0\ \cancel{3}\ 7 \\
-\ 1,6\ 8\ 2 \\
\hline
5\ 5
\end{array}
\quad
\begin{array}{r}
2\ \ 9\ 13 \\
3,\ \cancel{0}\ \cancel{3}\ 7 \\
-\ 1,6\ 8\ 2 \\
\hline
3\ 5\ 5
\end{array}
\quad
\begin{array}{r}
2\ \ 9\ 13 \\
\cancel{3},\ \cancel{0}\ \cancel{3}\ 7 \\
-\ 1,6\ 8\ 2 \\
\hline
1,\ 3\ 5\ 5
\end{array}
$$

Learn how to make change. Here's a problem to practice.

Alice buys a granola bar for 54¢. She gives the clerk a one-dollar bill. The clerk makes change by counting forward from the cost of the granola bar. She starts at 54¢. She adds one penny = 55¢, plus a dime = 65¢, plus another dime = 75¢, plus a quarter = $1.00. So the clerk gives Alice a penny, two dimes, and a quarter.

Alice can check her change with subtraction. $1.00 minus 54¢ is 100¢ − 54¢ = 46¢. So Alice will get 46¢ in change. A penny, two dimes, and a quarter add up to 46¢.

You make change by counting forward from the cost of what was bought to the amount paid for it. You should use as few coins or bills as possible when making change.

Always start with the coins or bills of least value, and work toward the coins or bills of greatest value. For example, a customer gives Roberta $20.00 for a book that costs $11.43. What change should Roberta give? Two pennies come to $11.45. A nickel comes to $11.50. Two quarters come to $12.00. Three one-dollar bills make $15.00. A five-dollar bill makes $20.00.

Practice making change using as few bills and coins as possible. You can make up your own examples, but here's one to get you started. How much change does Ron get from a hundred-dollar bill if his groceries cost $73.18?

Reading and Writing Graphs

A *graph* is a way of showing information in a diagram. Learn to read *line graphs* and *bar graphs*. Here is a bar graph.

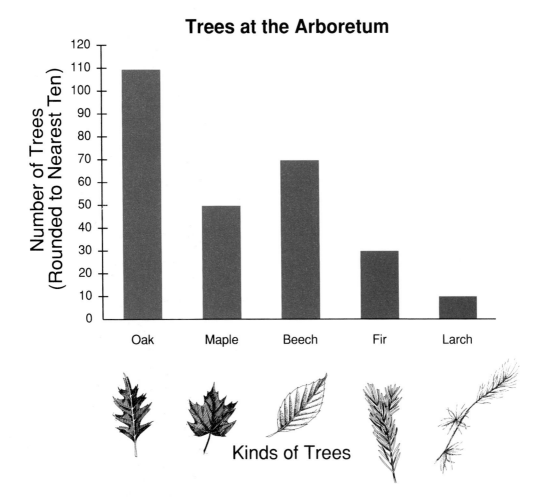

Trees at the Arboretum

This bar graph shows how many of each kind of tree there are at the arboretum, rounded to the nearest ten. Each bar, or rectangle, on the graph shows about how many trees of a certain kind there are. For example, there are about 70 beeches. About how many more oaks than maples are there? 60 more oaks, because 110 − 50 = 60.

Here is a line graph.

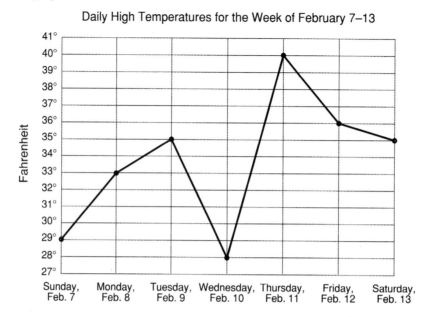

Daily High Temperatures for the Week of February 7–13

This line graph shows the daily high temperatures for the week of February 7–13. Each point shows the high temperature on that day. The line segments connect the points to show how the high temperature changed from day to day. The change in high temperature from Wednesday to Thursday was 12°F. How much warmer was the high temperature on Friday than on Sunday? 7°F, because 36 − 29 = 7.

You can make a graph, too. Here is a bar graph we made when we tossed a penny in the air twenty times and recorded how it fell each time. First we recorded how each toss fell.

Nine tosses came up heads, and eleven tosses came up tails. Then we wrote the same information on a graph. For the number of heads that came up, we made one bar. For the number of tails that came up, we made a second bar.

heads: ⊬⊬ ⦀⦀

tails: ⊬⊬ ⊬⊬ ⎮

	1	2	3	4	5	6	7	8	9	10	11	12	13	14	15
Heads	■	■	■	■	■	■	■	■	■						
Tails	■	■	■	■	■	■	■	■	■	■	■				

Now you try it. Toss a penny into the air twenty or even thirty times, and record how many times it comes up heads or tails. Then make your own graph.

Geometry

Polygons

Remember these kinds of lines?

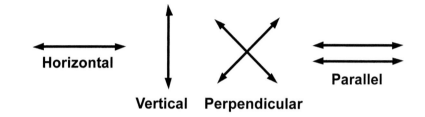

Remember the difference between closed figures and open figures?

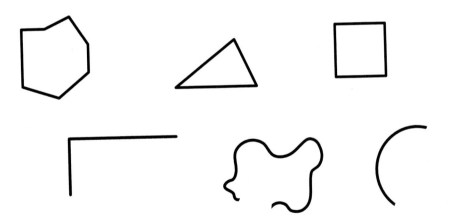

A closed figure can be formed entirely with line segments. Here is line segment TS or ST. A line segment gets its name from the letters assigned to its endpoints.

A closed figure that is formed by line segments is called a *polygon*. Triangles, rectangles, and squares are polygons; circles are not polygons.

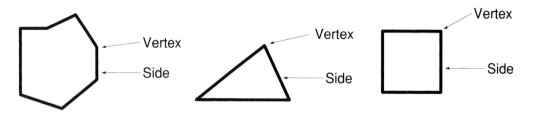

In a polygon, each side is a line segment. The point where two line segments meet is called a *vertex*. (The plural of "vertex" is *vertices* or *vertexes*.)

Like all points, vertices are named by letters. You name a polygon by starting at one vertex and naming all the other vertices in order. Here are two examples.

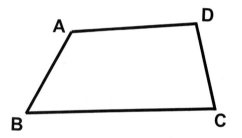

Starting at point B, you could name this figure polygon BADC; you could also name it by naming the vertices in the other direction: polygon BCDA. Or you could start with any of the other points and name the vertices in order in either direction. Altogether there are eight possible names for this polygon. Can you write all of them?

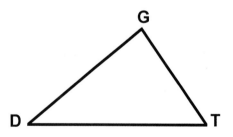

Here are the six possible names for the triangle above: triangle DGT, triangle DTG, triangle TGD, triangle TDG, triangle GTD, triangle GDT.

Have fun with polygons. Draw a polygon with a certain number of sides—let's say five. Now draw another polygon with five sides that looks very different. See how many polygons you can make with five sides.

Now do the same thing with a ten-sided polygon.

Angles

Whenever two sides of a polygon meet, they form an *angle*. Here's an example of an angle.

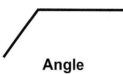

Angle

This polygon has four sides, four vertices, and four angles.

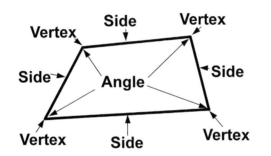

A *right angle* is an angle that forms a square corner.

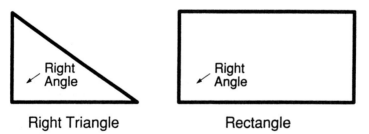

Right Triangle   Rectangle

Squares and rectangles have four right angles.

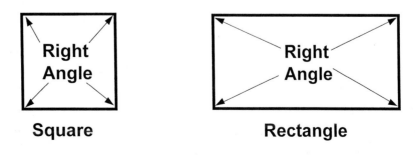

Square   Rectangle

Congruent and Symmetric Figures

Two figures that are exactly the same shape and size are said to be *congruent*. Sometimes you have to turn one figure around to see if it is congruent with another.

These two triangles are congruent.

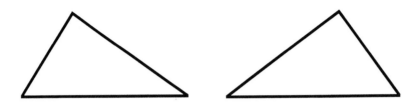

These two triangles are not congruent. They have the same shape but not the same size.

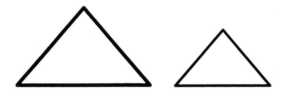

When a figure can be folded in half and both halves match, the figure is said to be *symmetrical*. The fold line is called the *line of symmetry*. Sometimes figures have more than one line of symmetry. For example, a square has four lines of symmetry.

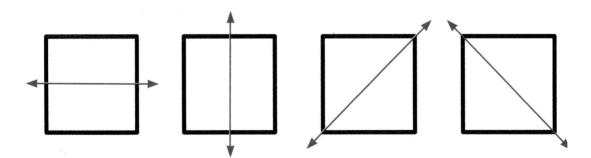

A circle has more lines of symmetry than you can count. Think how many different folds you can make down the center of a circle. Every time you do it, the two halves match.

You can fold figures to see if they are symmetric. If they are symmetric, you can see how many lines of symmetry they have.

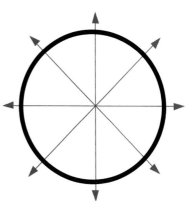

Make a Geometry Mobile

Make four or five symmetrical shapes out of construction paper. What sorts of symmetrical figures would you like to see floating in the air? All triangles, or an assortment of hearts, circles, and cones? Use a hole puncher or poke a hole in each. Then cut string or thread into 12-centimeter lengths and tie the threads through the holes in your figures. You can use twigs or Popsicle sticks to hang the figures. The hard part is finding the right lengths for each string to make the pieces balance each other in a pattern you like.

Perimeter

Perimeter is the distance around a figure. To find the perimeter of a figure, add the lengths of its sides together.

Practice measuring the sides of polygons to the nearest inch or centimeter; then add the lengths together to find the perimeter of the polygon in inches or centimeters. Here is an example in centimeters.

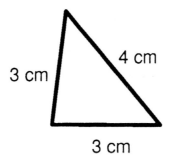

3 cm + 4 cm + 3 cm = 10 cm. The perimeter of the triangle is 10 cm.

Area

The *area* of a figure is the number of square units that cover its surface. A square unit has sides that are each one unit long. For example, this is a square centimeter:

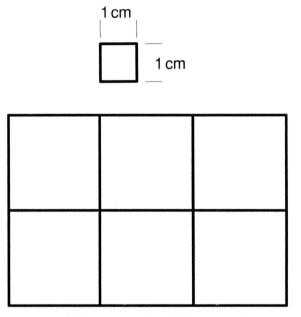

This rectangle has an area of 6 square inches. You write 6 square inches as 6 in^2.

This polygon has an area of 11 square centimeters. You write 11 square centimeters as 11 cm^2.

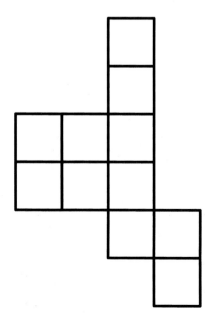

Learn to find the area of a figure by counting square units. Make sure always to write your answer in square units, such as in^2 or cm^2.

Solids

Three-dimensional objects are often called *solids*.

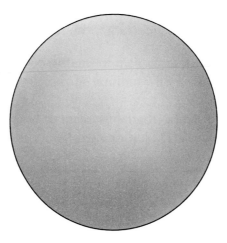

Some solids have curved surfaces, and some solids have flat surfaces. A flat surface on a solid is called a *face*. The line segment where two faces meet is called an *edge*. Edges come together at a *vertex*.

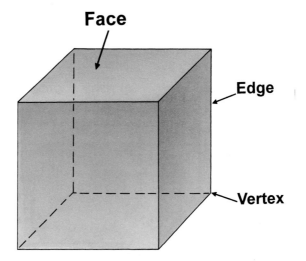

Here are three examples of changes between units in a system.

1. Since 1 ft = 12 in, to find out how many inches are in 3 feet, you can add 12 in and 12 in and 12 in. 12 + 12 + 12 = 36, so 3 ft = 36 in.

2. You can find out how many quarts are in 6 gallons of cider by multiplying.

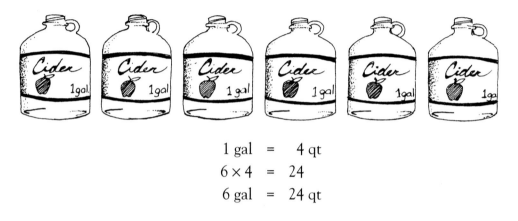

$$1 \text{ gal} = 4 \text{ qt}$$
$$6 \times 4 = 24$$
$$6 \text{ gal} = 24 \text{ qt}$$

3. To find out how many pints are in 8 cups, you can divide by 2, since 2 c = 1 pt.

$$8 \div 2 = 4$$
$$8 \text{ c} = 4 \text{ pt}$$

In the metric system, it is even easier to change units because it is just like working with place value. Here are some equations for changing units in the metric system.

$$1 \text{ m} = 100 \text{ cm} \qquad\qquad 1 \text{ kg} = 1,000 \text{ g}$$
$$1 \text{ cm} = 10 \text{ mm}$$
$$1 \text{ km} = 1,000 \text{ m}$$

Each meter is 100 centimeters. So 5 meters are 500 centimeters, because 5 × 100 = 500. Each kilometer is 1,000 meters. So 6 kilometers are 6,000 meters, because 6 × 1,000 = 6,000. In the same way, 9 kg = 9,000 g.

Measurement Word Problems

Learn how to solve problems that involve units of measurement. For example, Mrs. Johnson has a kilogram of flour. She uses 500 grams to make two loaves of bread. She uses another 250 grams to make some brownies. How many grams of flour does she use, and how many does she have left?

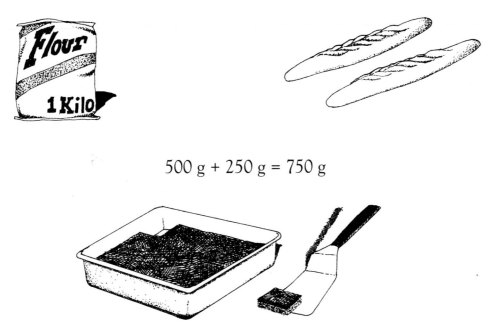

$$500 \text{ g} + 250 \text{ g} = 750 \text{ g}$$

So Mrs. Johnson uses 750 grams of flour. She started with 1 kilogram of flour. 1 kg = 1,000 g.

$$
\begin{array}{r}
\scriptstyle 0\ \ 9\ \ 10 \\
1,\,\cancel{0}\,\cancel{0}\,0\,\text{g} \\
-\ \ \ \ 7\,5\,0\,\text{g} \\
\hline
2\,5\,0\,\text{g}
\end{array}
$$

So Mrs. Johnson has 250 grams of flour left.

Practice problems like these, in which you first have to add, then subtract. Be careful in measurement problems to remember which units you are working with. Always write the units you are working with in your answer.

Measure and Draw Line Segments

You've learned what a line segment is. Now you can learn to measure the lengths of line segments in metric and U.S. customary units.

To measure the line segment AB to the nearest inch or the nearest centimeter:

1. Line up one end of the segment with the 0 mark on your ruler.
2. Look at the other end of the segment. Find the closest inch mark or centimeter mark.

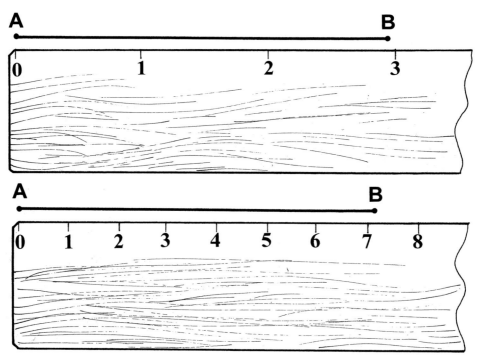

You can also measure line segments to the nearest half inch ($\frac{1}{2}$ in) or quarter inch ($\frac{1}{4}$ in).

1/2 Inch

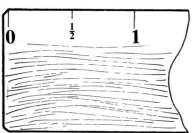

1/4 Inch

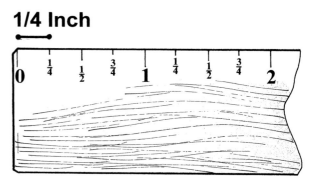

Here are some line segments. Measure each to the quarter inch and to the nearest centimeters.

Q _____ R W ___ X Y _____ Z

U _____ V S _____ T

Now draw line segments of the following lengths.

$4\frac{1}{2}$ in $5\frac{1}{2}$ cm   20 cm   5 mm

10 cm $3\frac{3}{4}$ in $11\frac{1}{2}$ in   5 in

Estimating Linear Measurements

When you are familiar with measuring inches, feet, centimeters, and meters, you can begin to estimate linear measurements. See the word "line" in "linear"? That's because linear measurements mean measuring on a straight line.

Would you use feet or inches to measure this turtle? Why would inches or centimeters work better for measuring the turtle than feet, yards, or meters? Estimate how many inches long this drawing of a turtle is. Estimate how many centimeters it is.

What about the chair you're sitting in? What measurement would work best to tell how tall it is?

Estimate the height of your chairback. Then measure your chair and compare your answers.

Estimate and then measure five real objects of different sizes. Why did you choose each measurement you used?

Measuring Weight

When you measure how heavy something is, you are measuring weight. Have you ever learned how to use a balance scale for measuring weight? Look at the balance scales in these pictures. When one side of the balance is lower than the other, which object weighs more?

Look at the balances again. Which is heavier: the pumpkin or the two apples? Which is heavier: the pumpkin or one apple?

Measuring Ounces, Pounds, Grams, and Kilograms

If you have a scale to use, you can practice measuring weight. Some scales measure in ounces; some measure in pounds. Some measure in grams and kilograms. What does your scale show?

Find five objects that feel as if they weigh different amounts. Weigh your objects and write a list of them with their weights, from lightest to heaviest.

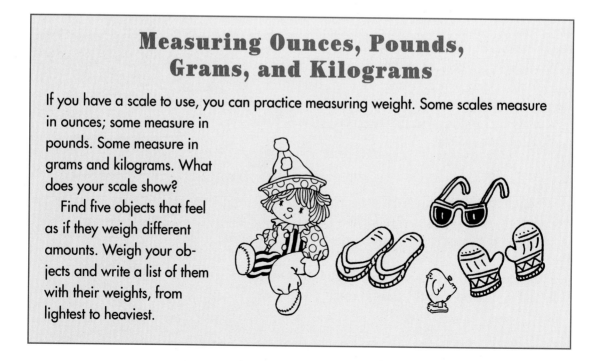

Measuring Volume

There is a system of measurement used just for liquids (like milk, juice, water, or paint). In the U.S. customary system, we use ounces, cups, pints, quarts, and gallons. In the metric system, we use liters and milliliters. A liter is a little more than a quart.

Use this table to help you answer the following questions.

Units of Measurement for Liquids

U. S. Customary Units	Metric Units
8 ounces = 1 cup	
16 ounces = 1 pint	
2 pints = 1 quart	1,000 milliliters = 1 liter
4 quarts = 1 gallon	

1. If you pour 1 gallon of milk into quart bottles, how many quart bottles will you fill?

2. Two pints equal 1 quart. How many ounces are in a quart?

3. How many milliliters are in 3 liters?

EXTRA: About how many liters are in a gallon?

Measuring Temperature

Do you remember the graph, earlier in this section of the book, on page 252, that showed the daily high temperatures during a week in February? To describe the temperature, we used units called *degrees*, and we used a little circle to stand for that unit. The highest temperature we plotted on that graph was 40°, and the lowest temperature was 28°.

When talking about temperatures, it is best to tell whether you are using the U.S. customary or the metric system. The U.S. customary system measures temperature in degrees Fahrenheit. The metric system measures temperature in degrees Celsius. You use the initials of those words, F and C, to show which scale of measurement you are using.

What kind of weather is it when the thermometer looks like this? Can you read the temperature in degrees Celsius? In degrees Fahrenheit? Is it very hot, or very cold, or just right?

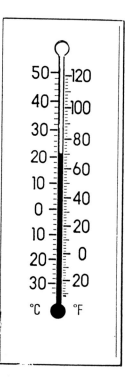

Here is a thermometer that shows temperatures using both scales of measurement. Let's use it to tell the temperature at which water freezes, in both Celsius and Fahrenheit.

A thermometer that measures temperature in degrees Celsius will read 0°C (zero degrees Celsius) when the temperature is just cold enough for water to freeze. At this same temperature, the freezing point of water, a thermometer that measures temperature in degrees Fahrenheit will read 32°F (thirty-two degrees Fahrenheit).

Sometimes you have to use negative numbers to talk about cold temperatures. On a fall day, a Celsius thermometer might read 10°C in the middle of the afternoon, but in the middle of the night, the temperature might go down to − 2°C. This temperature can be described as "negative two degrees Celsius," but people also say "two degrees below zero, Celsius."

Multiplication—Part Two

Multiplying Tens, Hundreds, and Thousands

It is easy to multiply tens, hundreds, and thousands. Use the multiplication facts you already know.

3×2 **tens** $= 6$ **tens** 4×7 **hundreds** $= 28$ **hundreds**

$3 \times 20 = 60$ $4 \times 700 = 2800$

$$
\begin{array}{r}
20 \\
\times\ 3 \\
\hline
60
\end{array}
\qquad\qquad
\begin{array}{r}
700 \\
\times\ 4 \\
\hline
2{,}800
\end{array}
$$

3×6 **thousands** $= 18$ **thousands**

$3 \times 6{,}000 = 18{,}000$

$$
\begin{array}{r}
6{,}000 \\
\times\qquad 3 \\
\hline
18{,}000
\end{array}
$$

Practice solving problems like these quickly. Remember that you are multiplying tens, hundreds, or thousands. Be sure to keep the right number of zeros in the product!

A Way to Multiply

One way to multiply 3 by 16 is to break 16 into smaller numbers. Graph paper can help show how this works. On graph paper, draw a rectangle with 3 rows and 16 columns.

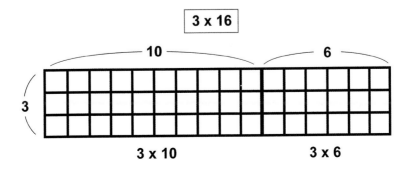

You can see from the picture that 3×16 is the same as $(3 \times 10) + (3 \times 6)$. So you can multiply 3×16 like this:

$$3 \times 16 = (3 \times 10) + (3 \times 6) = 30 + 18 = 48$$

You can also write this multiplication problem vertically, like this:

$$\begin{array}{r} 16 \\ \times\ 3 \\ \hline \end{array}$$

When you multiply vertically, you start with the ones and move to the left to the greater values.

Multiply the ones.   Multiply the tens.   Add.

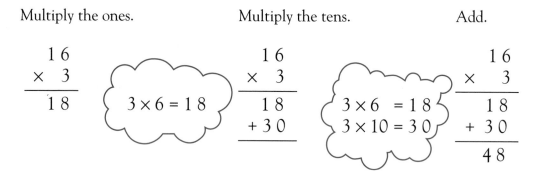

Notice how you write in the 0 to show that 3×10 is 3 tens, not 3 ones.

You can multiply 6×28 in the same way. First draw the problem on graph paper in rows and columns. Then write it vertically and multiply. Notice that first you multiply 6 by the ones, then you multiply 6 by the tens.

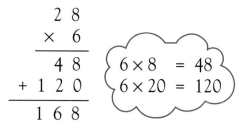

Practice multiplying this way, making a separate product for the ones and the tens, then adding.

The Short Way to Multiply

Now learn the short way to write multiplication. In this method, you write the products on the same line. Let's use 23×3 as an example.

First
we write
it vertically.

$$\begin{array}{r} 2\,3 \\ \times\ \ \ 3 \\ \hline \end{array}$$

Next
we multiply
3 by the ones
in 23.

$$\begin{array}{r} 2\,3 \\ \times\ \ \ 3 \\ \hline 9 \end{array}$$

Next we multiply
3 by the tens in 23
and write the product
on the same line.

$$\begin{array}{r} 2\,3 \\ \times\ \ \ 3 \\ \hline 6\,9 \end{array}$$

Often when you multiply this way, you need to regroup. See what happens when you multiply 6 by 28 this way.

Multiply 6 by 8 ones.
Regroup 48 as 4 tens 8
ones. Carry the 4 to the
top of the tens' place

$$\begin{array}{r} 4 \\ 2\,8 \\ \times\ \ \ 6 \\ \hline 8 \end{array}$$

Multiply 6 by 2 tens,
then add the 4 tens.
$(6 \times 2) + 4 = 12 + 4 = 16$

$$\begin{array}{r} 4 \\ 2\,8 \\ \times\ \ \ 6 \\ \hline 1\,6\,8 \end{array}$$

Multiplying Three-Digit and Four-Digit Numbers

You can multiply a three-digit number by a one-digit number by writing separate products for the ones, tens, and hundreds. Then you can add the separate products.

$$\begin{array}{r} 2\,8\,4 \\ \times\ \ \ \ \ 7 \\ \hline 2\,8 \\ 5\,6\,0 \\ +\ 1,4\,0\,0 \\ \hline 1,9\,8\,8 \end{array}$$

$7 \times 4 = 28$
$7 \times 80 = 560$
$7 \times 200 = 1,400$

The product of 7×284 is 1,988.

Practice multiplying three-digit numbers this way. Then learn to multiply a three-digit number the quick way, writing the products on one line

Multiply 7 by the ones. Regroup 28.	Multiply 7 by the tens. Add the 2 tens Regroup 58 tens.	Multiply 7 by the hundreds. Add the 5 hundreds

$$\begin{array}{r} 2 \\ 2\,8\,4 \\ \times\ \ \ 7 \\ \hline 8 \end{array} \qquad \begin{array}{r} 5\,2 \\ 2\,8\,4 \\ \times\ \ \ 7 \\ \hline 8\,8 \end{array} \qquad \begin{array}{r} 5\,2 \\ 2\,8\,4 \\ \times\ \ \ 7 \\ \hline 1{,}9\,8\,8 \end{array}$$

Here is an example where one of the digits in the number you are multiplying is 0. Remember that the product of any number and 0 is 0.

$$\begin{array}{r} 4 \\ 5\,0\,7 \\ \times\ \ \ 6 \\ \hline 3{,}0\,4\,2 \end{array}$$

In this example, 6×0 tens = 0. You add 0 and the 4 tens you carried to the tens' place.

Learn to multiply a four-digit number. You multiply from right to left. First you multiply the ones, then the tens, then the hundreds, then the thousands. Often you have to regroup. Here is an example.

$$\begin{array}{r} 5\ \ \ 3 \\ 1{,}7\,0\,4 \\ \times\ 8 \\ \hline 1\,3{,}6\,3\,2 \end{array}$$

The process of regrouping, multiplying in the next place, and then adding takes time to learn, and you need to practice it a lot. Practice multiplying one-digit numbers by two-digit, three-digit, and four-digit numbers. You can make up your own numbers to multiply. Be sure to practice with numbers that have zeros in them.

Checking Multiplication

One good way to check multiplication is to estimate, to see if the product is about right.

When you are multiplying a two-digit number, find the two tens that the number is between. You found that $8 \times 26 = 208$. To check this product, think: 26 is between 20 and 30. So 8×26 should be between 8×20 and 8×30. $8 \times 20 = 160$. $8 \times 30 = 240$. 208 is between 160 and 240.

You can write this check like this:

$$8 \times 20 < 8 \times 26 < 8 \times 30$$

$$160 < 208 < 240 \quad ✔$$

A number statement like $8 \times 20 < 8 \times 26 < 8 \times 30$ is called a *double inequality* because there are two inequality signs.

When you are multiplying a three-digit number, check the product by finding the two hundreds that the number is between.

To check $6 \times 507 = 3,042$, you can think: 507 is between 500 and 600.

$$6 \times 500 < 6 \times 507 < 6 \times 600$$

$$3,000 < 3,042 < 3,600 \quad ✔$$

When you are multiplying a four-digit number, find the two thousands that it is between to check. Does $8 \times 1,704 = 13,632$?

$$8 \times 1,000 < 8 \times 1,704 < 8 \times 2,000$$

$$8,000 < 13,632 < 16,000 \quad ✔$$

Check each multiplication problem by estimating in this way.

Another Way to Write Expanded Form

Remember that the expanded form of 7,836 is 7,000 + 800 + 30 + 6. Now that you know how to multiply tens, hundreds, and thousands, you can write the expanded form of a number in another way.

$$7,000 = 7 \times 1,000$$

$$800 = 8 \times 100$$

$$30 = 3 \times 10$$

So you can write 7,000 + 800 + 30 + 6 like this:

$$(7 \times 1,000) + (8 \times 100) + (3 \times 10) + 6$$

Practice writing numbers in this new expanded form. For example, write 3,604 as $(3 \times 1,000) + (6 \times 100) + 4$. Write 9,078 as $(9 \times 1,000) + (7 \times 10) + 8$.

Solving Word Problems Using Multiplication

Solve these word problems using multiplication:

1. At the beach, Andrea found 8 shells. Jeff found 5 times as many shells. How many shells did Jeff find?

2. Megan's truck gets 21 miles per gallon of gasoline. How far can she drive on 9 gallons?

Division—Part Two

Remainders

Mrs. Hughes wants to divide 33 sheets of construction paper among 7 students, so that each student has the same number of sheets. If she gave each student 4 sheets, she would use 28 sheets ($4 \times 7 = 28$). If she gave each student 5 sheets, she would use 35 sheets ($5 \times 7 = 35$). She only has 33 sheets: she has enough to give 4 sheets to each student, but not enough to give 5 sheets. Since $33 - 28 = 5$, there will be 5 sheets left over if she gives 4 to each student. Here is how you write this division problem.

Mrs. Hughes wants to divide 33 sheets of construction paper among her 7 students.

$$7 \overline{)\ 33}$$

What is 33 divided by 7? 7 doesn't go into 33 evenly. The closest we can come is $7 \times 4 = 28$. So we write 4 in the ones' place for the quotient. Then we put 28 below the 33 (or the dividend) and subtract it, to show how many we have left over: 5. Our remainder is 5. So we write R5 next to the quotient 4, like this:

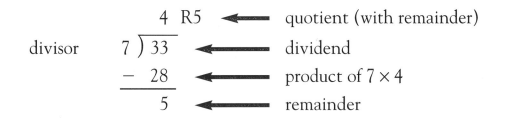

Notice how you multiply the divisor and the quotient, then subtract this product from the dividend to find the remainder.

When you do a division problem like this, make the quotient as big as you can. If the problem is 23 divided by 5, what would your quotient be? 3 or 4? It would be 4, because $3 \times 5 = 15$ and $23 - 15$ gives you 8 left over. Since you can subtract 5 from 8, you know that your quotient can be 1 greater. $4 \times 5 = 20$ leaves you 3 left over. Because you can't take 5 away from 3, you know you've found the largest possible quotient.

When you find the quotient, multiply the divisor by the quotient, then subtract this product. The result is the remainder. You can always check your work by making sure that the remainder is less than the divisor. If the remainder is not less, you need to try again, with a larger quotient. Here is an example.

$$\begin{array}{r} 5\ R9 \\ 8\overline{)\,49} \\ -\,40 \\ \hline 9 \end{array}$$

Subtract 8×5

$9 < 8?$

NO

$$\begin{array}{r} 6\ R1 \\ 8\overline{)\,49} \\ -\,48 \\ \hline 1 \end{array}$$

Subtract 8×6

$1 < 8?$

YES

Practice doing problems like $41 \div 6$ or $58 \div 7$, finding the quotients and the remainders. Remember that $6\overline{)41}$ and $41 \div 6$ are the same problem.

Dividing Tens, Hundreds, and Thousands

Sometimes you can divide tens, hundreds, and thousands easily, using the division facts.

$9 \div 3 = 3$	$35 \div 7 = 5$	$18 \div 6 = 3$
and	and	and
$90 \div 3 = 30$	$3500 \div 7 = 500$	$18,000 \div 6 = 3,000$

Notice how the quotient has the same number of zeros as the dividend? Practice doing problems like these in your head.

Two-Digit Quotients

Sometimes when you divide a two-digit number, the quotient has two digits. Divide 64 by 2. Remember, in division, you start with the highest place value in the dividend and move right. So in $2\overline{)64}$, we first divide the tens.

$$2\overline{)\,64}$$

Subtract 2×3

$0 < 2$

$$\begin{array}{r} 3 \\ 2\overline{)\,64} \\ -\,6 \\ \hline 0 \end{array}$$

Make sure the remainder is less than the divisor.

Then bring down the 4 ones in 64. Divide the ones.

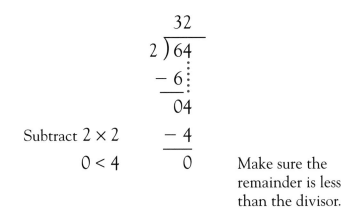

$$\begin{array}{r} 32 \\ 2\overline{)64} \\ -6 \\ \hline 04 \end{array}$$

Subtract 2×2 $-\ 4$

$0 < 4$ $\overline{0}$ Make sure the remainder is less than the divisor.

You can tell that $64 \div 2$ will have a two-digit quotient because you can divide the 6 by 2. In the same way, $84 \div 5$ has a two-digit quotient because you can divide the 8 by 5. $47 \div 8$ has a one-digit quotient because you cannot divide 4 by 8. You need to divide 47 by 8 instead.

Here is a problem with a two-digit quotient and a remainder.

Divide the tens.   Divide the ones.

$$\begin{array}{r} 1 \\ 5\overline{)84} \end{array}$$

Subtract $\ \ 5 \times 1$ $-\ 5$

Check $3 < 5$ $\overline{3}$

$$\begin{array}{r} 16 \text{ R4} \\ 5\overline{)84} \\ -5 \\ \hline 34 \end{array}$$

Subtract 5×6 $-\ 30$

Check $4 < 5$ $\overline{4}$

Recognizing Fractions from $\frac{1}{2}$ to $\frac{1}{10}$

Look over this list of fractions. You should learn to recognize these fractions just the way you recognize the numbers 1 to 10.

$$\frac{1}{2} \qquad \frac{1}{3} \qquad \frac{1}{4} \qquad \frac{1}{5} \qquad \frac{1}{6} \qquad \frac{1}{7} \qquad \frac{1}{8} \qquad \frac{1}{9} \qquad \frac{1}{10}$$

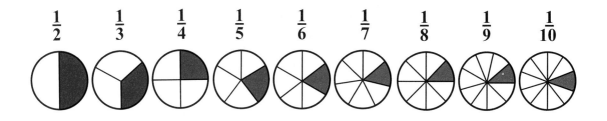

Equivalent Fractions

Sometimes fractions with different numerators and denominators name the same amount. Fractions that name the same amount are called *equivalent fractions*.

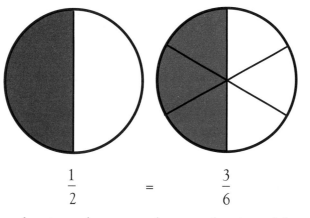

$$\frac{1}{2} \qquad = \qquad \frac{3}{6}$$

$\frac{1}{2}$ and $\frac{3}{6}$ are equivalent fractions: they name the same fraction of the circle.

Learn to recognize equivalent fractions. For example, from the picture you should know that $\frac{2}{4} = \frac{4}{8}$.

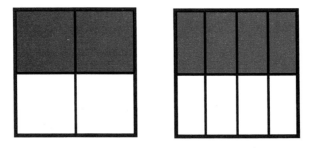

Comparing Fractions

Learn to compare fractions that have the same denominator by using the signs >, <, and =.

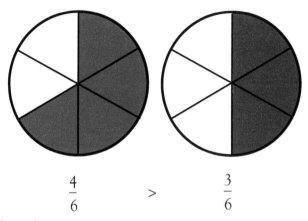

$$\frac{4}{6} \qquad > \qquad \frac{3}{6}$$

$\frac{4}{6}$ is greater than $\frac{3}{6}$. In $\frac{4}{6}$, there are 6 equal parts and you are talking about 4. In $\frac{3}{6}$, there are 6 equal parts and you are only talking about 3.

Rule: When two fractions have the same denominator, the one with the greater numerator is the greater fraction.

Without using a picture, you should know that $\frac{5}{9} > \frac{3}{9}$; $\frac{2}{7} < \frac{3}{7}$; $\frac{1}{6} = \frac{1}{6}$.

Mixed Numbers and Whole Numbers

The numbers 0, 1, 2, 3, 4, . . . are called the *whole numbers*. By calling them "whole numbers," we mean that they are not fractions and that they name a whole.

A number like $1\frac{1}{2}$ is called a *mixed number*. It has a part that is a whole number and a part that is a fraction. You read $1\frac{1}{2}$ as "one and one-half." When you read a mixed number, you always put an "and" between its whole-number part and its fractional part. Here are some more mixed numbers: $2\frac{1}{4}, 6\frac{1}{8}, 5\frac{7}{9}, 3\frac{3}{4}$.

On a number line, $1\frac{1}{2}$ is between 1 and 2. It is 1 *plus* $\frac{1}{2}$ more. In the same way, $5\frac{1}{4}$ is between 5 and 6. It is 5 plus $\frac{1}{4}$ more. $5\frac{1}{4}$ is more than 5, but less than 6.

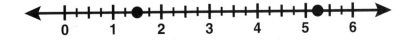

You often use mixed numbers when you measure in inches. Practice measuring to the nearest half inch or quarter inch using a ruler divided into quarter inches. For example, draw a line segment $5\frac{3}{4}$ inches long.

Decimals: Tenths

You can write the fraction $\frac{1}{10}$ as the decimal 0.1. You read both the same way. You say, "one-tenth."

The period to the left of the 1 is called a *decimal point*. The decimal point shows that the value of the digits to its right is anywhere between 0 and 1, like a fraction. A *decimal* is any number that uses places to the right of the decimal point to show a fraction.

The first place to the right of the decimal point is the tenths' place.

ones		tenths
1	.	7

You can write the mixed number $1\frac{7}{10}$ as the decimal 1.7. You read both the same way: "one and seven-tenths."

Decimals and Hundredths

The second place to the right of the decimal point is the hundredths' place. The fraction $\frac{1}{100}$ can also be written: 0.01

ones		tenths	hundredths
0	.	0	1

You read both the same way: "one-hundredth."

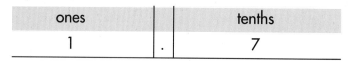

$2\frac{47}{100}$ =	ones		tenths	hundredths
	2	.	4	7

You read both as "two and forty-seven hundredths."

Notice that when there are both tenths and hundredths in a decimal, you read the tenths and hundredths together in terms of the hundredths. Also remember to put an "and" between the whole-number part and the fractional part of a decimal, just as in mixed numbers.

Decimals and Fractions of 100

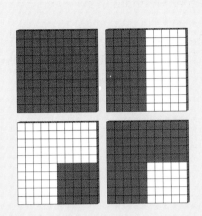

Each of these squares contains 100 smaller squares. The shaded areas can be represented by decimal numbers. The square at the top left, with all 100 squares shaded, is represented by 100 hundredths, or 1.00. The square at the top right, with 50 squares shaded, is represented by 500 hundredths, or 0.50. What proportion of the square at the top right is shaded? Half of it. It shows you clearly that $0.50 = \frac{50}{100} = \frac{1}{2}$.

What can we say about the square at the bottom left? Of its 100 squares, how many are shaded? 25. The decimal number representing that proportion is 0.25. Those smaller squares make up one-fourth of the full square, showing how $0.25 = \frac{25}{100} = \frac{1}{4}$.

What about the square at the bottom right? How many smaller squares are shaded? 75. What proportion of the total is shaded? $\frac{3}{4}$. This shows that $0.75 = \frac{75}{100} = \frac{3}{4}$.

Multiplying and Dividing Amounts of Money

Now that you've learned about decimals, you can multiply and divide amounts of money the same way you multiply and divide other numbers. Here are two examples.

$$
\begin{array}{r}
3\,2 \\
\$9.97 \\
\times \quad 4 \\
\hline
\$39.88
\end{array}
$$

$$
\begin{array}{r}
\$3.31 \\
5\,\overline{)\$16.55} \\
-15 \\
\hline
15 \\
-15 \\
\hline
05 \\
-5 \\
\hline
0
\end{array}
$$

Remember to write the dollar sign and the cents point in your answer.

Word Problems

In word problems, the important step is deciding what mathematical problem you need to solve. Once you can write the problem in numbers, then you can solve it.

You have already done problems that ask you to add, subtract, multiply, or divide. Sometimes you have to do two different operations in the same problem. These are called two-step problems.

A Two-Step Word Problem

Lisa has saved up $28.50. For a party, she buys 8 party favors. Each favor costs her $2.39. How much money does she have left after buying the favors?

First you have to multiply, to find out how much the party favors cost her in all.

You multiply amounts of money the same way you multiply other numbers. Include the cents point and the dollar sign in the product when you are done.

$$
\begin{array}{r}
3\ \ 7 \\
\$2\,.\,3\,9 \\
\times\quad 8 \\
\hline
\$1\,9\,.\,1\,2
\end{array}
$$

Then you have to subtract, to find out how much money she has left.

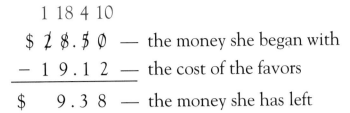

1 18 4 10

$ 2 8 . 5 0 — the money she began with

− 1 9 . 1 2 — the cost of the favors
_____

$ 9 . 3 8 — the money she has left

An Estimation Problem

Sometimes you do not need to know an exact answer for a word problem. You can estimate. Here is an example.

Kim has $20.00. She wants to buy a purse for $13.49 and a bracelet for $8.98. Does she have enough money?

Estimate: $8.98 is about $9.00 $ 9.00

$13.49 is about $13.00   + 13.00
_____

$ 22.00

The purse and the bracelet together cost about $22.00. So Kim does not have quite enough money.

If your answer is close when you estimate, you need to figure the problem out exactly. For example, if the cost of the purse and the bracelet came to about $19.00 or $20.00, you would have to add up exactly how much they cost to answer the problem.

A Problem Where You Need to Guess

Black mollies cost 85¢ and goldfish cost 99¢. Lewis buys some black mollies and some goldfish, 5 in all. He pays $4.53. How many of each kind of fish does he buy?

You must make a guess to start. Guess that he buys 2 black mollies. Then he must buy 3 goldfish. How much will these cost?

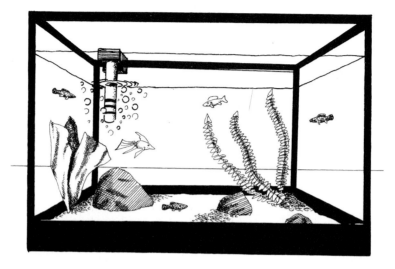

$$(2 \times 85¢) + (3 \times 99¢) = 170¢ + 297¢ = 467¢ \text{ or } \$4.67$$

$4.67 is too much. Try another guess. Lewis buys 3 black mollies and 2 goldfish.

$$(3 \times 85¢) + (2 \times 99¢) = 255¢ + 198¢ = 453¢ \text{ or } \$4.53$$

The second guess is correct. He buys 3 black mollies and 2 goldfish.

VI.

Science

INTRODUCTION

Children gain knowledge about the world by linking reading with observation and experience. They should be encouraged to view the world scientifically: to ask questions about nature; to seek answers through observation and study; to collect, count, measure, and make qualitative observations.

As children amass information, their hypotheses may be based on intuition more than solid knowledge. Balancing a child's personal observations with well-expressed scientific fundamentals will guide his or her understanding in the right direction. Book learning also provides knowledge not likely to be gained by simple observations, such as the nature of the planets and the universe or the structure of a cell.

The topics that follow are consistent with those offered to children in countries that have had outstanding results from teaching science in the elementary grades. Also included are biographies of people who have contributed to our advancement in science, from the Renaissance astronomer Copernicus to the modern astronaut Mae Jemison. A list of further resources can help you take your child's investigations of science even further.

Suggested Resources

Catherine Headlam, ed., *Kingfisher Science Encyclopedia* (Kingfisher Books). Third graders will need some help with the language in this book, but ample illustrations complement every entry.

Let's Read and Find Out series (HarperCollins). These inexpensive yet attractive books, categorized according to level of reading difficulty, reliably convey information on a wide range of scientific topics.

Classifying Animals

What Do They Have in Common?

An owl isn't much like a goldfish, and you would never mistake a whale for a butterfly! Even though these creatures are very different, they all have something in common. They are all living creatures that move and breathe and have babies. They are all animals.

Now, name a kind of bird. Eagle, robin, blue jay, flamingo, ostrich, duck—there are so many different kinds of birds. They come in different sizes and different colors. Some are dull brown, and some are brightly colored. But whatever their size or color, they all have feathers and wings, and they all lay eggs. That is what makes them all birds.

Name a kind of insect. You have many to choose from: ants, honeybees, ladybugs, flies, crickets. Do you remember what insects have in common? All insects have six legs, three main body sections, and a tough exoskeleton. No matter whether they are black or green, or whether they have dots or stripes, or whether they have wings or no wings—as long as they have six legs, three body sections, and an exoskeleton, they are insects.

Whenever you group things that have a lot in common, you are *classifying*. When we classify things, it helps us understand and talk about them. Many living things can be classified as animals: horses, dogs, cats, monkeys, robins, flies, whales, jellyfish, worms, and even you! But what about pine trees or rosebushes or blades of grass? They're not animals. They are plants.

When scientists want to classify the living things in the world, they begin by dividing things into these two very big groups: animals and plants. (They use other big groups as well, which you'll learn about in a later grade.)

Does It Have a Backbone?

When we classify things, we often need to take a big group, such as animals, and break it into smaller groups. Scientists classify animals into two smaller groups by examining their skeletons. Reach your hand around behind you and run your fingers up and down the center of your back. That long, bumpy ridge you feel is your backbone, which is also called your spine. It is made of a stack of small bones, each one called a *vertebra* [VUR-tuh-bra]. That is why animals with backbones are called *vertebrates* [VUR-tuh-bruts].

Where is the backbone on this child's skeleton?

You have a backbone. So does a horse, a dog, a cat, a fish, a bird, and a frog. Many animals have backbones, but many do not. An animal that does not have a backbone is called an *invertebrate*, a word that means "no backbone." Can you think of an animal with no backbone? How about a little creature that droops like a noodle and slithers through the dirt? That's right, an earthworm does not have a backbone. Neither does a moth, an oyster, or a spider. They are all invertebrates.

Now you know how scientists divide animals into two big groups: invertebrates (which have no backbone) and vertebrates (which do have a backbone).

Classifying the Vertebrates

Now let's see how scientists divide the vertebrates into five smaller groups, called *classes*. The five classes of vertebrates are:

fish   amphibians   reptiles   birds   mammals

Let's learn about what makes a fish a fish, what makes a bird a bird, and so on. As you learn about the different features of each class, try to name some animals in that class.

Cold-Blooded and Warm-Blooded

Fish, amphibians, and reptiles are *cold-blooded*. Birds and mammals are *warm-blooded*. What do we mean by cold-blooded and warm-blooded?

Snakes are cold-blooded animals, which means that their body temperature changes according to the temperature around them.

Some animals get the warmth they need from the air or water around them. When it's hot outside, their body temperatures rise. When it's cold, their body temperatures drop. These animals are called *cold-blooded*. It doesn't mean that their blood is always cold. It means their body temperatures go up or down depending on the temperature around them.

Other animals stay nearly the same temperature no matter whether the air around them is hot or cold. These animals are called *warm-blooded*. Mammals and birds are warm-blooded.

Are you cold-blooded or warm-blooded? On winter days, you might shiver with cold, and on summer days, you might feel like you're about to melt, but your body temperature normally stays right around 98.6° Fahrenheit. So that makes you warm-blooded.

Fish

- Fish are cold-blooded.
- Fish live in water.
- Fish use gills to take oxygen from the water.
- Most fish are covered with scales.
- Most fish hatch from eggs laid by the female outside her body.
- Goldfish, trout, and sharks are different kinds of fish.

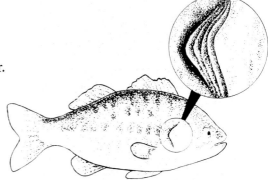

This picture shows the gills of a fish. With their gills, fish get oxygen from the water.

Amphibians

Baby frogs, or tadpoles, live underwater.
Frogs live on land when they grow up.
See how the tadpole is growing into a frog?
Frogs are amphibians.

- Amphibians are cold-blooded.
- Amphibians live part of their lives in water and part on land. (The word "amphibian" means "living in two places.")
- When they are young, amphibians have gills to take oxygen from the water. When they grow up, most amphibians develop lungs that allow them to take oxygen from the air.
- Amphibians usually have moist skin with no scales.
- Frogs, toads, and salamanders are amphibians.

Reptiles

This sea turtle is a reptile.

- Reptiles are cold-blooded.
- Reptiles have dry, thick, scaly skin.
- Reptiles breathe with lungs.
- Reptiles hatch from eggs.
- Snakes, lizards, and turtles are reptiles.

Birds

Most birds feed their young until they are big enough to leave the nest and survive on their own.

- Birds are warm-blooded.
- Birds have feathers and wings.
- Most birds can fly.
- Birds breathe with lungs.
- Birds hatch from eggs. Most birds build nests in which to lay their eggs.
- Robins, cardinals, chickens, and eagles are birds.

Mammals

- Mammals are warm-blooded.
- Mammals have hair on their bodies.
- Mammals breathe with lungs.
- Baby mammals need care and feeding

Pigs are mammals. Mother pigs produce milk for their babies.

- Female mammals produce milk for their young. (Mammals are the only animals that do this.)
- Horses, cats, dogs, monkeys, and humans are mammals.
- Most mammals live on land, although some mammals live in water. Whales and dolphins live in the water, but they are not fish. They breathe with lungs, not gills, and they need to come to the surface to breathe air. They are mammals.

Some mammals, like this humpback whale, swim deep underwater. Whales breathe with lungs, so they swim up to the surface for air.

The Human Body: The Skeletal and Muscular Systems

Muscle and Bone

Imagine that you're eating a nice golden fried chicken drumstick. (Or, if you're a vegetarian, imagine someone else eating that drumstick!) The drumstick has skin, muscle, and bone. When you eat the meat, do you know what you're eating? You are eating muscle.

See all the muscles in this picture?
Can you feel any of them in your own body?

Do you know what part of a chicken the drumstick is? It's the lower leg. Now touch your own lower leg, which is also called your calf, between your knee and your ankle. Your calf has skin, muscle, and bone, too. You can see and touch the skin. You can feel your muscles when you flex your foot. You can feel the hard bone of your shin.

There are two big bones in your lower leg, called the *tibia* and the *fibula*. The bone you feel along your shin is the tibia, the larger of the two lower leg bones. The fibula is deeper inside your muscle.

Bones and Connections

Most of your body is soft and squishy, but not your bones, which are very hard. Your bones give your body its shape, the way a stiff clothes hanger gives shape to a floppy shirt. Your bones also protect the soft organs inside your body.

Is Your Skeleton Inside or Out?

Insects have an *exoskeleton,* which means that their bodies are made of a tough outer layer surrounding softer insides. Human beings have an *endoskeleton,* which means that their soft skin and muscles surround the hard bones inside their bodies.

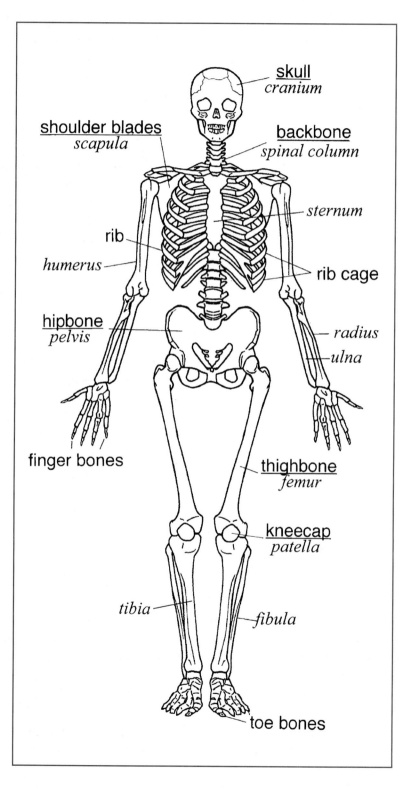

skull
cranium

shoulder blades
scapula

backbone
spinal column

sternum

rib

humerus

rib cage

hipbone
pelvis

radius

ulna

finger bones

thighbone
femur

kneecap
patella

tibia

fibula

toe bones

All your bones put together make up your skeleton. From head to toe, your skeleton is made up of 206 bones. No matter how big or small we are, we all have 206 bones in our body.

Bones come in many shapes and sizes. The biggest bone in your body is your thighbone, also called your *femur* [FEE-mer]. The smallest bone in your body is a tiny little bone inside your ear, called the *stirrup*. It's about the size of a grain of rice!

The front of your knee joint looks like this. Can you see where you bend your knee?

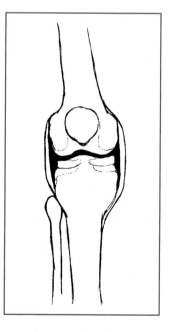

Lift your arm and bend it. Your arm bends at your elbow. Your elbow is a *joint*. A joint is a place where your bones come together. At each joint, the bones are connected by strong, stretchy tissue, like big rubber bands, called *ligaments*. Joints make it possible for you to bend, twist, run, chew, kick a ball, touch your toes, and hold a pencil. Can you point to some other joints in your body?

Touch the tip of your nose. That tough stuff you feel is called *cartilage*. In some places in your body, such as in your knee, cartilage keeps bones from rubbing together. When you were born, your skeleton was made of cartilage. But as you grew up, hard bone replaced the soft cartilage.

Let's learn about your most important bones.

The Skull

The bones in your head are called your *skull*. Your skull surrounds and protects one of the most important organs in your body, your brain. The top part of your skull is called the *cranium*. It is made up of eight bones that fit tightly together to act like a helmet around your brain.

The Spinal Column

Run your hand gently down the center of a friend's back and feel how bumpy it is. Those bumps are your twenty-four *vertebrae*, stacked on top of one another. Stretchy ligaments join the vertebrae into a long, flexible chain of bones called the *spinal column*, the spine, or the backbone. A thick pad of cartilage provides a cushion between each vertebra.

When someone tells you to stand tall and strong, you straighten your spinal column. Your spinal column helps hold up your head and upper body. Your spine can bend forward, back, and sideways. It can swivel in both directions. All of these movements are possible because of the way the bones, ligaments, and cartilage join.

The Ribs

Start just under your armpits and run your fingers along your sides. Do you feel *ribs*? Your ribs connect with cartilage to a hard bone in the center of your chest called the *sternum*, or breastbone. From your sternum, your ribs curve around and connect to your spinal column in the back. You have twelve ribs on each side of your body, and together they form your *rib cage*. Your rib cage is a strong yet flexible set of bones that protects your lungs, heart, and stomach.

The Scapula

How many ways can you move your arms? You can point down to the ground. You can lift your arms above your head. You can swing your arms forward and back. Your arms can move in all these directions because of the way they are attached to your body at the shoulder bone, or *scapula* [SKAP-yuh-luh]. The word "scapula" comes from the Latin word for "shovel." Your scapula looks sort of like the blade of a shovel. It's a big, flat, triangle-shaped bone that joins the arm to the spine. People often call the scapula the shoulder blade.

The Pelvis

When you sit down, stand up, walk, or run, you are moving your *pelvis*. The pelvis is a set of bones at your hips. Your legs connect to your upper body at the pelvis. The word "pelvis" comes from the Latin word for "basin" or "sink." If you look at the pelvis on a skeleton, you can see why that name fits. The bones that make up the pelvis come together in a shape like a big bowl. The bowl shape of the pelvis protects your intestines and other digestive organs. When a baby is growing inside a mother's body, the mother's pelvis cradles the baby until birth.

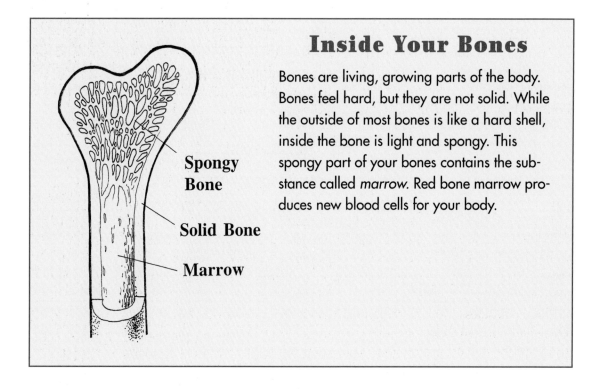

Inside Your Bones

Bones are living, growing parts of the body. Bones feel hard, but they are not solid. While the outside of most bones is like a hard shell, inside the bone is light and spongy. This spongy part of your bones contains the substance called *marrow*. Red bone marrow produces new blood cells for your body.

Spongy Bone

Solid Bone

Marrow

Will You Sign My Cast?

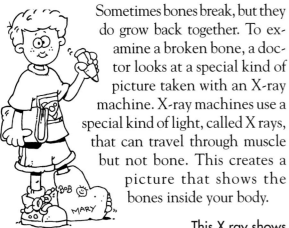

Sometimes bones break, but they do grow back together. To examine a broken bone, a doctor looks at a special kind of picture taken with an X-ray machine. X-ray machines use a special kind of light, called X rays, that can travel through muscle but not bone. This creates a picture that shows the bones inside your body.

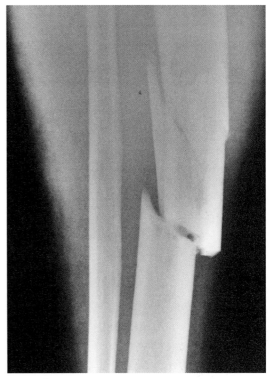

This X ray shows a broken tibia, which is the larger of the two bones in the lower leg.

Here's an X ray of Harry's leg after he broke it. To help it heal, Harry's doctor carefully lined up the broken pieces of bone. Then she put a cast around his calf. Harry had to wear the cast for six weeks to hold the bone in place and protect it while new bone cells were growing.

Many Muscles

Let's pretend that you're a powerful Olympic athlete. Now, show me your muscles—stand up, stretch out your arms, then bend them at the elbow as you curl your fists toward your head.

When you do that, you are tightening the muscles on the upper part of each arm, called the *biceps* [BIE-seps]. So you've shown me two of your muscles. But did you know you have about 650 muscles in your body?

Some muscles, such as the ones in your ears, are as tiny as a thread. Other muscles, such as the hamstring muscles in the back of your leg, are thick and wide. Where do you think your biggest muscle is? It's called the *gluteus maximus* [GLOO-tee-us MAX-i-mus], and it's the muscle you sit down on (your rear end).

You use hundreds of different muscles when you play baseball or any other sport. Exercise helps keep your muscles strong.

You use your muscles when you walk, run, jump, swim, skate, play soccer, or ride a bicycle. Every time you move, you use your muscles.

Even when you're not exercising, you use muscles. When you read, your neck muscles hold your head up and your eye muscles move your gaze across the page. When you smile, you use about fifteen different face muscles. When you frown, you use more than forty different face muscles. So smile—it's easier than frowning!

When you bend your arm, your biceps muscle tightens. See it in the picture? Bend your arm and feel your own biceps tighten. When you straighten your arm, your biceps relaxes and your triceps muscle tightens. Can you point to the triceps in this picture? Can you feel it in your arm?

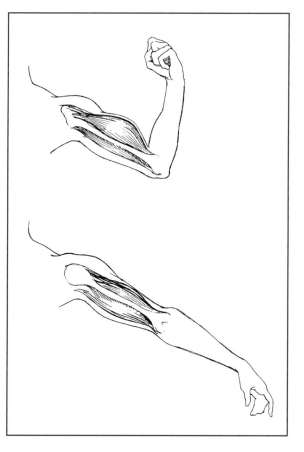

When you move, your muscles work in pairs. When you bend your arm, you tighten your biceps, while another muscle on the lower part of your arm, called the *triceps*, relaxes. When you stretch your arm out straight again, the opposite occurs: the biceps relaxes and the triceps tightens.

That's how many muscles work in your body. When one pulls tight, a companion muscle relaxes.

Voluntary and Involuntary Muscles

When you tighten your biceps, you use *voluntary* muscles. Voluntary muscles are the ones you can control. You can choose whether to kick a ball or raise your hand or sit down. Whenever you do these things, you are using voluntary muscles.

But your body also depends on many muscles that move whether or not you want them to. These are called *involuntary* muscles. For example, your heart is an involuntary muscle. It keeps on pumping blood without your telling it when to do so. Involuntary muscles in your intestines work automatically to help you digest the food you eat. Involuntary muscles work all the time, whether you're awake or asleep, and whether or not you think about them.

Connecting Muscles and Bones

Muscles make you move by pulling on the bones of your skeleton. To do this, the muscles must be attached to the bones. Throughout your body, strong fibers called *tendons* connect muscles to bones.

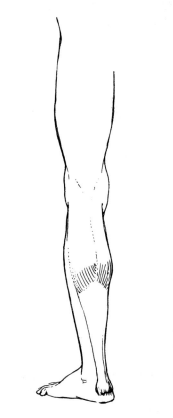

Your largest and strongest tendon is called the *Achilles* [ah-KIL-eez] *tendon*. It connects your calf muscle to your heel bone. It's easy to find your Achilles tendon. Gently pinch the back of your foot, just above your heel. Do you feel something like a strong, tough rope? Wag your foot up and down and feel how the Achilles tendon stretches and relaxes.

The Achilles tendon stretches from the calf to the heel.

Why is it called the Achilles tendon? A myth from ancient Greece tells of a boy named Achilles who would become a great warrior. When he was a baby, his mother dipped him in the river Styx. She believed its water would protect him from all harm. But when she dipped him, one part of his body never touched the water—his heel.

Achilles grew up to become a great hero in the Trojan War. It seemed that no sword, spear, or arrow could harm him. But when a poisoned arrow pierced his heel, he died. Today people still use the phrase "Achilles' heel" to refer to a person's special weakness.

The Human Body: The Brain and Nervous System

Your Powerful Brain

Inside your body there's an organ that you use to think, talk, listen, look, hear, smell, taste, dream, feel, decide, and remember. Sounds like a computer, a telephone, a camera, a television, and a scrapbook all wrapped up in one, doesn't it? It's your brain, which connects with your nerves to do all these things.

Your brain is in charge of everything you do. It's sort of like the president of your body. It keeps your heart beating. It makes sense of the information coming to it from your sensory organs—your eyes, ears, nose, tongue, and skin. It sends orders all over your body. It stores information in memory, such as the aroma of orange peel, your best friend's favorite color, or the way to solve the math problems you learned last week.

The human brain has three main parts.

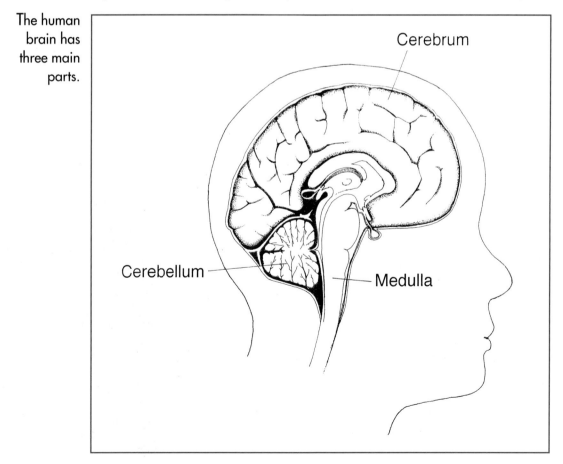

A groove runs down the middle of your cerebrum and divides it into two halves, right and left. Here's a curious fact: The right half of your cerebrum controls the left half of your body, while the left half of your cerebrum controls the right half of your body.

The human brain is a pinkish-gray, wrinkled, spongy organ. An adult's brain weighs about three pounds. The brain is divided into three main parts, which you can see in the picture. The *cerebrum* [suh-REE-brum] is by far the biggest section, about nine-tenths of your brain. Most brain activity takes place in the outer layer of the cerebrum, called the *cerebral cortex*. It's full of deep, wiggly grooves. Different parts of the cerebrum do different things. Some parts understand speech, other parts store memories, others control appetite, others control eye movements, and so on.

Deep in the back of your brain lies the *cerebellum* [ser-uh-BELL-um]. It coordinates your balance and movements. When you first ride a bicycle, for example, you have to concentrate really hard. Soon you learn to balance and move your body easily, without even thinking about what you're doing. When that happens, your cerebellum is in control.

The *medulla* [me-DOO-la], or brain stem, lies even deeper than the cerebellum. It controls involuntary body functions. These are the functions that go on without your choosing to do them, such as your heartbeat, breathing, and digestion.

You've Got Nerves

You've probably seen telephone wires running from pole to pole, carrying messages back and forth from homes and businesses all over. If you imagine your brain as your central communications headquarters, then you can think of your nerves as the wires running throughout your body.

What signals might be traveling through this boy's nervous system?

The medulla connects your brain to a thick bundle of nerve fibers called your *spinal cord*. The spinal cord runs through your backbone, through a hole in each vertebra. The spinal cord connects to many nerves that stretch throughout your body, branching out to your legs, arms, toes, and fingers.

Your nerves carry messages back and forth to and from your brain. How does this work? Let's see what happens in the nervous system when you lean down toward a rose. First your eyes send signals along special nerves to the brain. Your brain recognizes the image of a flower, then compares the image with others in your memory and recalls that this kind of flower often has a pleasant smell. Your brain sends signals through your spinal cord and nerves to many muscles, giving the orders that make you bend toward the flower. Your brain then sends a message to breathe in deeply. The scent of the rose comes into your nose, then signals of that scent travel through nerves to your brain. Ah, the sweet smell of a beautiful rose!

Reflex Responses

Imagine that you've just sniffed that lovely rose. You reach to bring the flower close to you when suddenly a sharp thorn pricks your thumb. Without thinking, you jerk your hand away.

When this happens, it is called a *reflex action*. Reflex actions happen almost instantly, without the brain's sending a message to perform the action.

When you touched the sharp thorn, a signal of pain raced from your finger to your spinal cord, which then sent back an immediate command to your muscles, saying, "Pull back!" Your body didn't wait for your brain to receive the pain message and respond to it. Instead, your reflexes took over and saved you from feeling even more pain. Your reflexes will work the same way if, for example, you accidentally touch something hot, such as a pan that's just been taken out of the oven.

A doctor may use a soft rubber hammer near your knee to test your reflexes.

Has a doctor ever tested your reflexes? Try this. Sit in a chair and cross one leg loosely over the other. Ask someone to give you a *gentle* "karate chop" just below the kneecap. If the chop comes gently in just the right place, your leg will kick out automatically. You didn't have to think about it—it's a reflex.

Other common reflex actions are blinking and sneezing.

Light and Vision

Fast and Straight

You walk into a dark room, flip on the light switch, and *presto*, the room instantly fills with light. It seems to happen all at once. That's because light travels fast—*amazingly* fast! The speed of light is 186,000 miles *per second*. Light travels so fast that in the time it takes you to blink your eyes three times, light could travel to the moon and back.

Rays of light travel in straight lines. You can see this by making shadows. In a darkened room, shine a desk lamp or flashlight at a wall. Now hold this book in front of the light. What happens? The light doesn't bend or curve around the book. Instead, the book blocks the rays of light, which are traveling in straight lines. That's why you see the shadow of your book on the wall.

Do you like to make shadow figures? How does it happen? The light rays don't bend. Your hand blocks the rays of light coming from the lamp and casts a shadow.

Your book does not let light pass through it because it is *opaque* [oh-PAKE]. Opaque materials block light. A wooden door is opaque. So is a metal can. Can you name some other things that are opaque?

Some materials are the opposite of opaque: they are *transparent*. Transparent materials are clear. You can see through them. They let light pass through almost unchanged. Glass and water are transparent.

Mirrors Flat and Curved

When you need to look your best, you wash your face, comb your hair, then look at your reflection in a mirror.

A mirror *reflects* light, which means that it bounces back the light that hits it. How does this happen? First the light passes through the transparent glass part of a mirror. The back of the glass is coated with a special silver paint. When the light hits the silver surface, it bounces back through the glass. Shine a flashlight at a mirror, and you can see how almost all the light is reflected.

The mirrors that hang on the walls at home or school are flat mirrors. A flat mirror is also called a *plane* mirror. When you look in a flat mirror, you see a reflection that looks almost exactly like yourself. But even though you see a clear image of your smiling face,

Lenses can make things look bigger or smaller. Have you ever looked through a pair of binoculars? Binoculars use lenses to make faraway things look bigger. But what happens when you look through binoculars backward? They make things appear smaller.

Because of lenses, we can see the world better than we ever could with only our eyes. Lenses in telescopes help us see far away, as far away as the moon, planets, and stars. Lenses

in microscopes help us see tiny things close-up, including things we cannot see with our eyes alone, such as the cells in our body or the little creatures that live in a drop of pond water.

Lenses, lenses everywhere! How many different lenses do you see in this picture?

What Color Is Light?

What color is sunlight? You might think it has no color at all. But scientists call the light that comes from the sun *white light*. What's amazing is, the white light of sunshine is actually made up of all the colors in the rainbow!

You can prove it if you have a wedge-shaped piece of clear glass called a *prism*. If you hold the prism near a sunny window, the light will shine through and make a rainbow-like band of colors. This shows that even though light may appear to be white or color-less, light is really made up of *all* colors.

When light goes through a prism, the glass slows it down and changes its path. The process is called *refraction*. A prism refracts the light. A lens refracts the light. Remember the glass of water with the pencil in it? Both the water and the glass are refracting the light.

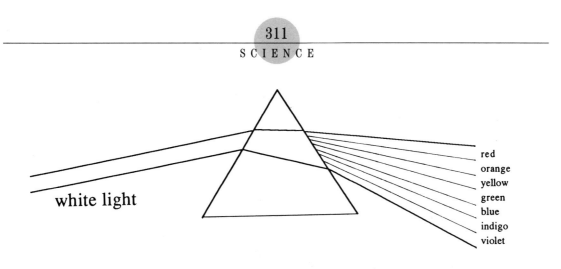

A prism separates white light into the spectrum of colors.
The prism bends the rays of light, but rays of each color bend differently.
Red bends the least. Violet bends the most.

Raindrops in the sky refract the light, which is what causes a rainbow. When light is refracted, it often separates into a combination of colors called the *spectrum*. The colors of the spectrum always appear in the same order: red, orange, yellow, green, blue, indigo, and violet. You can use a funny name to help you remember that order: "Roy G. Biv."

How Your Eyes See

Close your eyes and what do you see? Nothing, of course! But why? You might say, "Because my eyes are closed, silly!" Or you could answer, "Because no light is coming into my eyes."

Somewhere Over the Rainbow

Is there a pot of gold at the end of a rainbow? Rainbows are so unusual and beautiful that you almost want to believe the magical stories about them.

When you see a rainbow in the sky, you see sunlight reflected off water droplets in the sky. The droplets work like prisms to refract the sunlight and separate it into colors. If you've been lucky enough to see a rainbow more than once, you might have noticed that rainbow colors always come in the same order as the color of the spectrum, from red to violet. On a sunny day, you can make a little rainbow by turning on a hose and putting your thumb over the end to make the water come out as a mist. When the light bounces off the droplets of mist, you should see your own little rainbow.

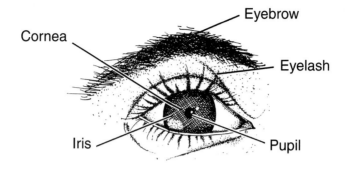

The parts of an eye.

You see things because light bounces off them, and then this light enters your eyes. Another way of saying this is that things reflect light, and we see the reflected light. But that's just the beginning. Let's find out what happens when you see.

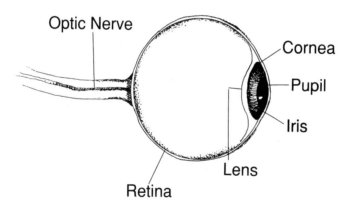

A cross section of the eyeball.

Look at the picture of the eyeball and its parts. Rays of light first pass through your *cornea* [KOR-nee-uh], a transparent covering on the outside of your eye. (Remember, "transparent" means "clear" or "see-through," like glass.) Next the light goes through the *pupil*, which is a hole in the middle of the *iris*. The iris, the colored part of your eye, helps the pupil open and close. On a bright sunny day, the iris makes the pupil grow smaller to let in less light. In a dark room, such as a theater, the iris makes the pupil grow wider to let in more light. (By the way, the iris is an *involuntary* muscle—it works without your thinking about it.)

After light rays pass through the iris, they go through the *lens*. Muscles attached to the lens change its shape just a little bit, to help the lens focus. The lens focuses the light rays onto the surface at the back of the eyeball, called the *retina* [RET-in-ah].

Inside the retina, light rays change into electrical signals. These signals travel along the *optic nerve* to your brain. The brain makes sense of the signals and recognizes the image as, for example, a tree, cat, car, or the letters on this page. It all happens so fast you don't even notice. All you do is open your eyes and see.

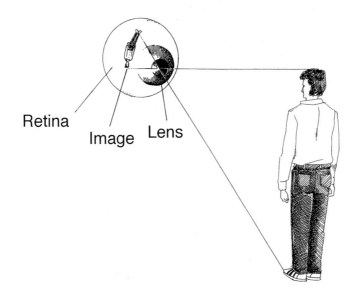

Retina

Image   Lens

Light passes through the lens in the eye and makes an upside-down image on the retina. Then why don't we see things upside down? Because the brain turns that image right side up. Smart brain!

Getting in Focus

In some people's eyes, the lenses don't change and focus as well as they should. Those are the people who need glasses. A person who can see things close-up but needs glasses to focus on things far away is called *nearsighted*. A person who can see things far away but needs glasses to focus on things close-by—in order to read, for example—is called *farsighted*. Glasses made of differently shaped lenses correct each of those seeing problems.

There are even glasses designed to help people see both far away and close-up. They are called *bifocals*. Can you guess why? Here's a hint: The prefix "bi-" means "two." Bifocal glasses are made from two differently shaped lenses. They help a person's eyes focus in two different ways, to see close-up and to see far away.

Look Deep into My Iris

The iris, the colorful part of your eye, gets its name from Iris, the goddess of the rainbow in ancient Greek mythology. Look at your eyes in a mirror. What color are they? Brown, blue, green? The parts of your eye that you can see make up only a small portion of the entire eyeball. Much of the eye is inside the skull, protected behind hard bone.

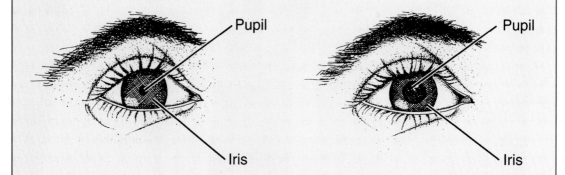

The pupil opens and closes to let more or less light into the eye, responding to the amount of light coming into it. Which picture shows the eye on a bright, sunny day? Which shows the eye in a dark room?

Want to see your iris at work? Go into the bathroom and turn the light on. Look at your eyes in the mirror and see how small the pupil is (the black circle in the center of your eye). Now turn the light off and count slowly to twenty. Flip the light back on and—quick!—look at your pupils. They grew larger in the dark, because of the work of the iris muscle.

Sound and Hearing

Good Vibrations

An alarm clock rings, a dog barks, a voice calls, "Time to get up!" Every day is full of familiar sounds. But what exactly *is* sound?

Sound is caused by a back-and-forth movement called *vibration*. Try this. Close your lips and hum. While you're humming, feel your throat under your chin. Do you feel a tingling? It is caused by something moving back and forth very fast. When you hum, the vocal cords in your throat are vibrating back and forth, which makes the air around them vibrate. These vibrations of air strike your eardrums and make them vibrate, to create the sound you hear.

Here's a way you can see how sound makes the air vibrate. Stretch a piece of plastic wrap over the surface of a bowl and fasten it tightly with a rubber band. Sprinkle a few grains of dry sand or rice on the plastic. Now take a big pan, hold it near the bowl, and strike it with a spoon a few times. Do you see the grains jump when you hit the pan? That is because the pan is vibrating, which causes the air and then the plastic to vibrate. We call the vibrating air *sound waves*. When you hit the pan, sound waves travel through the air and cause the plastic to vibrate, which in turn makes the grains jump.

Sound waves move out from a vibrating object in all directions, making the air move back and forth in a way that we can't see. Sounds *compress* and *decompress* the air, pushing and then relaxing, making invisible vibrations. Those back-and-forth vibrations spread out from the source that made them, getting weaker as they get farther away. That's why you hear your friend standing right next to you more clearly than you hear someone calling from across the street.

What Does Sound Travel Through?

Sound can travel through all kinds of matter: through gases, through liquids, and through solids. Every time you speak, you prove that sound travels through gases, since the sound of your voice is traveling through air, which is made of gases like oxygen.

Can you think of an example that proves sound travels through liquid? Have you ever heard someone's voice underwater in a swimming pool? It sounded funny, but you could hear it. That sound was traveling through a liquid. Some animals, like whales and dolphins, depend upon sound that travels through the water. Whales sing underwater and can hear each other from more than a mile away.

At first, you might not think that sound travels through solids, since we build walls to keep out sounds. But in your room, sometimes you hear laughter or talking from the room next door, don't you?

Lightly touch your fingertips to the side of a radio, television, or stereo speaker when the sound is coming out. Do you feel the vibrations?

Try this. Drum your fingers on a table. Now rest your ear right on the table's surface and drum your fingers on it again. Doesn't it sound louder? That's because the sound is traveling through the solid table.

When the Native Americans of the Great Plains hunted for buffalo, they would sometimes put their ears to the ground. Why do you think they did this? Think about how sounds travel through solids. The hunters might not hear the sound of faraway hoofbeats in the air, but they could hear the sound as it traveled through the solid earth.

The Speed of Sound

Remember how fast light travels? Faster than anything else—an amazing 186,000 miles per second. Sound travels much more slowly than light. In air, sound travels at about 1,086 feet per second, or about 740 miles per hour. Of course, that's still very fast compared to a car going 55 miles per hour on the highway! But there are jets that can fly as fast as the speed of sound. When these jets go even faster than the speed of sound, we say that they have "broken the sound barrier."

Voices from a Distance

Our word "telephone" comes from two old Greek words: *tele,* which means "at a distance," and *phone,* which means "sound."

You can make your own telephone that will let you hear a friend's voice at a distance. You'll need two paper or plastic cups, two paper clips, and about twenty feet of string or strong thread. Have an adult help you poke a small hole in the bottom of each cup. Stick one end of the string into each hole, and knot it tightly around a paper clip. You take one cup and your friend takes the other. Walk apart from one another until the string stretches out straight and tight. Now when you talk into your "telephone," your friend should be able to hear you.

How does this work? Remember, sound can travel through solids. When you talk into the cup, you make it vibrate. The vibrating cup makes the string vibrate. The vibrating string makes the bottom of the other cup vibrate. Those vibrations go into your friend's ear, and that's when your friend hears the sound of your voice.

Here's an example that shows how light travels faster than sound. During a thunderstorm, a crash of thunder and a bolt of lightning happen at the same time. When you're far away, though, you see the lightning before you hear the thunder. Why? Because the light traveled faster to your eyes than the sound did to your ears.

Loud and Quiet

If you're listening to the radio and a favorite song comes on, you might say, "Turn it up!" and reach for the knob marked VOLUME.

When you turn up the volume, you are making the sound louder. A scientist might say that you are increasing the sound's *intensity*. How far away you can hear a sound depends on its intensity. A quiet sound, like a whisper, doesn't travel very far. But a really loud sound can travel for hundreds of miles. More than a hundred years ago, when a volcano exploded on the island of Krakatoa, the sound could be heard in Australia, almost three thousand miles away!

How would you arrange these sounds in order of intensity, from quietest to loudest?

a doorbell
a lawn mower
a whisper
a rocket blasting off
a dog barking

High and Low

How high is the highest pitch you can sing?

Pretend that you're an opera star. Sing the highest note you can sing. Now sing the lowest. When we describe how high or low a sound is, we are talking about the sound's *pitch*. A bird singing makes a high-pitched sound. A dog growling makes a low-pitched sound. Think of a flute and a tuba. Which instrument makes high-pitched sounds? Which makes low-pitched sounds?

When you sing a high note, your vocal cords vibrate very fast. When you sing a low note, your vocal cords vibrate more slowly. Faster vibrations make a sound with a higher pitch. Slower vibrations make a sound with a lower pitch.

Try this. Take a large rubber band and loop it around a drawer knob. Pull it tight and pluck it. Now loosen it and pluck it again. Can you hear the difference? When it's pulled

318

WHAT YOUR THIRD GRADER NEEDS TO KNOW

> You carry a noisemaker around with you wherever you go. It's called your *larynx* [LAIR-inks], or voice box, and it's in your throat. When you felt your throat and hummed, you were feeling the vibration of your larynx.
>
> How does your body make a sound? Air travels from your lungs and past your vocal cords, which stretch open and shut like two thick rubber bands inside your larynx. You use muscles to relax or tighten your vocal cords, which changes the pitch of your voice from low to high. You use your tongue, teeth, and lips to form words.

tight, the rubber band makes a higher-pitched sound. Is the rubber band vibrating faster when it's loose or when it's pulled tight?

How the Ear Works

Let's find out what happens when sound waves enter your ears.

If you look at someone's head, you see the *outer ear*. The outer ear is made of cartilage. Nature has cleverly designed the outer ear to catch and direct sound waves through an opening into the *ear canal*.

The vibrations travel through the air inside the ear canal to the *eardrum*. Like a drum, the eardrum is made of thin tissue stretched tightly across an opening. Each of your eardrums is only about as big as the fingernail on your little finger. Sound waves enter the ear and make the eardrum vibrate.

Eardrum: Handle with Care

The eardrum is a delicate, airtight seal. *Never* poke anything long or sharp into your ear, because it could damage your eardrum. Extremely loud sounds can damage the eardrum, too. Try not to stand close to loudspeakers, and if you listen to music through headphones, don't turn up the volume too loud. Damaged eardrums are hard to heal. Without healthy eardrums, you won't hear well.

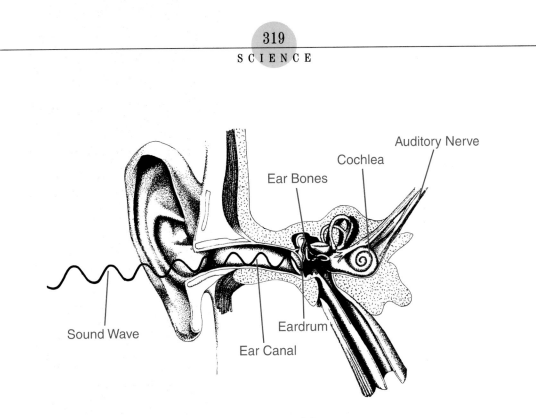

A cross section of the ear.

Next, those vibrations travel through three bones deep inside the ear. They're called the *hammer, anvil,* and *stirrup.* These are the tiniest bones in your body. They get their names from their shapes. The hammer looks like a tiny hammer. The anvil looks like an anvil, the heavy iron surface that a blacksmith uses. And the stirrup is shaped like a stirrup, the metal ring for a horseback rider's foot.

Vibrations are passed from the hammer to the anvil to the stirrup, and then on to the *cochlea* [CAH-clee-uh]. The cochlea is spiral-shaped. Can you find it in the picture? Does its shape remind you of a certain animal? ("Cochlea" comes from the Latin word for "snail.")

The cochlea is filled with liquid, which vibrates as sound enters. When the liquid vibrates, it shakes tiny hairs inside the cochlea. The hairs are connected to nerves that send signals to a big nerve called the *auditory nerve.* The auditory nerve carries the signals to the brain and, *ta-dah!* you hear the sound.

Astronomy

The Universe: Big and Getting Bigger!

On a clear night, go outside and look up at the sky. What do you see? Is the Moon shining? Are the stars twinkling?

There you are, a single small person on this planet called Earth, looking up into the vastness of space. It seems to go on forever. But for every star you see, there are billions more you can't see. On and on the universe goes, stretching out in all directions, farther and bigger than anyone can imagine.

The stars in the universe are grouped into huge *galaxies*. Some galaxies, like ours, are spiral-shaped, like pinwheels. Others look like big oozing blobs of light.

Our Sun is only a single star among the billions of stars that make up the galaxy we live in, which is called the Milky Way. Why is it called the Milky Way? On a dark night, you can sometimes see a fuzzy, milky-white stripe running across the sky. That white stripe is made up of the billions of stars in the Milky Way.

The Andromeda galaxy, as seen through a telescope.

We call the science of outer space, planets, and stars *astronomy*. That word comes from the Greek word *astron*, which means "star."

Beyond the Milky Way, there are billions more stars in the galaxies that are our closest neighbors. One of our close neighbors is the Andromeda galaxy, but don't expect to travel there soon. Even though Andromeda is closer to us than most other galaxies, it is almost 2 million light-years away. That means that light traveling from Andromeda to Earth takes nearly 2 million years to arrive!

Beyond Andromeda, there are still billions more galaxies. Astronomers—the scientists who study outer space—have made an amazing discovery. All these billions of galaxies seem to be flying out and away from each other. In other words, the universe is *growing bigger!*

When astronomers observed how galaxies seem to be flying away from each other, they came up with a theory—an idea, an explanation, based on the evidence—for how the universe began. Their idea, which most scientists accept, is called the Big Bang theory. Many scientists think that about 15 billion years ago all the matter in the universe was packed into a super-dense ball. No one knows exactly what it was or why it happened, but something caused this ball to explode with a big bang. The explosion sent chunks of matter flying out into space. Eventually, this matter became the stars, planets, and everything else in our universe.

Just think—if the Big Bang theory is correct, then all matter came from that super-dense ball that exploded billions of years ago. And since you are made of matter, that means you are made of the stuff of stars!

How Do We Learn About Outer Space?

The biggest telescopes need to be in special buildings in faraway places, where city lights don't make it hard to see out into the night sky. These buildings on the top of a mountain in Arizona house four different telescopes at the Kitt Peak National Observatory.

Astronomers learn about distant planets, stars, and galaxies by looking through powerful *telescopes*, made of lenses and mirrors that let the human eye focus on objects far, far away. As soon as the first telescopes were invented, in the 1600s, people began to observe the stars and planets. What they learned also taught them a lot about this planet of ours called Earth.

Today's astronomers also use another kind of telescope, called a *radio telescope*. Radio telescopes use sound, not sight, to learn about the universe. They collect faint signals from outer space. They gather information that might not be seen through telescope lenses.

The Hubble Space Telescope.

In 1990, the space shuttle put the Hubble Space Telescope into orbit about 370 miles above the earth. The Hubble Space Telescope is about as big as a school bus. It weighs twelve tons. It uses a concave mirror eight feet across to collect light from faraway stars, then radios information about that light back to Earth.

Astronomers also learn a great deal from

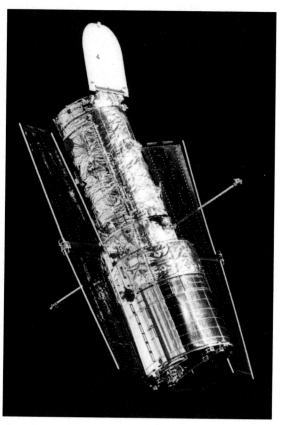

unmanned space probes. These spacecraft carry cameras, computers, and scientific instruments far into space. They send radio signals back to Earth. Sometimes astronomers turn those signals into pictures, like postcards sent from outer space!

Our Solar System

When we say "solar system," what do we mean? We mean all the planets, moons, and other heavenly bodies that circle around our Sun. "Solar" comes from the Latin word *sol*, which means "sun." "System" means a group of things that move and interact with each other. So the "solar system" is the group of planets that move in circles around our Sun.

Hundreds of years ago, people believed that the Sun, the stars, and the other planets circled Earth. Some Greek astronomers guessed that Earth circled the Sun, but their ideas didn't take hold. Then, in the 1500s, a Polish astronomer named Nicolaus Copernicus argued that the Sun, not Earth, was at the center of our solar system. Not many people believed Copernicus during his lifetime, but today no one would argue with him. (You can read more about Copernicus and his ideas on page 345 in this book.)

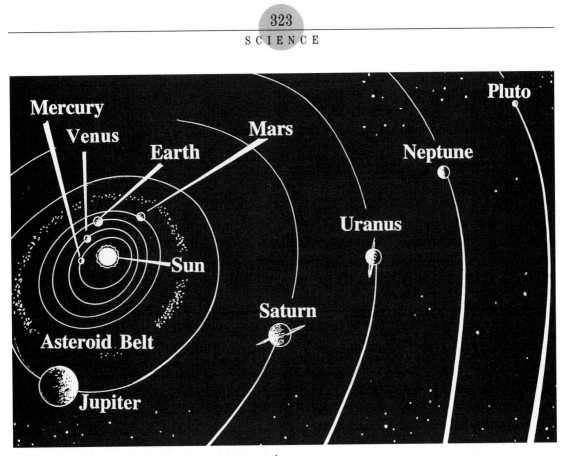

Our solar system.

The Sun is a star like other stars you see at night. The Sun looks bigger and brighter than other stars because it is closer to us. Even though it's the closest star, the Sun is still 93 million miles from Earth.

You know that light travels fast. When you turn on a lamp, think how fast its light reaches your eyes. For the Sun's light to travel 93 million miles to reach us here on Earth, it takes about eight minutes.

How big is Earth compared to the Sun? Picture this: If the Sun were the size of a basketball, Earth would be about as big as the seed of an orange!

Like other stars, the Sun is a giant ball of churning, glowing, exploding gas. On a very hot day on Earth, the temperature might reach 100 degrees Fahrenheit. The surface of the Sun can reach 10,000 degrees Fahrenheit, and astronomers believe that the deep core inside the Sun might be as hot as *27 million degrees!*

The natural world depends upon the energy that comes from the Sun. Without the light and heat we get from the Sun, life simply wouldn't exist. But don't worry. The Sun isn't going anywhere. It's been around for billions of years and will still be around billions of years from now.

Planets in Motion: Orbit and Rotation

Around the Sun travel the nine planets: Mercury, Venus, Earth, Mars, Jupiter, Saturn, Uranus, Neptune, and Pluto. The word "planet" comes from an old Greek word that means "wanderer." But the planets do not wander around the solar system. They travel around the Sun in fixed paths called *orbits*.

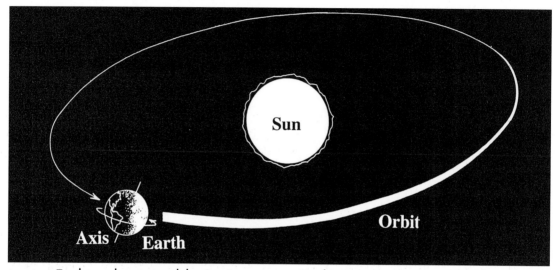

Earth revolves around the Sun in one year. Earth rotates on its axis in one day.

As the planets orbit (go around) the Sun, they also *rotate*. That means they spin around like a top. Like the other planets, Earth both orbits the Sun and rotates. We say that Earth rotates around an *axis*, which is an imaginary pole running through the planet from the North Pole to the South Pole.

If you were to spend a day keeping track of the position of the Sun in the sky, it might appear as though the Sun is moving. Get up early some morning and notice where you see the Sun. A few hours later Earth has rotated so that it looks as though the Sun has moved to a different place in the sky. But really, the Sun isn't moving. It only appears to move because Earth is rotating. When evening comes, notice where the Sun sets. It always sets in the west and rises in the east. We talk about the Sun "rising" and "setting" because that's what the Sun appears to do. But remember: It only looks that way. Earth is moving, not the Sun.

It takes a day for Earth to make one complete spin around its axis. When the place where you live is turned toward the Sun, it is day for you, while it is night for people on the opposite side of Earth. As Earth continues to rotate, the place where you live turns away from the Sun, and it becomes night for you.

Do you know how long it takes for Earth to make one complete orbit around the Sun?

In other words, do you know how long it takes Earth to go around the Sun and come back to where it started? It takes one year (365 days) for Earth to orbit the Sun.

Happy Leap Year

Actually, it takes Earth $365\frac{1}{4}$ days to make one complete orbit around the Sun. To make up for those quarter days, we have *leap years* every fourth year, when the month of February has 29 days instead of 28. That extra day makes up for four quarter days.

The Earth doesn't stand straight up and down on its axis as it spins. It tilts slightly, and this tilt causes the different seasons. When we have summer, our part of Earth is tilting toward the Sun. The tilt means that sunlight shines more directly on us, bringing warm weather. When we have winter, our part of Earth is tilting away from the Sun. This position makes the sunlight shine less directly on us. The areas tilted away from the Sun receive less sunlight. Winter is cold because we get less heat from the Sun.

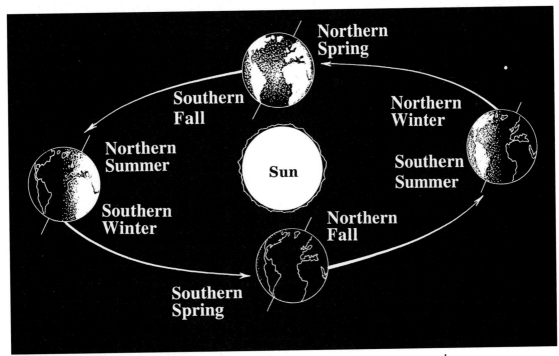

People living in different parts of the globe experience winter and summer in different months of the year. Can you see why?

Try this with a globe and desk lamp. Shine the desk lamp at the equator. Holding the globe at the poles, tilt the top (north) slightly toward the lamp. That's summer for the continents in the Northern Hemisphere, like North America and Europe, when they receive sunshine more directly. Now tilt the top of the globe slightly away from the lamp. This makes the continents in the Southern Hemisphere, like Africa and Australia, receive more direct sunshine. Did you know that when people in North America are enjoying sunny summer days, people in Australia are shivering because it's the middle of winter? Now you know why.

Earth's Satellite: The Moon

Earth orbits the Sun. And what orbits Earth? The Moon. Another way of saying this is that the Moon is a *satellite* of Earth. You may think of a satellite as a device that gets blasted into space by a rocket and then orbits Earth, sending down radio signals and scientific measurements. That's one kind of satellite. In astronomy, the word "satellite" can mean any heavenly body that orbits another. The word "satellite" comes from the Latin for "attendant," meaning someone who waits on an important person.

On some nights, you might look up at the sky and say, "Look, the Moon is shining so brightly!" The Moon may look bright, but it does not make its own light, as the Sun does. The Moon reflects the light cast on it by the Sun.

Moon Shapes

Ask a friend to hold a ball (about the size of a softball) up in the air. Have another friend stand a few feet away and shine a flashlight at it. Now look at the ball. See how one side lights up and the other has a darker shadow? The Moon has a lit-up and a shadowy side, too.

Find a position to stand in where you see half a lit-up ball and half a ball in shadow. That's a way to think about what you're seeing when the half-moon appears in the sky.

Can you find the position to stand to see a crescent of light? That's what you're seeing when the crescent moon appears.

There are nights when no moon appears in the sky at all, even if the sky is clear. That's the time we call the new moon. Of course, the Moon is out there, but you can't see it. In fact, when there's a new moon, the Moon is overhead during the day, but the bright sunlight makes it impossible to see from Earth.

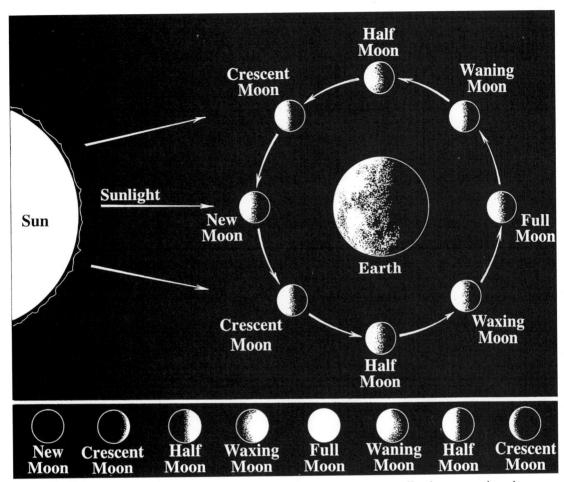

The Moon appears to change shape, but the Moon doesn't actually change. What does happen? The Moon reflects the light of the Sun. Depending on the position of the Moon and Sun to our eyes, we on Earth see all, part, or none of the Moon. With your finger, trace how the Sun's light travels from the Sun to the Moon and then to Earth, where we see it.

Over the course of a month, the Moon may look as if it is changing shape and size, but what changes is the way the Moon reflects sunlight to our eyes on Earth. It takes twenty-nine days for the Moon to go through all its *phases*, from new moon to full moon and back to new moon again. When more of the Moon is becoming visible each night, we say the Moon is *waxing*. When less of the Moon is becoming visible each night, we say it is *waning*. It's fun to pay attention to the Moon every night for a few weeks, to notice how it waxes and wanes.

What is the Moon made of? Not green cheese! The Moon is mostly a big ball of rock. There is no atmosphere on the Moon—no air, no water, no clouds, no rain. Nothing grows on the Moon. All you can see on the lunar landscape are rocks and moon dust.

("Lunar" is a word for anything that has to do with the Moon. It comes from *luna*, the Latin word for the Moon.)

When you were little, did you ever look up at night and see the face of "the Man in the Moon"? It is fun to imagine a face there, even though what you are seeing are huge mountains and craters on the surface of the Moon.

Apollo 11 astronauts Neil A. Armstrong and Edwin E. "Buzz" Aldrin, Jr., left footprints and a flag on the Moon.

Human beings have visited the Moon and walked on its surface. In July of 1969, three American astronauts—Michael Collins, Buzz Aldrin, and Neil Armstrong—blasted off from Cape Kennedy on the Apollo 11 space mission to the Moon. On July 20, Neil Armstrong became the first person to set foot on the Moon. As he stepped from his spacecraft onto the Moon's surface, he said, "That's one small step for a man, one giant leap for mankind."

The Force of Gravity

What keeps the Moon orbiting around Earth instead of floating off into space? *Gravity*. Gravity is a force between bits of matter, attracting every bit to every other bit.

Gravity is the force that keeps your feet on the ground. You may not feel it, but gravity affects you all the time. When you throw a ball up into the air, what happens? No matter how high you throw the ball, it always comes back down. The *gravitational force* between the earth and the ball pulls the ball down to the ground. If it were not for the pull of gravity, the ball would just keep going up. In fact, without gravity, if you jumped, you would keep moving out into space!

Earth's gravity pulls on the Moon, the Moon's gravity pulls on Earth, and those forces keep the Moon in orbit around Earth. In the same way, the Sun's gravity pulls on Earth and the other planets and keeps them in their orbits around the Sun.

The power of the pull of gravity between objects depends on two things: how far apart the objects are and the *mass* of each object—that is, how much matter each object contains. Objects that are close together and objects that have lots of mass attract each other strongly. Things that are far apart and things with small mass attract only weakly.

Gravity is the force of attraction between any two objects that have mass.

Let's think about what these rules mean. If you were on the Moon, you could jump much higher than you can when you are on Earth. You could jump high and slam-dunk a basketball as easily as a seven-foot-tall basketball star. Why? Since the Moon is much smaller than Earth and contains much less matter than Earth, its gravitational pull is weaker than Earth's. With gravity pulling more weakly, you can jump higher. You would even weigh less on the Moon—only about one-sixth of what you weigh here on Earth. Can you figure out, then, how much you would weigh on the Moon?

Although the Moon has less gravity than Earth, its gravity still affects us. The gravity of the Moon (with just a little help from the gravity of the Sun) pulls on the waters of the oceans here on Earth. That gravitational pull causes the *tides*, which are the regular patterns by which the ocean's water level rises and falls.

If you've spent a day at the beach, you've probably noticed the difference between low tide and high tide. At low tide, you can play on a broad, sandy beach. But when high tide comes, the ocean's water level rises and covers part of the beach, leaving less room for you to play. So if your sand castle gets washed out by the tide, blame the Man in the Moon!

Astronomers think there are some places in the universe where the force of gravity is so strong that it captures everything that comes near it. These super-dense places pull in everything—nothing can escape. Their pulling power is so strong that not even light can escape from them, which is why astronomers call these places *black holes*.

When Day Becomes Night: A Solar Eclipse

It's dangerous to look at a solar eclipse, but telescopes can take pictures like this one.

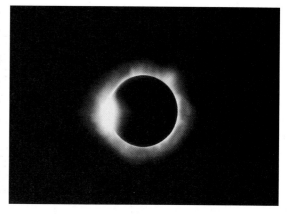

As the Moon orbits Earth, it sometimes moves right between Earth and the Sun. Then the Moon blocks our view of the Sun and casts a shadow on Earth. And when that happens, we on Earth see a *solar eclipse*.

As a solar eclipse begins, it looks as if a dark disk is creeping slowly across the face of the Sun. The disk—which is the Moon—seems just as big as the Sun, but that's because the Moon is so much closer to Earth than the Sun. As more and more of the Moon blocks the light of the Sun, day seems to turn to night, no matter what time it is. The sky darkens. Stars become visible. Some animals curl up and go to sleep.

During a solar eclipse, the Moon passes between Earth and the Sun.

A solar eclipse lasts only a few minutes. The Moon moves out of its position between the Earth and the Sun. The sky brightens. Roosters crow as if it were dawn! Hundreds of years ago, before people understood about the solar system, they were terrified by solar eclipses. They didn't understand why the Sun seemed to be getting darker in the middle of the day.

Even when you're studying the Sun, **never** look directly at it, either with your eyes alone or through binoculars or a telescope. You could damage your eyes or even blind yourself. If you happen to be somewhere where you can see a solar eclipse, here's a simple way to view it safely. Poke a little hole in an index card. Hold it about three feet above a white piece of paper. A little image of the sun will be projected by the hole onto the paper.

When Earth moves between the Moon and the Sun, what do you think will happen? Remember that the Moon does not make its own light. It just reflects the light of the Sun. If Earth blocks sunlight from reaching the Moon, Earth will cast a shadow on the Moon. When that happens, it's called a *lunar eclipse*.

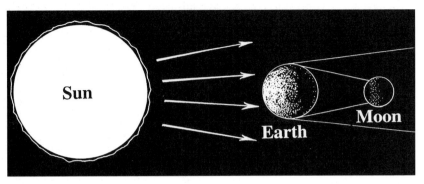

During a lunar eclipse, Earth passes between the Sun and the Moon.

The Inner Planets

Let's take a quick tour of the solar system. We'll visit all nine planets, but let's start with the four planets closest to the Sun—Mercury, Venus, Earth, and Mars. These four are often called the inner planets.

Mercury

The closest planet to the Sun, Mercury, was named after the Roman god Mercury, the swift and speedy messenger of the gods. The name fits because compared to Earth, Mercury orbits the Sun quickly. A year on Mercury—one complete orbit around the Sun—takes only 88 of our Earth days.

In 1974, the spacecraft *Mariner 10* flew by Mercury and sent back pictures of its surface. We learned that Mercury gets very hot and very cold—almost 800 degrees Fahrenheit when facing the Sun and down to almost 300 degrees below zero when facing away from the Sun.

Venus

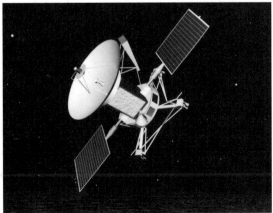

In 1993 and 1994, this unmanned spacecraft, called *Magellan*, orbited the planet Venus and sent back pictures by radio.

The second planet from the Sun, Venus, gets its name from the ancient Roman goddess of love and beauty, perhaps because it appears to shine so brightly and beautifully in the sky. In the morning or the evening, you can often see Venus. It has been nicknamed the "morning star" and "evening star" because you can see it, brighter than any star, just above the horizon at dawn or dusk. But Venus isn't a star. It's a planet. Thick clouds always cover Venus. Those clouds reflect sunlight, making the planet look bright.

Earth

The Apollo 17 spacecraft took this photograph of Earth from space. Look closely and see if you recognize the continent of Africa through the clouds. Can you see Antarctica, too?

As you sit at your desk or lie in your bed, it's hard to think of Earth as a huge round planet spinning on its axis and orbiting the Sun. But like the other eight planets in our solar system, Earth is always moving in relation to the Sun. It moves in a nearly round path, speeding around the Sun at more than sixty thousand miles per hour!

If you were an astronaut looking back at Earth from your spacecraft, you would see a blue and white ball. What do you think the white is? Clouds, lots of clouds. And the blue is water, lots of water. Nearly three-fourths of Earth is covered with water. All that water is one of the main reasons there is life on Earth.

Calvin and Hobbes   by Bill Watterson

As far as we know now, Earth is the only planet with life on it. But with all those billions of other galaxies out there, you can't help but wonder.

Mars

If you were in a spaceship 2,500 kilometers (or about 1,500 miles) above the planet Mars, it would look like this. See all the craters?

The fourth planet from the Sun is Mars, named after the Roman god of war. Sometimes you can see Mars in the night sky, even without a telescope. Mars is nicknamed the "red planet" because of its orange-red color. That color comes from the large amount of rusty iron on the planet's rocky surface.

For many years, people thought that, among all the other planets in the solar system besides Earth, Mars was the one most likely to have life. In 1976, two *Viking* space probes, launched by the United States, landed on the surface of Mars and found no life. The *Viking* probes sent back pictures of a bare, rocky, dusty planet.

In 1898, an English writer named H. G. Wells wrote a book called *The War of the Worlds* that told a story about Martians invading Earth. Forty years later, on Halloween night, 1938, an American radio station broadcast a play based on Wells's story. Thousands of people tuned in to the broadcast without knowing it was a play. They were terrified—they believed Martians were really attacking!

The Asteroid Belt

Between Mars and Jupiter, the fifth planet from the Sun, is the *asteroid belt*, which is made up of thousands of chunks of rock and metal that are orbiting the Sun. Some asteroids are as small as a basketball. Others are as big as a mountain. The biggest is one-fourth the size of our Moon!

Where did the asteroids come from? Some scientists think they are bits and pieces left over from the time of the Big Bang, when the solar system was first formed.

Sometimes asteroids escape from the asteroid belt and wander toward the inner plan-

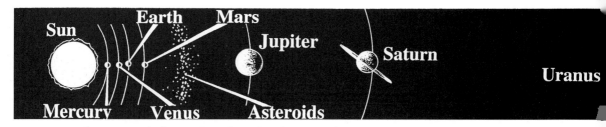

This picture helps to show how far the nine planets and the asteroid belt
are from the Sun. Which planet is closest to the Sun? Which is farthest from it?
Which planets are closest to Earth?

ets. Some scientists think that a huge asteroid might have hit Earth about 65 million years ago, creating tidal waves, fires, and a thick cloud of dust that blocked out the sunlight for years. These scientists think that this terrible disaster wiped out much of the life on our planet, including the dinosaurs.

The Outer Planets

Now you have learned about the four inner planets in the solar system. Can you name them? They are Mercury, Venus, Earth, and Mars. The inner planets are all solid and rocky. But when we move to the outer planets, we find that four of them are made mostly of liquid and gas. These four, called the *gas giants*, are Jupiter, Saturn, Uranus, and Neptune. After them comes the farthest planet from the Sun, tiny Pluto.

Jupiter

This *Galileo* space probe took off from Earth in 1989 and arrived near Jupiter in 1995.

Jupiter, the largest planet in our solar system, was named for the Roman king of the gods. Jupiter is so big that more than a thousand Earths could fit inside it. Jupiter is mostly made of hydrogen, in liquid form inside the planet and as gas on the surface. Strong winds swirl that gas into colorful clouds of red, orange, yellow, and brown.

Imagine looking up and seeing *many* moons in the sky. Galileo, the great Italian astronomer who lived around 1600, looked through a telescope and discovered four moons around Jupiter. Since then, astronomers have found twelve more moons. In the 1990s, a space probe traveled toward Jupiter. It was called the *Galileo*—can you guess why? In 1995,

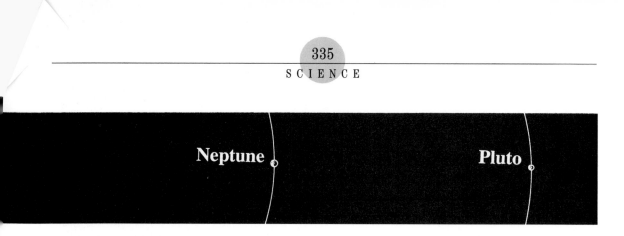

Neptune

Pluto

Galileo reached Jupiter. In 1999, it flew past one of Jupiter's moons, called Io, and sent back amazing pictures.

Saturn

The Hubble Space Telescope took this picture of the planet Saturn and its distinctive rings.

Saturn, the second largest planet in our solar system, was named for the Roman god of the harvest. This planet looks different from all the rest because of its spectacular rings. Astronomers know that the rings are made of ice, dust, and rock, but they aren't sure where all that stuff came from. Some think the rings may be the remains of a moon that shattered long ago. At least eighteen moons still orbit Saturn.

Uranus

The farther we get into outer space, the less we know about the planets. Uranus, the seventh planet from the Sun, was named for the father of all the Greek gods. Uranus has rings as well, but they are much fainter than Saturn's. Until 1986, only five moons were known to circle Uranus. Then the *Voyager II* spacecraft flew by and sent back information showing ten more moons around the planet.

Neptune

The last of the four gas giants, Neptune is the eighth planet from the Sun. It was named for the Roman god of the sea. This planet is so far away that it takes about 165 Earth years to complete one orbit around the Sun. We learned a lot about Neptune when the *Voyager II* space probe flew by the planet in 1989. *Voyager* revealed Neptune to be a frozen and stormy world, bluish in color, with the strongest winds in the solar system—up to twelve hundred miles per hour!

Pluto

Far out in the dark, cold reaches of space, you'll find the smallest planet of our solar system, Pluto, named after the Roman god of the underworld. Most of the time, Pluto is the farthest planet from the Sun. Its orbit follows a strange path, though, that sometimes swoops inside the orbit of Neptune—but not until the twenty-third century. Mark that on your calendar!

Only the most powerful telescopes on Earth can see Pluto. Astronomers did not even discover this planet until 1930. In 1978, astronomers found one moon around Pluto and named it Charon, after the man in Greek mythology who took souls to the underworld. Charon is so big that some astronomers consider Pluto and Charon a "double planet."

Dirty Snowballs and Shooting Stars

Chunks of matter called *comets* and *meteors* are zipping through space. Astronomers think that, like asteroids, these heavenly bodies may be left over from the beginnings of the solar system.

Comets are sometimes called dirty snowballs because they're made of ice, rock, and dust. When a comet passes near the Sun, the Sun's rays melt some of the ice, which causes a huge tail of gas and dust to form. The tail of a comet can stretch out for hundreds of thousands of miles!

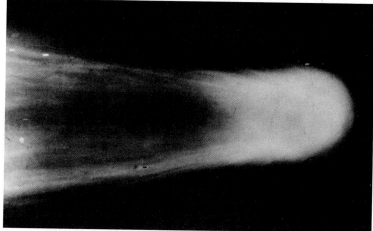

Halley's Comet orbits the Sun and comes into view from Earth every seventy-six years.

Millions of comets orbit the Sun. Sometimes a comet that passed close enough to Earth for people to see will come back hundreds of years later and be visible again. The English astronomer Edmund Halley predicted that a big comet, seen in 1531 and 1607, would return in the 1750s. He was right, and scientists named the comet after him. Halley's comet last came into view in 1986. It takes about seventy-six years for it to return to Earth's view. You can look forward to seeing it in the year 2061.

Comets don't appear very often, but on many nights you might be able to see something bright streak across the night sky. These shooting stars, as they're often called, are not really stars at all. They are meteors, bits of matter that soar through space and sometimes cross

the path of Earth. When a meteor falls through Earth's atmosphere at a super-fast speed, it gets so hot that it burns up and makes the fiery streak you might see in the sky.

Scientists estimate that several hundred million meteors enter Earth's atmosphere every day! Most burn up and never reach the ground. A meteor that makes it through to the ground is called a *meteorite*.

Most meteorites are made of iron and rock. Scientists are very eager to collect and study all the meteorites they can find. What might these scientists be hoping to find?

Constellations: Shapes in the Stars

Long ago, when the earliest humans looked up into the night sky, what thoughts do you think passed through their minds? As they stared at the stars, they began to see shapes and patterns—bears and lions, maidens and hunters. These "connect the dot" pictures that people have imagined in the stars are called *constellations*. They have names like Leo (the Lion), Taurus (the Bull), and Orion (a mighty archer).

One star pattern you can easily see is called the Big Dipper, which looks like a cup with a long handle. The Big Dipper is part of the constellation called Ursa Major, or the Great Bear.

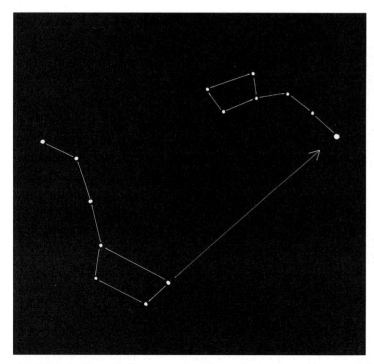

Follow the line formed by the outer two stars in the Big Dipper to the North Star, a bright star in the handle of the Little Dipper.

If you live in a region where you can view the Big Dipper, you can use its stars to figure out which way is north. Find the two stars that form the front of the Big Dipper's cup. Let your eyes follow an imaginary line starting at the bottom star, going through the top one, then moving out into space. The first bright star you see, brighter than any others around, is Polaris, or the North Star. Polaris is part of another constellation. It's the first star in the handle of the constellation called the Little Dipper.

In the days before radio and satellites, stars and constellations were important to sailors, who used them to determine compass directions. You can do that, too. When you look at the North Star, you are facing north. Once you know where north is, you can find your way south, east, or west.

The Space Shuttle

It wasn't so very long ago that people first blasted off into space. In the spring of 1961, the Union of Soviet Socialist Republics (which has since become Russia and other countries) sent the first man into space. About a month after that voyage, an American astronaut, Alan Shepard, climbed into the *Mercury* space capsule, which was attached to a powerful rocket. The rocket blasted off and sent the capsule 116 miles into space, making Shepard the first American in space. He stayed in space for fifteen minutes, then his capsule fell back through Earth's atmosphere and into the ocean, where he was picked up by a U.S. Navy ship.

In 1962, John Glenn became the first American astronaut to orbit Earth. Many more flights led to that exciting moment in 1969 when Neil Armstrong took the first steps on the Moon.

Today American astronauts fly in the space shuttle. Unlike the old space capsules, which could only fly once, the space shuttle can fly many times. So far, five different shuttles have flown in space, named *Atlantis, Columbia, Discovery, Endeavour,* and *Challenger.*

Here is the space shuttle *Discovery,* with a crew of five people aboard, lifting off for a mission in space.

As many as seven people travel together on the space shuttle, and their missions can last for many days. During one shuttle mission, the astronauts fixed the Hubble Space Telescope. Several times, an American shuttle and a Russian spacecraft named *Mir* met in space so that astronauts from the two ships could work together.

Almost every shuttle mission carries an experiment designed by students. Students have designed experiments to see what happens to mold, fungus, plant seeds, and yeast in outer space. What experiment would you like to send into space on the shuttle?

Ecology

The Natural World

Close your eyes and imagine it's a cool summer day, and you're sitting on a dock that juts out into a little pond. Look around in your imagination. How many different living things are in this pond environment?

You might see frogs and toads, turtles and salamanders. You might see dragonflies skimming the surface of your imaginary pond. Hear that buzz? Is it a fly or a mosquito? Both of them can be found near a pond. If the water is clear and still, you might be able to see the fish that live underwater.

If you were walking at the edge of this pond, what living things would you hear and see? They all share the pond environment.

And don't forget all the plants. Plants are living things, too. Think how many plants live near, and even in, a pond. Little plants grow right up to the pond's edge, and some plants may even grow underwater.

There are also beings, so tiny you can't see them, living in the mud and in the water. All these living things depend on each other, and on the kind of world a pond setting provides. In other words, these plants and animals share the pond as their *habitat*.

Living Things Depend on Each Other

Let's see how some of the creatures living in and near the pond depend on one another. Green ferns grow at the edge of the pond. The ferns absorb light from the sunshine. Their roots take in water and nutrients from the muck underwater. The ferns use sunlight, water, and nutrients to grow big and healthy.

A tadpole swims up and nibbles on one of the roots. But watch out, little tadpole! What's that coming up behind you? It's a hungry bass. Chomp! The bass eats the tadpole in one gulp.

A few months later the bass grows old and dies. Its body sinks to the bottom of the pond. Down under the water, tiny worms and bacteria, those creatures so tiny you can't see them, break down the dead bass's body as they use it for food. Nutrients from the decaying flesh and bones of the bass settle into the soil at the bottom of the pond. Those nutrients are absorbed by the roots of the ferns growing at the water's edge. And so we're back where we started.

Look how many ways the living things of this pond depend on each other—and we haven't talked about how big fish eat little fish, or how raccoons and bears catch fish to eat them, or how deer graze on the plants at the pond's edge! All these creatures, living together, are part of a *cycle of nature*.

How Natural Cycles Work

The pond's cycle of nature depends on three groups of living things, called

    producers
    consumers
    decomposers

Producers make their own food. Can you name a kind of living thing that makes its own food? Not your mother in the kitchen, but something in nature that uses sunshine and water and nutrients from the soil? A plant produces its own food. Plants are producers. In our pond, the plants at the pond's edge are producers.

Can you trace the cycle of consumers and decomposers in this pond?

All living things need energy to live, and all living things need food for energy. In our pond, the tadpole eats the plants. Then the fish eats the tadpole. The tadpole and the fish are *consumers*, since both of them consume (or eat) other living things. Are you a consumer? Yes, indeed. You eat plants and you may eat other

animals. If you eat a bacon, lettuce, and tomato sandwich, you are eating plants (the lettuce, tomato, and the wheat in the bread) and animals (the bacon). You and all the other animals in the world are consumers, because you consume food to get the energy you need.

When plants and animals die, they provide food for the *decomposers*. To "decompose" means to break something down into smaller pieces. In the pond, the little worms and bacteria are decomposers because as they seek food to eat, they decompose the body of the dead fish and break it into smaller pieces. They eat some, but they drop some, too. Those pieces become part of the soil at the bottom of the pond.

You can see how producers, consumers, and decomposers connect in a kind of natural cycle. Plants produce food. Animals eat plants, or they eat other animals that have eaten plants. When plants and animals die, decomposers break down their remains, leaving nutrients in the soil. Plants use those nutrients to produce their own food. And so, like a circle, this cycle of nature goes on and on.

Depending on Each Other

In northern Arizona, when farmers killed wolves to protect their cows and sheep, they changed the balance of nature.

If one part of the cycle of nature changes, other parts may feel the change. This happened not long ago in the southwestern United States, in Arizona. For centuries, wolves and deer had lived side by side in the forests in northern Arizona. The wolves, which are carnivores (meat eaters), killed and ate the deer. The deer, which are herbivores (plant eaters), ate moss, leaves, fruits, and twigs. Then people moved in and began farming in that part of Arizona. The wolves started eating the cows and sheep on the farms. To protect their animals, the farmers killed the wolves. They kept on hunting the wolves until there were no wolves left.

What do you think happened? Without the wolves to eat some of the deer, more deer lived. More and more deer went looking for food, and they ate all the green plants they could find. They even ate the very young trees. As the years passed, no trees grew big enough to make seeds from which new trees could grow. Finally, there were no plants left for the deer to eat. The forest was destroyed, and the deer began to starve.

People did not realize that the wolves were an important part of the natural cycle in their habitat. When this link disappeared, the balance of nature changed. Since then,

people have brought wolves back to northern Arizona and set them free. The number of deer is decreasing, and the trees are beginning to grow again.

A Web of Living Things

You have been learning about cycles of nature. You've read about producers, consumers, and decomposers, and how they all depend on each other. You read about the farmers, wolves, and deer in Arizona, and you saw what happens when part of a natural cycle changes.

In learning about these things, you have been studying *ecology*. Ecology is the study of the relations between living things and their *environment*—the world around them. (The word "environment" comes from a French word for "all around.")

In nature, living things depend on each other in an *ecosystem*, which is another word for "environment." The pond you have been thinking about is an ecosystem. It includes the pond itself, the stream that flows into it, and the surrounding forest, as well as the community of creatures living in and near the pond, all affecting each other and depending on each other.

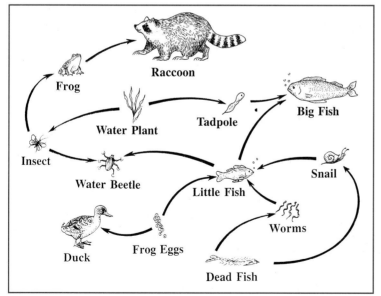

These animals all share an ecosystem.
Who eats what? See how many ways one kind of animal depends on another.

You can imagine an ecosystem as being something like a delicate, invisible web that holds life together for a group of living things. It changes whenever anything new comes into the web or anything old leaves it. If one or two strands of the web get damaged, the web might still hold together. But if too many strands are broken, that web changes its shape altogether. That is what happened in the Arizona ecosystem when the farmers got rid of the wolves.

As you can see from the example of the wolves in Arizona, human beings are part of ecosystems, too. People are part of the world of nature, and we can do things to affect it. Let's look at some of the things people do to the environment.

Hold Your Breath!

Have you ever smelled the exhaust coming out of a truck or school bus? Have you ever seen thick smoke pouring from a factory's smokestack?

Smoke from this paper factory pollutes the air.

Exhaust and smoke often contain unhealthful chemicals that pollute the air. To "pollute" means to make something dirty or impure or unsafe.

Cars, trucks, and buses are one cause of air pollution. Their engines burn fuel, usually gasoline. From their exhaust pipes these vehicles put out unhealthful emissions. (Emissions are what cars and other vehicles put in the air as a result of burning fuel in their engines.) Now imagine a city full of cars, trucks, and buses, every one of them burning fuel and releasing emissions. That's one big reason why the air in many big cities is polluted. When city air gets so dirty that the sky starts looking brown, it is called *smog*, a word made up from the two words "smoke" and "fog." If people breathe in too much smog, it can hurt their lungs.

Should You Drink the Water?

Go to a sink, turn on the faucet, and out comes a nice clear stream of water. Do you know where that water comes from?

People get most of their water from lakes, rivers, and water under the ground. If you live in the country, your water may come from an underground well. This water is often very pure because it has passed through layers of sand and soil and rock that help to filter out particles and leave the water clean and clear.

Cities often get their water from rivers and lakes. The city engineers use man-made filters to clean it. Then they add small amounts of chemicals, such as chlorine, to kill germs. (You've probably smelled chlorine in the water of a swimming pool.)

Litter pollutes the environment, too.

Of course, we only want to drink water that is clean and pure. But water can get polluted. Sometimes factories pollute water by dumping chemicals and waste products into lakes and rivers. Sometimes farmers put chemicals, such as fertilizers and insect-killers, into the soil, and then the rain washes these chemicals into nearby rivers, lakes, and underground water supplies. These chemicals and other particles pollute the water, which can make it unhealthful for people and other animals to drink.

Conservation and Recycling

Do you help recycle in your neighborhood?

You can help fight pollution. Do you have any ideas how?

One way is by *conserving*, which means using something carefully and not wasting it. When you don't leave the bathroom faucet dripping, you are conserving. Lights and the TV use electricity, and electricity is often made by factories that burn fuel and send emissions into the air. When you turn off the lights and the television when you're not using them, you are conserving, and you're helping to fight pollution.

Are you practicing conservation at home or school? For example, do you recycle? When you recycle something, it will be used again.

Recycling can help reduce water and air pollution. If you recycle glass and aluminum containers, for example, factories won't have to burn as much fuel to make new containers. If a factory burns less fuel, it puts fewer unhealthful chemicals into the air and water.

Maybe you have seen this symbol on a bottle, a cardboard box, or a trash can. It means "Recycle!" It reminds us that instead of throwing things away, we can use them, or the materials they are made from, again.

Lots of stuff can be recycled: aluminum cans, tin cans, glass bottles, plastic bottles, cardboard, newspapers, even junk mail. Recycling helps make sure we don't use up what nature has to offer.

The Lives of Famous Scientists

Nicolaus Copernicus

Today we know the real reason why the Sun seems to go around Earth every day. It's because Earth spins on its axis, and the view of the Sun from any one point of Earth changes as it spins. It's Earth that moves.

But five hundred years ago, people believed that Earth was still and the Sun moved around it. Nicolaus Copernicus [nic-o-LAY-us co-PER-ni-cus] was brave enough to question that belief.

Copernicus was born in Poland in 1473. He studied astronomy at a Polish university. Then, wanting to learn more, he traveled to Italy. If you can find Poland and Italy on a map, you will see that he had to cross the Alps to make that journey. Some say he and his brother walked the whole way across the Alps, just to get to Italy to study. In the Italian city of Bologna [ba-LO-nya], he studied not only astronomy but also medicine and law.

Nicolaus Copernicus (1473–1543).

Copernicus was nineteen years old in 1492—a big year for people who were interested in science. What happened in 1492? Christopher Columbus sailed across the Atlantic to North America. Why would that matter to an astronomer, like Copernicus? Because Columbus's experience helped more people understand that Earth is a sphere-shaped planet that orbits the Sun.

Columbus's voyage must have set Copernicus thinking. By then, he had traveled home to Poland, where his work kept him from studying astronomy all the time. He was a canon (or priest) in the church, and he also helped run the government in the part of the country where he lived. No matter what work he did, though, he kept thinking and studying about the planets.

Copernicus wrote down his proofs for why Earth must revolve around the Sun and sent them to the pope. Other people heard about his ideas as well. Friends told Copernicus he should publish his ideas in a book so that more people could read them. But Coper-

nicus was not ready. He knew that rumors about his ideas were upsetting some people, who didn't want to change their minds about the importance of Earth in the universe.

Finally, a younger man named Rheticus came to work with Copernicus on a book. The book was called *De revolutionibus orbium coelestium*, which is the Latin for "about the revolutions of the planets in the sky." Copernicus waited so long to write and publish his book that not long after he got a printed copy in his hands, he died, at the age of seventy. Now we consider that book to be an important step toward our modern understanding of how Earth and the other planets in our solar system revolve around the Sun.

John Muir

John Muir [MYOOR] loved wild places. He spent years of his life in the American wilderness, recording what he found. He is remembered as one of the foremost defenders of our natural heritage.

Muir and his family came to the United States from Scotland in 1849, settling on a farm in Wisconsin. He was interested in machines and enrolled in engineering classes at the University of Wisconsin. Soon, though, he decided that instead of human inventions, he wanted to "study the inventions of God," by which he meant the world of nature. He set out on foot with only a compass, a small bag of clothes, and a wood press for collecting flower specimens. For his first adventure, he walked from the Midwest to the Gulf of Mexico. Here's how John Muir described the way he studied nature.

> *I drifted about from rock to rock, from stream to stream, from grove to grove. Where night found me, there I camped. When I discovered a new plant, I sat down beside it for a minute or a day, to make its acquaintance and hear what it had to tell.*

He arrived in California's Yosemite [yo-SEM-i-tee] Valley in 1868. He spent six years there, studying, writing, and making sketches of the valley. Legend has it that he once climbed a hundred-foot pine tree in a windstorm and clung there, swaying in the gale, to get a better sense of the forest in a storm.

John Muir (1838–1914).

John Muir understood how important it was to observe details. He measured California's giant sequoia trees, one of which he estimated was four thousand years old. Noticing deep scratches on some rock walls, he formed a hypothesis that the mountains and valleys of the Sierra Nevada had been formed by *glaciers*—slow-moving rivers of ice. Muir went on to explore other regions of western North America, including Nevada, Utah, and Alaska. He wrote his observations in personal journals, and using those journals, he wrote articles and books.

John Muir believed that people needed the solitude and pleasure they could find in nature. He began to think that the United States should set aside large, beautiful natural areas for all Americans to enjoy. Although most of us agree with this idea today, in Muir's time few people did. Most of them viewed nature as a wild thing that needed to be tamed.

When he was forty-two, Muir stopped traveling and started working as a fruit farmer. But every year he took four months for a retreat in the wilderness. He was more and more disturbed by how logging, farming, and other human projects were destroying the natural woodlands and river valleys. He wrote and spoke publicly about preserving the wilderness. Thanks to his ideas and work, the United States now protects millions of acres as national parks and forests, such as Yellowstone, Yosemite, and Sequoia National Parks. If you ever visit one of these places, remember to think about John Muir.

Alexander Graham Bell

Even as a boy, Alexander Graham Bell was fascinated by sound. "How do the vocal cords make noise?" he asked. "How does the ear hear?" He and his brother dissected the larynx of a sheep, then built a machine of tin and rubber, designing it to work like the sheep's vocal cords. When they blew through the machine, it made a noise.

Bell was born in 1847. His father and his grandfather were teachers who taught students who could not speak or hear. Many of their students had been deaf all their lives. Bell's father and grandfather invented "visible speech," which showed deaf people how to move their mouths to pronounce different letters.

The young Bell learned that when air vibrations come into the ear, we hear sounds. A friend of his father's had demonstrated that principle to him by scattering sand on top of a drum, then playing the violin nearby—just like the demonstration mentioned on page 315. Vibrations from the violin made the drumhead vibrate. The sand, in turn, vibrated and shifted around.

In those days, around 1860, people had two ways to communicate over long distances. They could write letters or use the telegraph, which had been invented by Samuel Morse in 1840. The telegraph worked by sending electrical pulses through long wires. By following a code, now called *Morse code*, the pulses spelled out words.

Aleck Bell wondered whether wires could carry more complicated signals. Could they

carry the sounds of the human voice? In an electrical shop in Boston, Bell and another inventor named Thomas Watson began building machines to test the idea.

Bell designed a machine with two parts that worked like the voice box and the ear, connected by electrical wire. One part of the machine, the *transmitter,* turned sounds into electricity and sent them through the wire. The other part, the *receiver,* turned the electrical signals back into sound.

In March 1876, the invention finally worked. Alexander Graham Bell spoke into the transmitter: "Mr. Watson! Come here—I want to see you!" Thomas Watson, sixty feet away in the next room, heard the words quite clearly.

Alexander Graham Bell (1847–1922).

In June 1876, Bell showed his invention at America's Centennial Exhibition in Philadelphia. The emperor of Brazil was there. He held the receiver to his ear, and from the far end of the hall, Alexander Graham Bell spoke into the transmitter, reciting words from Shakespeare's *Hamlet:* "To be, or not to be: that is the question."

For his new invention, Bell received the Centennial Prize. Later that year, Bell and Watson attached their instruments to telegraph wires and spoke to each other between Boston and Cambridge, Massachusetts, two miles apart. It didn't take very long before people wanted telephones. Within a year, hundreds of households in Boston were connected by telephone wires.

Throughout the rest of his life, Alexander Graham Bell continued experimenting. He worked on early versions of phonograph records, air conditioners, and X-ray machines. He even designed a circular kite. But he will always be remembered for his most important invention: the telephone.

Women on the Final Frontier

In the 1500s and 1600s, the New World of the Americas was the great frontier. Today outer space is our New World, with many places yet to be discovered. There's one big difference between then and now. Five hundred years ago, few women took part in explo-

ration. Today women work together with men, making discoveries in space. Some women even lead the teams as they travel into space, making scientific discoveries.

Almost as soon as flight began, women flew airplanes. Bessica Raiche was America's first woman aviator, flying in 1910, only seven years after the Wright brothers' first flight. One year later Harriet Quimby was the first American woman to earn a pilot's license. Amelia Earhart became the first woman to fly alone across the Atlantic, in 1932, and the first person, man or woman, to fly alone from Hawaii to California, in 1935.

The first woman to go into space was from Russia. Her name was Valentina Tereshkova, and she flew as a cosmonaut in 1964. In 1978, six of the people chosen to be American space shuttle astronauts were women. They all studied hard, becoming experts in science and engineering. They were physically fit and eager to put their learning to the test by flying in the space shuttle.

Five years later the first of those female astronauts was assigned to be part of the space shuttle crew. On June 18, 1983, the seventh shuttle mission took off from the Kennedy Space Center in Florida with a crew of five, including Sally Ride. Sally Ride grew up in California and studied physics. She was the first woman assigned to the space shuttle mission. She flew on one other space shuttle mission, then she decided that she wanted to go back to work as a scientist. Now she teaches physics at a university in California.

Kathryn Sullivan was the first woman to walk in space, in 1984. She and fellow astronaut David Leestma spent three and a half hours outside the shuttle, testing whether they could refuel a satellite in space.

A tragic accident happened in 1985. The space shuttle *Challenger* was set to take off, carrying a crew of seven. Among those seven was Christa McAuliffe, an elementary school teacher from New Hampshire. She was the first person chosen for a shuttle mission who had not spent years training as an astronaut. The plan was for her to send messages from the space shuttle to all the schoolchildren in America.

Only seventy-three seconds after takeoff, the *Challenger* exploded. All the astronauts, including Christa McAuliffe, died. It was a horrible time for all the schoolchildren who had been hoping to hear from Christa McAuliffe in outer space, and for all the people around the world who were excited about space travel. Engineers spent months determining what went wrong in the machinery of the shuttle. After three years and three hundred changes in shuttle design, it was ready to fly again.

During the 1990s, one out of every four American astronauts was a woman. Many shuttle crews have included at least one woman. In 1992, Mae Jemison flew her first shuttle mission on the *Endeavour*, making her the first African American female astronaut. A physician and a scientist, she helped conduct experiments in space.

How did Mae Jemison grow up to become such a special person? Science—especially astronomy—fascinated her all her life. She attended Stanford University in California and studied chemical engineering and African American history. Then she decided to become a doctor. While still a medical student, she traveled far, helping in places where

Mae Jemison, the first African American woman to become an astronaut, flies on space shuttle missions and conducts scientific experiments in space.

there aren't enough doctors, like Cuba, Kenya, and Thailand. She worked as a doctor in the Peace Corps in West Africa. The first time she applied to be an astronaut, she was not chosen. She worked hard and tried again, and in 1987 she became an astronaut. It took five more years of hard work and study before she was ready for her first space flight.

In 1993, Ellen Ochoa became the first Hispanic woman among the American astronauts. She and her crewmates flew on the *Discovery*, named after the last ship that Henry Hudson sailed from England to the New World in search of a Northwest Passage.

In 1995, Eileen M. Collins took the helm of the space shuttle, becoming the first woman pilot in the U.S. space program. Collins had been a pilot for the air force. She knew how to fly thirty different kinds of jets and planes. Before becoming an astronaut, she taught mathematics and piloting to air force cadets. She flew the space shuttle during two flights in which it met and hooked up with the Russian spacecraft *Mir*.

Women take on many important jobs in the space shuttle missions nowadays. In 1993, Kathryn Thornton stepped out of the space shuttle and worked in outer space, twice during one shuttle mission, repairing the Hubble telescope. In 1996, Shannon Lucid launched with crew members on the shuttle *Atlantis*. They docked with Russia's *Mir* spacecraft, and Lucid moved onto the *Mir*, where she stayed for six months. At the end of that space flight, Shannon Lucid had traveled 75 million miles over 188 days—the longest any American astronaut, male or female, has ever stayed in space.

Illustration and Photo Credits

Text Credits and Sources

Poems

"Adventures of Isabel," from *The Bad Parents' Garden of Verse* by Ogden Nash. Copyright © 1936 by Ogden Nash. Reprinted by permission of Little, Brown and Company.

"By Myself," from *Honey, I Love* by Eloise Greenfield. Copyright © 1978, by Eloise Greenfield. Used by permission of HarperCollins Publishers.

"Catch a Little Rhyme," from *Catch a Little Rhyme* by Eve Merriam. Copyright © 1966 by Guy Michel. Used by permission of Marian Reiner.

"Dream Variations," from *Collected Poems* by Langston Hughes. Copyright © 1994 by the estate of Langston Hughes. Reprinted by permission of Alfred A. Knopf, a division of Random House, Inc.

"Jimmy Jet and His TV Set," from *Where the Sidewalk Ends* by Shel Silverstein. Copyright © 1974 by Evil Eye Music, Inc. Used by permission of HarperCollins Publishers.

"Knoxville, Tennessee," from *Black Feeling, Black Talk, Black Judgment* by Nikki Giovanni. Copyright © 1968, 1970 by Nikki Giovanni. Reprinted with permission of HarperCollins Publishers, Inc.

Stories

"Gone Is Gone," adapted from *Gone Is Gone, or The Story of a Man Who Wanted to Do Housework*, retold and illustrated by Wanda Gag (Coward, McCann & Geoghegan, 1935). Reprinted with permission.

"The Hunting of Great Bear," from *Iroquois Stories* by Joseph Bruchac. Copyright © 1975. Reprinted with permission from Crossing Press, Freedom, Calif.

"The River Bank," from Kenneth Grahame's *The Wind in the Willows*, adapted by Bob Blaisdell, 1995. Reprinted with permission from Dover Publications, Inc.

Index

Page numbers of illustrations appear in italics.

About the Author

E. D. Hirsch, Jr., is a Professor Emeritus at the University of Virginia and the author of *The Schools We Need*, *The Dictionary of Cultural Literacy*, and the bestselling *Cultural Literacy*. He lives in Charlottesville, Virginia.